S0-BRQ-323

INTERNATIONALIZATION OF HIGHER EDUCATION IN THE UNITED STATES OF AMERICA AND EUROPE

Recent Titles in
Greenwood Studies in Higher Education Series

Academic Staff in Europe: Changing Contexts and Conditions
Jürgen Enders, editor

Higher Education in the Developing World: Changing Contexts and Institutional Responses
David Chapman and Ann Austin, editors

Academic Pathfinders: Knowledge Creation and Feminist Scholarship
Patricia J. Gumport

INTERNATIONALIZATION OF HIGHER EDUCATION IN THE UNITED STATES OF AMERICA AND EUROPE

A Historical, Comparative, and Conceptual Analysis

Hans de Wit

Greenwood Studies in Higher Education
Philip G. Altbach, Series Editor

GREENWOOD PRESS
Westport, Connecticut • London

Library of Congress Cataloging-in-Publication Data

Wit, Hans de, 1950–
    Internationalization of higher education in the United States of America and Europe : a historical, comparative, and conceptual analysis / Hans de Wit.
        p.   cm.—(Greenwood studies in higher education, ISSN 1531–8087)
    Includes bibliographical references and index.
    ISBN 0–313–32075–6 (alk. paper)
    1. International education—United States—Cross-cultural studies.   2. International education—Europe—Cross-cultural studies.   3. Education, Higher—United States.   4. Education, Higher—Europe.   I. Title.   II. Series.
    LC1090.W594   2002
    378′.016′0973—dc21   2001040557

British Library Cataloguing in Publication Data is available.

Library of Congress Catalog Card Number: 2001040557
ISBN: 0–313–32075–6
ISSN: 1531–8087

First published in 2002

Greenwood Press, 88 Post Road West, Westport, CT 06881
An imprint of Greenwood Publishing Group, Inc.
www.greenwood.com

Printed in the United States of America

The paper used in this book complies with the Permanent Paper Standard issued by the National Information Standards Organization (Z39.48–1984).

10 9 8 7 6 5 4 3 2 1

Published in cooperation with the Center for International Higher Education and the Program in Higher Education, Boston College, Chestnut Hill, Massachusetts.

To my parents

Contents

Figures

Series Foreword

Greenwood Studies in Higher Education publishes current research and analysis on higher and postsecondary education. Higher education in the twenty-first century is a multifaceted phenomenon, combining a variety of institutions and systems, an increasing diversity of students, and a range of purposes and functions. The challenges of expansion, technology, accountability, and research, among others, require careful analysis. This series combines research-based monographs, analysis, and reference books related to all aspects of higher education. It is concerned with policy and practice in a global perspective. Greenwood Studies in Higher Education is dedicated to illuminating the reality of higher and postsecondary education in contemporary society.

Higher education is a central enterprise of the twenty-first century and a key part of the knowledge-based economy. Universities are the most important source of basic research, and are therefore key to the development of technology. They are also the repositories of the wisdom of society—their libraries and other facilities are in many ways the institutional memory of civilization. University faculty provide not only education and training, but are involved in the creation and interpretation of knowledge. Universities are central to the civil society. Higher education is a key to the social mobility and progress of large numbers of people.

Universities and other postsecondary institutions are increasingly complex. They are large and multifaceted. Academe is also diverse, with a wider range of institutions, a less homogenous student population, and a mixture of public and private support. This series is dedicated to illuminating these complexities. It is also committed to the improvement of one of the most important parts of society—postsecondary education.

Philip G. Altbach

Acknowledgments

This study provides a critical *tour d'horizon* of the internationalization of higher education. It is based on my twenty years of experience with, and study of, the internationalization of higher education as an institutional director and vice president for international affairs, a national and international administrator in a great variety of organizations, and as consultant, researcher, and editor. My previous publications on the subject are reflected in its content, along with the results of a careful study of the existing literature and the knowledge I have gained through my active involvement in developing and assessing strategies for internationalization in the Dutch, European, and international contexts. Although I am solely responsible for the analysis presented and the opinions expressed, I am deeply indebted to the many organizations and colleagues, both administrators and researchers, with whom I have debated and interacted on the internationalization of higher education over the past two decades.

First and foremost I am indebted to the Universiteit van Amsterdam. The people with whom I have worked have always stimulated me to combine my work for the university with an active involvement in the international arena of higher education. The late JanKarel Gevers, president, and Ruud Bleijerveld, the secretary general of the university, in particular demonstrated their support and interest in my work, generously providing me with time and space for my involvement in the foundation of the European Association for International Education (EAIE), my activities in other organizations, my role as editor of the *Journal of Studies in International Education*, and my research.

I wish to thank my many friends and colleagues in international education for their inspiration over the years. Without excluding others, the International Management of Higher Education (IMHE) program of the Organization for Economic Cooperation and Development (OECD), the European Association for International Education (EAIE), and the Council on International Educational Exchange (CIEE) have played important roles in the realization of my work. It is impossible to name all those individuals who have in one way or another contributed to the completion of this work, but I extend to them all my grateful thanks. I also would like to thank my friends and colleagues at Boston College, in particular Seymour and Paula Leventman and Marian St. Onge, who helped me lay the foundation for this study during my visiting lectureship in 1995.

I am indebted to Philip Altbach (Center for International Higher Education, Boston College), Ulrich Teichler (Wissenschaftliches Zentrum für Berufs- und Hochschulforschung Universität Gesamthochschule Kassel, Germany), Marijk van der Wende (Center for Higher Education Policy Studies, Twente University) and Rob Kroes (American Studies, Universiteit van Amsterdam), who through their interests and research work have paved the way for the development of research on the internationalization of higher education, and whose work and discussions have inspired me in my own work. I would also like to thank Mariam Assefa (World Education Services), who gave me the confidence to believe that this was an endeavor I could bring to a successful end, Belinda Stratton, who assisted with the editing of the English, and Jacomijn Baerts, who has supported me in managing the combination of my work as vice president for international affairs with the work on this book.

In particular, I am grateful to my dear friend and colleague Jane Knight of the University of Toronto (previously of Ryerson Polytechnic University) for the inspiring walks and talks on the internationalization of higher education, which we have had over the past five years. Our cooperation on projects, publications, seminars, and workshops in different parts of the world, and the time this has provided us for long discussions, has been an inspiring force in my work on this publication.

For the past twenty years I have divided my love for, and life in, international education with that for Ingrid, Jacob, and Katja. Ironically, the eight months that I was a visiting lecturer at Boston College in 1995—the start of my workplan—and the eight months dedicated in the year 2000 primarily to the writing of this publication were a small but pleasant compensation for the previous nineteen years of sharing me with the world of travel and work.

I dedicate this publication to my parents. I am glad that I am able to give something back to them for their continuous love and attention.

Introduction

Internationalization has become an important issue in the development of higher education. Sven Groennings (1987b) describes it as "one of the most powerful substantive developments in the history of American higher education" (p. 2). It is perceived "as one of the laws of motion propelling institutions of higher learning" (Kerr 1990, 5); as "one of the important features of contemporary universities" (Smith, Teichler, and van der Wende 1994, 1); as "a pressure no one who teaches can be unaware of" (Halliday 1999, 99); as "a major theme for the next decade" (Davies 1997, 83); and as "one of the most important trends of the last decade" (Teichler 1999, 6), if not of the past half century (Altbach 2000c, 2).

At the same time, the internationalization of higher education is still a phenomenon with a lot of question marks regarding its historical dimension; its meaning, concept, and strategic aspects; its relationship to developments in society and higher education in general, in particular the movement to globalization and regionalization; and regarding its status as an area of study and analysis.

The questions addressed in this book are the following:

- What has been the historical development of the internationalization of higher education, in particular in the United States of America and Europe, and how are the differences in development between these two regions to be explained?

- What are the rationales behind this internationalization of higher education, its meaning and approaches, and the different strategies and organizational models?
- How can we interpret some of its key manifestations at the turn of the century?

One of the fundamental problems we face when dealing with the internationalization of higher education is the diversity of related terms. Sometimes they are used to describe a concrete element within the broad field of internationalization, but terms are also used as *pars pro toto* and as a synonym for the overall term "internationalization." Each term has a different accent and reflects a different approach, and is used by different authors in different ways. For a better understanding of the internationalization of higher education it is important to place that term in perspective to approaches and other terms used and to provide a working definition of its meaning, and this is the purpose of one of the chapters. These issues are mentioned here to warn the reader of this complexity. In this study three terms will mainly be used: "international dimension," "international education," and "internationalization of higher education," each referring to a specific phase of development.

Peter Scott (1998) observes and at the same time questions that "in a rhetorical sense, internationalism has always been part of the life-world of the university" (p. 123). In this book it will be argued that the international dimension of higher education, prior to the twentieth century, was more incidental than organized. It will also be argued that this international dimension as an organized activity, referred to in general by the term "international education," is a product of the twentieth century, at first mainly in the United States for reasons of foreign policy and national security. The third argument is that, around the end of the Cold War, this international dimension evolved into a strategic process, referred to as the "internationalization of higher education," and became increasingly linked to the globalization and regionalization of our societies and the impact of this on higher education. In addition, it will be argued that with the further development of globalization the international dimension will evolve into an integrated element of higher education and move away from its present position as an isolated set of activities, strategies, or processes. This is manifested in a shift in emphasis from more traditional forms of international education to strategies that are more directly related to the core functions of the university, and in a shift in emphasis from political to economic rationales. Implications of these shifts are the increasing importance of quality assessment of internationalization strategies, the emergence of English as the common language in higher education, the increasing relevance of international networks and strategic alliances, and the gradual acceptance of the internationalization of higher education as an area of research.

Little research has been done on the historical roots of the present wave of internationalization of higher education. It is nonetheless important to relate the generally acknowledged focus on the internationalization of higher education in today's world to the original roots of the university, and to place the present developments in historical perspective. Only in this way is it possible to identify the specific character of the internationalization of higher education as currently encountered.

In Part I, the historical development of the international dimension of higher education is analyzed. This historical dimension is mentioned in many documents and studies on internationalization, but if one takes a more careful look the references, with some exceptions, are rather limited. Most studies refer in general terms to the supposed international dimension of universities in medieval times, and before that in the Arab era. In Chapter 1, therefore, a historical context for the development of the internationalization of higher education is given, mainly using examples from Europe, but with reference to other parts of the world.[1] In Chapters 2 and 3 this historical development is elaborated further, with a detailed analysis of the European and American cases. In Chapter 4, a comparison is made between the development of the internationalization of higher education in the United States and Europe.

A historical analysis of the internationalization of higher education makes clear that at certain moments different answers have been given to the why (rationales), what (meanings and approaches), and how (strategies and organization models) of this phenomenon. In Part II a conceptual framework for the internationalization of higher education is presented as an update and extension of previous work (de Wit 1995b; Knight and de Wit 1997). Chapter 5 deals with the why, the rationales for internationalization, and relates these rationales to the different stakeholders in higher education. In Chapter 6, an overview is given of the debate on the meaning and definition of "international education" and "internationalization of higher education" (the what), a working definition is presented for it, and different approaches to internationalization are summarized. In Chapter 7, the focus is on institutional strategies for the internationalization of higher education, followed by an overview of organizational models.

The historical and conceptual analysis as presented in the first two parts of this book are the basis for the study of developments in the internationalization of higher education today. In Part III, five key issues that are relevant to the study of internationalization of higher education at the turn of the century are discussed. It is not the intention to present these as the only issues of importance, but as relevant examples to illustrate the impact of internationalization on higher education.[2]

In Chapter 8 the development of internationalization of higher education is placed in the context of globalization and regionalization in our societies. In Chapter 9 the link between quality assurance and internationalization is analyzed. In Chapter 10 special attention is paid to an issue that illustrates the growing link between the internationalization of higher education and globalization: the emergence of English as the new common language for higher education. In Chapter 11 a second illustration of this link is discussed: the development of regional and global academic networks and alliances.

In Chapter 12 the internationalization of higher education as an area of research is analyzed, following the argument of Ulrich Teichler (1996b) that "we might consider internationalization of higher education as the next theme, which gives rise to a new focus of both higher education policy and higher education research" (p. 435).

In the last chapter, Chapter 13, a summary and conclusions are provided. Although recently the number of studies on the internationalization of higher education has been growing, few provide a historical and comparative analysis of this phenomenon. In de Wit (1995b) and Knight and de Wit (1997) an attempt to present such a study has been made, stimulated by the program on Institutional Management of Higher Education (IMHE) of the Organization for Economic Cooperation and Development (OECD). Other studies have followed on national or regional policies for internationalization, but an overall analysis is still lacking.[3]

While making ample reference to the internationalization of research, this study focuses on that other core function of higher education, teaching. This is true for most studies on the internationalization of higher education. The notion of higher education as being "international" by nature refers primarily to the research function. Although in recent years several studies have been published on universities and the knowledge economy, these studies refer more to research and globalization than to teaching and internationalization.[4]

This book presents a critical *tour d'horizon* of the internationalization of higher education: in its historical dimension, by comparing the United States of America and Europe, and as a conceptual framework. This analysis is based on the author's twenty years of experience with and study of the internationalization of higher education as an institutional director and vice president for international affairs, a national and international administrator in a great variety of organizations, and a consultant, researcher, and editor. The study is also based on previous publications by the author, an ample study of the literature, and active involvement in developing and assessing strategies for internationalization in the Dutch, European, and international contexts. This book can be considered the first full-scale analysis of the literature on, debates on, and experience with the internationalization of higher education.

NOTES

1. See, for instance, Altbach (1998), Kerr (1994b), Neave (1997), and Scott (1998).

2. For instance, the internationalization of the curriculum as analyzed by van der Wende (1996), Mestenhauser and Ellingboe (1998b), and others is another important issue not touched upon in detail in this study.

3. On national policies, see, for instance, on Australia, Back, Davis, and Olsen (1996); and on Canada, Knight (2000); on regional policies, see, on Europe, Kälvermark and van der Wende (1997).

4. See, for instance, Etzkowitz and Leydesdorff (1997) and Slaughter and Leslie (1997).

Part I

The Historical Development of the Internationalization of Higher Education: A Comparative Study of the United States of America and Europe

Chapter 1

The Historical Context of the Internationalization of Higher Education

Little research has been done on the historical roots of the present wave of internationalization of higher education. It is nonetheless important to relate the generally acknowledged focus on the internationalization of higher education in today's world to the original roots of the university, and to place the present developments in historical perspective. Only in this way is it possible to identify the specific character of the internationalization of higher education as currently encountered.

Stephen Muller (1995) states that we have entered the information age and seem to be "on the road toward a single global marketplace of ideas, data, and communication" (p. 65). He comes to the conclusion that "knowledge as understanding is the province of the university, and as of now knowledge has outrun understanding by far. Higher learning must now restore understanding" (p. 75). His reference to a supposed restoration of the universal character of science and education is based on the assumption that higher education in the past has gone from a transnational to a more isolationist national period, and that the globalization of current society requires a renewal of its universal role. In similar words, Philip Altbach (1998) calls the university the one institution that has always been global: "With its roots in medieval Europe, the modern university is at the center of an international knowledge system that encompasses technology, communications and culture" (p. 347). These observations are not new. F. Brown wrote as early as 1950, "The universities of the world are today aspiring to return to one of the basic concepts of their origin—the universality of knowledge. Many are also seeking to discover and adopt procedures that will restore the desirable aspects of the itinerant character of scholars that was an accepted part of university education until growing nationalism created the barriers of language" (p. 11).

The observations of Muller, Altbach, and Brown come close to Clark Kerr's (1994b) statement that "universities are, by nature of their commitment to advancing universal knowledge, essentially international institutions, but they have been living, increasingly, in a world of nation-states that have designs on them" (p. 6). He notes a historical movement from a unified model of higher education, lasting until the end of the Reformation, to a diversified nation-by-nation system of higher education, accelerating in the nineteenth century and again after World War II (Kerr 1990, 6). Kerr sees at present a "partial reconvergence" of the cosmopolitan university. Until five hundred years ago, higher education could be typified by the "convergent" model of universal education. That model was replaced by a "divergence model," in which higher education came to serve the administrative and economic interests of the nation-state and also became an essential aspect of the development of national identity. Now he sees the emergence of a partial reconvergence, which Kerr calls the "cosmopolitan-nation-state university," a result of the fact that it has generally been to the advantage of nation-states to support the expansion of higher learning and its internationalization within and beyond their borders. He judges that we will finally come to the conclusion that "it will have been a century of transformation from nation-state divergences in higher education toward a more nearly universal convergence where universities best serve their nations by serving the world of learning" (Kerr 1994b, 26).

Scott (1998) criticizes the "myth of the international university" dating from the medieval ages. Not only were very few universities founded in that period and ultimately transformed by the modern world, but he classifies this myth as "internationalist rhetoric." The university of the middle ages could not be "international," given that nation-states did not yet exist:

Rather it shared an archaic notion of 'universalism,' within that narrow world of medieval Europe, with other institutions. . . . So the peregrinatio academica of the medieval scholar cannot be seen as a precursor of today's ERASMUS and SOCRATES student mobility programmes, or of junior year abroads, or of the (until recently) massive flows of international students . . . any more than the debates within medieval scholasticism, or (a bit later) the ideological wars of Reformation and counter-Reformation can be compared to the global flows of information exchange in the knowledge society. The contemporary university is the creature of the nation state not of medieval civilization. (p. 123)

This view is also present in Neave (1997), who speaks of a "myth," qualifying the notion of international mobility in the medieval period as "inaccurate," and of "de-Europeanisation" with the creation of the nation-state.

To provide a clearer insight into the international dimension of higher education in the medieval era, the twentieth century, and the period in between, an overview of the main international elements of the periods as mentioned by Kerr follows, ending with the present, post–Cold War context, which Kerr (1994b) describes as "an unsettled period, perhaps the most unsettled since the Reformation in Western Europe," and as a move in the direction of "partial reconvergence" (p. 9).

THE INTERNATIONAL DIMENSION OF HIGHER EDUCATION IN THE MIDDLE AGES AND RENAISSANCE

Most publications on the internationalization of higher education refer back to the days of the Middle Ages and up to the end of the eighteenth century. At that time, in addition to religious pilgrims, "pilgrims or travellers (peregrini) of another kind were also a familiar sight on the roads of Europe. These were the university students and professors. Their pilgrimage (peregrinatio) was not to Christ's or a saint's tomb, but to a university city where they hoped to find learning, friends, and leisure" (de Ridder-Symoens 1992, 280). The academic pilgrimage started long before the twelfth century, but became at that time a common phenomenon. According to de Ridder-Symoens, "In the twelfth and thirteenth centuries, when there were not many universities and they were not widely distributed over Europe, the 'happy few' who aspired to higher education had to leave home and travel long distances to the 'studium' of their (rather limited) choice" (p. 281). But even later, in the fifteenth century, when higher education was more widespread in Europe, short-term study abroad and migration for complete studies continued to be important factors. This was not so much because of numbers; owing to the creation of more universities recruitment of students became more regionalized and migration of students came nearly to a halt. By the end of the Middle Ages, three-quarters of all students went to a university in their region. The exception were those who wanted "to continue their studies in an internationally renowned university and in disciplines not taught in their own schools" (p. 287).

de Ridder-Symoens describes the impact of the mobility of students and scholars on higher education and society in that period in a way that reminds us of many of the arguments used to promote mobility today:

The use of Latin as a common language, and of a uniform programme of study and system of examinations, enabled itinerant students to continue their studies in one "studium" after another, and ensured recognition of their degrees throughout Christendom. Besides their academic knowledge they took home with them a host of new experiences, ideas, opinions, and political principles and views. Also—and this is important—they brought back manuscripts and, later on, printed books. They had become familiar with new schools of artistic expression, and with living conditions, customs, ways of life, and eating and drinking habits all previously unknown to them. As most itinerant scholars belonged to the élite of their country and later held high office, they were well placed to apply and propagate their newly acquired knowledge. The consequences of academic pilgrimage were, indeed, out of all proportion to the numerically insignificant number of migrant students. (pp. 302–303)

Reading this, it comes as no surprise that the European Commission chose the name of Erasmus, one of the best-known wandering scholars of that period, for their most important mobility program. However, according to Scott (1998), one cannot call it anything more than a myth or a symbolic expression, "a pleasant legend untroubled by the slightest relevance, save to the romantically inclined" (Neave 1997, 1). Field (1998, 8) sees a tension between this symbolism in the titles of the educational action programs of the European Commission, their attachment to the humanistic tradition of education, and the technological and instrumentalist tendency of these programs.

However, because nations as political units did not yet exist, one can speak of a medieval "European space," defined by this common religious credence and uniform academic language, program of study, and system of examinations (Neave 1997, 6). This medieval European education space, although limited and scattered in comparison to present mass higher education, is relevant to the current debate on the development of a new European education space. One expression of that is the gradual growth of the English language as the common academic language today, resembling the role of Latin—and later, although in a more moderate way, French—in that period. More than a superficial resemblance and reference between the two is not possible, however, because of the different social, cultural, political, and economic circumstances.

INTERNATIONAL ELEMENTS IN HIGHER EDUCATION IN THE PERIOD BETWEEN THE EIGHTEENTH AND NINETEENTH CENTURIES

With the emergence of the nation-state, universities became de-Europeanized and nationalized. This transition did not take place in a radical way. As Jan Kolasa (1962) notes, toward the end of the seventeenth century and in the eighteenth century, "European culture continued, to a considerable degree, its universalistic spirit. . . . National cultures became more differentiated but the most prominent savants and artists still belonged to the whole of Europe, and the French language was commonly spoken by cosmopolitan aristocracy, which managed all political and a good deal of non-political affairs" (p. 12). According to Kolasa, the Middle Ages, the Reformation, and the Enlightenment were periods of "natural, not organized or regimented, flow of culture, and of free wandering of the creators of that culture across political frontiers" (p. 12). This domain of international cultural relations was challenged in the second half of the nineteenth century, with the emergence of a strong sentiment of political and cultural nationalism.

Hammerstein (1996, 624) illustrates this with the following examples: prohibition of study abroad in many countries; displacement of Latin as the universal language by vernacular languages; and the disappearance of the "peregrinationes academicae" and its gradual replacement by the "grand tour," which differed in its emphasis on cultural experience compared to the academic objectives of the former. Universities became institutions that served the professional needs and ideological demands of the new nations in Europe. "Paradoxically perhaps," observes Scott (1998), "before it became an international institution the university had first to become a national institution—just as internationalization presupposes the existence of nation states" (p. 123). In that period, three international aspects of higher education can be identified: export of higher education systems, dissemination of research, and individual mobility of students and scholars.

The most important international element of higher education in this era was probably the export of systems of higher education. As Roberts, Rodrígues Cruz, and Herbst (1996) describe, by the end of the eighteenth century universities and other institutions of higher education could be found in North, Central, and South America, as implants from Europe. Altbach and Selvaratnam (1989) describe this phenomenon for Asia. This took the form of export from the colonial powers to their colonies, and later to the newly independent states. Higher education in Latin America has been, and still is to a large extent, modeled on higher education in the Iberian Peninsula. Higher education in India and other Asian, African, Caribbean, and North American countries belonging to the British Empire was modeled on British higher education. In the same way, the Asian, African, Caribbean, and North American universities in the former French colonies have been built according to the structure of French higher education. After independence these influences prevailed, and only more recently have other national and international influences had their impact on higher education in these countries.

Countries with a noncolonial heritage, such as Japan, China, and Thailand, were also affected and have largely Western university systems. Higher education in Japan, for instance, was seen as an important part of the modernization process, which took place in the nineteenth century under pressure of Western economic, political, and military power. First, the German university was used as a model, then, after World War II, American higher education ideas were imposed. To this day, contemporary higher education in Japan includes elements of German origin and of current American higher education (Altbach and Selvaratnam 1989, 10).[1]

Even higher education in the United States, often regarded today as the dominant model in international developments of higher education, was based on European influences and continued to reflect these for a long time. Oxford and Cambridge were the models for the first colleges established in the colony. Later, with the creation of Johns Hopkins University, the German model of research university was also imported. As a side effect, many students sojourned to the universities in Europe, on which these institutions were modeled, to pursue further studies. The American system of higher education, which emerged in its modern form between the 1860s and the 1900s, can be considered, according to Joseph Ben-David (1992) as "one of 'secondary reform' and belongs to the same category of externally inspired change as the establishment of modern systems of higher education in Russia, Japan and elsewhere in Asia, and Africa" (p. 25).

Peter Scott (1998, 124) calls this export of higher education models the first of two main forms of internationalization of higher education that went on well into the twentieth century. This can hardly be seen, however, as a process of integrating an international–intercultural dimension. It would be tempting to call it a primitive form of globalization of higher education or globalization of higher education *avant-la-lettre*, but that would ignore the role of the nation-state in the process, although it coincides with what Thomas Friedman (1999, xiv) calls an "area of globalization," the period from 1800 to 1920, with relatively similar volumes of trade and capital flows and Great Britain as the dominant global power. Nonetheless, it was different in degree and kind to the present area of globalization, and the adjective *avant-la-lettre* is therefore appropriate. The best description is "academic colonialism" and "academic imperialism."[2]

The second international element of higher education in the eighteenth and nineteenth centuries could be found in research and publications. Although much of the research in that period had a national focus and interest, the international exchange of ideas and information through seminars, conferences, and publications has remained a constant factor of international scholarly contact. To a certain extent, one can say that although this international scholarly cooperation and exchange did not have the intensive form as in the present period, for most academics international contacts in research have always been and still are the main if not the only reference when asked about the need for internationalization of higher education. Jan Kolasa (1962, 15, 163) notes that the international academic associations and societies of the nineteenth century were private in character and dedicated to individual and professional relationships. This element comes closest to the notion of "universalism" that has always been present in higher education.

Although there is very little statistical information on the mobility of students and scholars in the eighteenth and nineteenth centuries, mobility—the third international element of this period—never completely came to an end but changed character. de Ridder-Symoens (1996) describes this change as follows: "Renaissance teachers looked upon study abroad as the culmination of the humanist education of young members of the elite. In Renaissance times wandering students were strongly attracted by the renown of teachers" (p. 417), while most of the traveling students in early modern Europe were mainly concerned with the cultural and intellectual advantages of educational travel, the "Bildungsreise."

If the first decades of the sixteenth century were, according to de Ridder-Symoens (1996), "the golden age of wandering scholars" (p. 418), by the mid-sixteenth century the Reformation and counter-Reformation did have a strong negative impact on mobility. Study abroad was prohibited in many countries, based on the argument that foreign universities were "sources of religious and political contamination" (p. 419). As in present foreign student flows, economic and financial arguments were important. Emigration of students was seen as a loss for the sending cities and a threat to the development of their own universities. At the same time, the reduction in foreign student numbers affected the cities that most of them visited. In the seventeenth and eighteenth centuries, the Grand Tour did revive student mobility, at first in order to get a degree; later, in the period of Enlightenment, mainly for pleasure. All in all, de Ridder-Symoens (p. 442) concludes that until about 1700 student mobility was an important element of university life, and even afterward continued to influence intellectual and political life in Europe.

Until the twentieth century, in sharp contrast to the present situation, the mobility of students was greater in the direction from the United States to Europe than from Europe to the United States. For many Americans the pursuit of study in Europe was considered the final touch to their cultural integration into American society: the Grand Tour. The same can be said of Canadian and Australian higher education.

The last two elements, research and student flows, together relate to the second main form of internationalization that Scott (1998, 124) observes, transmitted via the Grand Tour, scientific academies, and literary salons. It is better to call it a primitive form of internationalization, more incidental than structured and strategic, as the present form of internationalization can be defined.

In summary, one can describe the period from the end of the Renaissance to the beginning of the twentieth century as being one of predominantly nationally oriented higher education. The main areas of international academic attention in that period were the individual mobility of a small group of well-to-do and academically qualified students to the top centers of learning in the world, the export of academic systems from the European colonial powers to the rest of the world, and cooperation and exchange in academic research.

This confirms the suggestion of Kerr (1994b), Altbach (1998), and Scott (1998) that the focus of higher education in that period became more directed to the development of a national identity and national needs and less to universal knowledge. This applies to Europe, but also to the United States, as will be shown later.

THE INTERNATIONAL DIMENSION
IN THE TWENTIETH CENTURY

Even before World War II, one can observe a certain shift in the direction of more international cooperation and exchange in higher education. Again, little research is available on this period, but, for instance, the creation of the Institute of International Education (IIE) in 1919 in the United States, the Deutscher Akademischer Austauschdienst (DAAD) in 1925, and the British Council in 1934 are indications of the growing attention to international cooperation and exchange. Academic cooperation at that time was more focused on scholars than on students. And, as will be shown in the following chapters, in the aftermath of World War I it was driven by political rationales of peace and mutual understanding. The International Committee on Intellectual Co-operation, created in 1921 under the auspices of the League of Nations and the predecessor of UNESCO, was a manifestation of that new emphasis. As Jan Kolasa (1962) observes, "The co-operation of intellectuals with politicians within the framework of the League of Nations is one of the most essential differences between the unofficial organizations of the nineteenth century and the League organization for intellectual co-operation" (p. 41).[3]

According to Tierney (1977), "Educational exchange as we know it is very much a product of the twentieth century" (p. 1505), and he sees two main factors that explain the rise of that phenomenon after World War II: the establishment of UNESCO and the Fulbright Act, both immediately after the end of the war. More than the creation of these two institutions, the political and cultural rationales behind them were crucial. As will be shown in later chapters, the international dimension was more present in American higher education than in Europe, and what international activities did take place were mainly between the two continents.

After World War II, international educational exchange expanded, first and foremost in the United States. Europe was still too heavily focused on recovering from the severe wounds of two world wars and on reconstruction to be able to invest in international educational exchange and cooperation. In the field of area studies it was barely able to maintain its historical strength in the knowledge of other cultures and languages. Many of its academics had either become victims of the wars or migrated to other parts of the world, mainly the United States, Canada, and Australia. The world of academia was turned upside down, as Goodwin and Nacht (1991) describe: "Views of the world in US higher education were transformed almost overnight by World War II. From a cultural colony the nation was changed, at least in its own eyes, into the metropolis; from the periphery it moved triumphantly to the center" (pp. 4–5). Cunningham (1991) describes the same phenomenon for Canada: "Until the Canadian higher education system was well established, Canadians often had to study in the United States and Europe to obtain their qualifications, particularly in the professions. Then, as our own infrastructure matured, students from other countries began to arrive here for advanced studies. But this phenomenon is quite recent. Students from overseas began arriving in Canada in significant numbers only after World War II" (p. 1).

At the same time, the Soviet Union, the other new superpower that was the result of the war, expanded its political, economic, social, and academic control over Central and Eastern Europe in a quite different and clearly repressive way, bringing academic freedom and autonomous cooperation and exchange almost to an end. Dennis Kallen (1991a) describes the situation of higher education in Central and Eastern Europe during the Communist period: "Higher education, as well as the educational system in general, had been made subservient to the political and economic interests of the State and in fact the Party. The universities were among the chosen and most prestigious instruments for transforming human minds and for providing the State economy with the right numbers and the right kind of highly qualified manpower" (p. 17). He recognizes at the same time that "some of them remained institutions of high intellectual and cultural prestige where, in contrast to what happened in many other walks of life, integrity, merit and individual academic performance remained important values" (p. 17). For academic cooperation, the Western world was not a priority:

Much higher importance was attached to co-operation with other socialist countries, whether in Central/Eastern Europe itself or elsewhere in the world. Large numbers of students with scholarships attended higher education in the USSR and in other socialist countries, and considerable numbers of staff were invited to teach or learn, particularly in the USSR. The Third World at large represented the second priority. Apart from receiving large numbers of students on state scholarships and inviting considerable numbers of staff, the Central/Eastern European countries carried out a vast programme of development assistance in Third World countries. (pp. 27–28)

Both powers had clear political reasons to promote international educational exchange and cooperation: to gain a better understanding of the rest of the world and to maintain and even expand their spheres of influence. Together with diplomacy, development aid, and cultural exchange, international exchange and cooperation in higher education became an important tool to reach these objectives.

In general, though, one can say that the international dimension was marginal, certainly at the institutional level. Most national governments did enter into cultural and academic agreements with other friendly nations, under which the exchange of faculty and students was made possible with national grants, mainly for research cooperation, language studies, and post-graduate training. But the numbers were small and the objectives more related to diplomacy than to academic and cultural cooperation. Guy Neave (1992a) characterizes the period between 1945 and 1964 with respect to mobility as follows: "Overwhelmingly voluntarist, unorganized and individual" (p. 15), and with respect to exchanges by "the relatively small numbers of students involved and though organized under the aegis of national agencies, whether public or private, continued in the main along a North–North axis, between North America and the United States in particular and Western Europe. Or, from the standpoint of the Eastern bloc, between the Soviet Union and its satellites" (p. 18).

In the 1960s and 1970s, the second phase in Guy Neave's (1992a) analysis of international cooperation after World War II (1964–1981), the situation changed, with developments such as the decolonialization of the developing world, expansion of higher education, and the changing role of universities as generators of human resources in addition to their traditional role as centers of scholarly study. In this period, internationalization was expressed predominantly in the growing one-way mobility of students from the South to the North.

After World War II and in particular in the 1960s and 1970s, the Third World, in itself not a factor in academic cooperation and exchange, became, ironically enough, the main battlefield of international academic cooperation. First, the Western models and systems of higher education continued to dominate, as in the previous era. This expressed itself in the influence of the English language, the impact of foreign training, the dominance of Western scientific products, and the impact of Western academic ideas and structures, neocolonialism, or imperialism (Altbach and Selvaratnam 1989, 12–15). Second, the role of the Third World manifested itself through development cooperation and technical assistance projects. "More than a few development projects in the Third World became something of a chess game between the superpowers," as Burkart Holzner and Davydd Greenwood (1995, 39) observe. Not only the USSR saw developing countries as an important region in which to expand their political and economic power and invested in development aid programs for universities, but the United States and soon after Western Europe, Canada, and Australia moved large development funds into higher education in Asia, Latin America, and Africa. Academic staff were sent to these regions for teaching, training, and curriculum development; students and junior staff received grants for postgraduate training in the donor countries; and equipment and books were sent to improve the infrastructure of the universities in the developing world. North–South relations dominated internationalization strategies in higher education in the period from 1950 to 1985, in Europe (East and West), the United States, Canada, and Australia. That relationship was a one-way relationship with different aspects—student flows from South to North, faculty and funds from North to South—and severe impacts, both negative (brain drain) and positive (better understanding and knowledge).

At first, development cooperation and technical assistance were the dominant factors in North–South relations in higher education. However, the massive mobility of students from South to North, in particular to the five most important receiving nations—the Soviet Union, Germany, France, the United Kingdom, and (in absolute numbers in particular) the United States—became increasingly prominent and has remained so to the present day.

This period, described by Kerr (1990, 6) as an acceleration of the process of divergency as a consequence of intensification of international military and economic competition, can be seen from the point of view of internationalization as a period in which the international dimension of higher education moved from the incidental and individual into organized activities, projects, and programs, based mainly on political rationales and driven more by national governments than by higher education itself. Kerr (1994b) notes that "it has been to the advantage of nation-states to support the expansion of higher education and its internationalization within and beyond their borders" (p. 20).

The Cold War played a central role in the development of internationalization in this period, in particular in the United States and the Soviet Union, but also elsewhere. The Cold War and the related increases in military expenditures provided opportunities to American higher education for research grants, fellowships, and new fields of study. Area studies, for instance, received a big push as a result of the Cold War, even though, as Wallerstein (1997) says, they did not always deliver the results the military had hoped.

THE INTERNATIONAL DIMENSION OF HIGHER EDUCATION AFTER THE COLD WAR

In the 1980s, the third phase in Guy Neave's analysis (1982–1991) and the period of partial reconvergence according to Kerr (1994a), the global context changed. The strengthening of the European Community and the rise of Japan as an economic world power challenged not only the political and economic dominance of the United States but also its dominance in research and teaching. Both Japan and the European Community invested in research and development (R&D) programs to compete with the United States. The European Community invested in programs of cooperation for R&D between the member states, with specific reference to the technological race with Japan and the United States. Following the example of countries such as Germany and Sweden, the European Commission decided to expand its role to the promotion of international cooperation in curriculum development, mobility of students, and faculty and university–industry networks.

The collapse of communism at the end of the 1980s and the beginning of the 1990s changed the map even further. The countervailing political and military superpower, the USSR, fell apart at a time when the United States was being increasingly threatened as the economic superpower by Japan and the European Union.

The end of the Cold War according to Shaw (1994) created an atmosphere of global anarchy, a contradictory context of growing nationalism based on the exclusivity of ethnic groups, in itself the result of "disintegration of nation-states and national societies," and the development of a global culture and society, a "global complex of social relations," both at the level of systems as in the value sense. This global society can be best understood

as a diverse social universe in which the unifying forces of modern production, markets, communications and cultural and political modernization interact with many global, regional, national and local segmentations and differentiations. Global society should be understood not as a social system but as a field of social relations in which many specific systems have formed some of them genuinely global, others incipiently so, and others still restricted to national and local contexts. (p. 19)

The global environment moved from one dominated by the superpowers to one characterized by Jonathan Friedman (1994) as "ethnicization and cultural pluralization of a dehegemonizing, dehomogenizing world incapable of a formerly enforced politics of assimilation or cultural hierarchy" (p. 100). This is a development that is expressed in the stronger emphasis on globalization of economics, social and political relations, and knowledge, but at the same time by tendencies toward ethnic conflicts and nationalism (most clearly at present in the former USSR and former Yugoslavia; or broader, the clash of civilizations, as Huntington, 1996, predicts), and isolation, a danger in the present United States. The last is evident, for example, in a reduction in international education, as Altbach and de Wit (1995) describe:

For a half century after World War II, American higher education has been the undisputed leader in higher education internationally. Cold War competition, a booming US economy, and rapidly expanding student population were contributing factors. American higher education remains very strong, but it is losing its competitive edge in the international marketplace. The slide has begun, and growing insularity will mean that the United States will fall behind its competitors. (p. 10)

This context is different from that prevailing after World War II and in the period from 1970 to 1980. The immediate postwar period was strongly influenced by the war and had a strong idealistic connotation of peace and mutual understanding. The second period, as mentioned, focused more on the developing countries, with North–North cooperation marginalized to a small sector within diplomatic relations. The third period is characterized by an emphasis on economic arguments to promote international cooperation and exchange in higher education. Richard Lyman (1995) describes this for the United States: "For too long, international education, especially exchange and study abroad programs, were justified by a vague sense that such studies were the path to mutual understanding and world peace, [but] today, internationalizing education in the US is proposed as a way to help restore our economic competitiveness in the world" (p. 4). Harari (1992, 57) also stresses the growing importance of the argument of economic competitiveness. Callan and de Wit (1995) have stated that the same applies for the arguments used by the European Commission for their programs to promote cooperation and exchange within the European Union and with the rest of the world. Van der Wende (1997a) also mentions a change in rationale from political to economic. Neave (1992a, 21) uses terms such as the "market ethic" and the "cash nexus" for this period.

A more analytical approach to the internationalization of higher education is needed, however, than simply assuming that the internationalization of higher education is now based only on money. As we have seen, Kerr analyses this development as a partial reconvergence, a hybrid situation of the "cosmopolitan-nation-state university." This might be considered an over-nostalgic approach. The end of the Cold War, the deepening of European integration, and the globalization of our societies started a process of strategic development of the international dimension of higher education. Although one could disagree with Callan's (2000) emphasis on the role of analysts in this process, her description of the change between the 1980s and 1990s is correct: "A dominant concern through the 1990s has been with internationalization as a process of strategic transformation of institutions. This concern makes a clear departure from earlier, piecemeal and limited, concerns with the management of student mobility. . . . 'Striving for strategy' has become a recurrent motif in the construction of internationalization, both descriptively and prescriptively" (p. 17).

Teichler (1999) argues that this period is one of substantial qualitative changes, referred to as the "three quantum leaps" in the internationalization of higher education. The first one is the leap from "a predominantly 'vertical' pattern of co-operation and mobility, towards the dominance of international relationships on equal terms." That leap coincides with the "piecemeal and limited" focus on internationalization as described by Callan. The second leap is "from casuistic action towards systematic policies of internationalisation." That leap refers to the emergence of a strategic perspective on internationalization, as mentioned by Callan. The third one is "from a disconnection of specific international activities on the one hand, and (on the other) internationalisation of the core activities, towards an integrated internationalisation of higher education" (pp. 9–10). This analysis is the more appropriate view of the developments in this period, where the third leap can be seen as the millennium leap, the leap we are just starting at the beginning of the twenty-first century. The leap in which internationalization as a strategic issue moves into an integrated part of the overall strategy of institutions of higher education. One should note, however, that the observations made by Callan and Teichler are based on the European context, while in the United States, as will be shown later, one can question such development of strategic analysis and implementation of internationalization.

CONCLUSION

From this description of the historical development of the international dimension of higher education, it becomes obvious that changes in the external and internal environments of higher education over the centuries have been extremely influential on the way in which this international dimension has manifested itself.

One can say that until the twentieth century this dimension was rather incidental and individual: the wandering scholar and student, the Grand Tour, the student flows from South to North. The export of higher education models in the eighteenth and nineteenth centuries, seen by some as an important manifestation of the internationalization of higher education, is difficult to understand as such and is better seen as academic colonialism. The notion of knowledge as universal applied mainly to research and it did not presuppose action; on the contrary, it assumed no need of action. Perhaps Davies's (1995, 4) description of the international character of universities as a "devolved way" is the appropriate expression.

Before World War II and immediately afterward, these incidents became more structured into activities, projects, and programs, mainly in the United States and only marginally in Europe (the Soviet Union, Germany, France, the United Kingdom). National scholarship programs for students and staff (Fulbright); institutional study abroad programs (the American junior year abroad); the development of area studies, international studies, and foreign language training (NDEA, HEA, Title VI); scientific and cultural agreements between countries; and the creation of national agencies (IIE, DAAD, and British Council) were manifestations of more organized activity-based approaches to internationalization, and in the literature are collectively referred to as "international education." They were driven in particular by the Cold War.

A second manifestation appearing in the 1960s was technical assistance and development cooperation, an area that in some countries, such as Australia, Canada, and The Netherlands, until the 1980s became the most dominant international program and is also strongly present elsewhere. In addition, though less organized, the international flow of students, mainly from South to North, continued and even expanded.

Major changes in internationalization took place in the 1980s. The move from aid to trade in Australia and the United Kingdom; the development of the European programs for research and development (the Framework programs and their predecessors) and for education (SOCRATES, LEONARDO, and their predecessors); the development of transnational education; and the presence of internationalization in mission statements, policy documents, and strategic plans of institutions of higher education were clear manifestations of these changes.

Globalization and the related knowledge society based on technological developments, as well as the end of the Cold War and the creation of regional structures (in particular the EU), influenced these changes. The need for an organized response by higher education to these external developments resulted in an internationalization strategy that was based on more explicit choices (rationales) and a more integrated strategy (process approach). It was only in the 1980s that the internationalization of higher education became a strategic process. Competitiveness in the international market became a key rationale. Incidents, isolated activities, projects, and programs were still present, both at the national and institutional level, but internationalization as a strategic process became more central in higher education institutions.[4] This relates to the first two quantum leaps identified by Teichler (1999).

However, this situation is one of transition, the beginning of a great transformation, according to Kerr (1994b, 9). The globalization of our societies and markets and its impact on higher education and the new knowledge society based on information technology will change higher education profoundly and will also change the nature of internationalization of higher education. Will that change be, as Kerr is convinced, "in the direction of the supremacy of the pure model of academic life consistent with reasonable guidance by the nation-state [and] a universal reconvergence where universities best serve their nations by serving the world of learning" (p. 26)? That would be too simplistic and naïve a conclusion. Internationalization will take place in the context of globalization processes, processes that, as Scott states, "cannot simply be seen as reiteration of the old internationalism, still dysfunctionally dominated by the West (or, at any rate, the developed world) but are now intensified by the new information (and knowledge) technologies" (Scott 1998, 124). It would be better to speak of a transition to an integrated internationalization of higher education; that is, a response of higher education to globalization and regionalization (see Chapter 8).

NOTES

1. For the influence of Western ideas on Chinese higher education and the role of returned foreign-educated students on Chinese higher education, see Yugui Guo (1998).

2. Although reference is made to the export of educational systems as the dominant international dimension during the expansion of European colonialism, it is also important to note the impact colonialism has had on the academic curriculum in

European higher education, in particular the study of foreign languages, anthropology, and geography, but also in other disciplines such as agricultural science, medicine, law, and economics. This impact can still be seen in the curriculum and, as will be indicated later, has had different implications in Europe for the development of area studies as compared to the United States, where area studies are a more recent phenomenon, a consequence of the role of the United States as a superpower during World War II and the Cold War.

3. The Netherlands Commission for International Academic Relations is another example of this period.

4. See also Davies (1995, 4–5) who links the need for institutional strategies for internationalization to these external changes.

Chapter 2

The International Dimension of Higher Education in the United States of America

The development of the international dimension of higher education in the United States of America will be described in order to clarify the specific characteristics of the international dimensions in that country when compared to Europe, examined in Chapter 3. As explained, in the period between the two world wars, as well as after World War II and during the Cold War, the United States determined to a large extent the development and characteristics of the international dimension of higher education, under the umbrella term of "international education." After the Cold War, Europe and to a certain extent also Australia and Canada have taken over the leading role in developing internationalization strategies for higher education.

The system of higher education in the United States includes community colleges, four-year colleges, and (research) universities. There are both state (including land-grant colleges), religiously affiliated, and private universities. There are over 3,500 institutions of higher education. The Carnegie Classification is the most commonly accepted system for classifying the heterogeneous higher education system of the United States. "One can hardly call it a system. No central body at the national level controls or even coordinates higher education in the United States, even with respect to international programs and activities," as Thullen and colleagues (1997, 3) remark. One has to keep in mind the specific, heterogeneous character of American higher education when analyzing the international dimension of its higher education in comparison with Europe, itself, as we will see, a far from homogeneous system. In addition, the fact that by constitution the government's role is limited in educational policy but extensive in foreign affairs, defense, trade, and commerce suggests that federal policy on international education will be more linked to these areas than to education itself.[1] That which Ulrich Littman (1996) describes for exchange in Germany and the United States is true for the whole of Europe: "American 'educational exchange' and German 'akademische austausch' reflect differences in what might be expected from mobility, and moreover reflect basic differences in the structures of higher education" (p. 16).

HISTORICAL ASPECTS OF THE INTERNATIONAL DIMENSION OF AMERICAN HIGHER EDUCATION

Although it will become clear that international education in the United States already existed at the end of World War I, after World War II it moved to a more structured level. Mestenhauser (1998b, 10–12) identifies three phases of international education since the late 1940s. The first phase, which he calls "euphoria," lasted from 1946 to the Vietnam War and the oil crisis in the 1960s and 1970s; the second, termed "darkening clouds," ran from the fiasco of the International Education Act of 1966 to the end of the 1970s; and the third, "defense through the associations," began in the early 1980s with a threat of enormous budget cuts to international education programs by the Reagan administration. At the end of the 1990s there were signs of a new phase, in which the internationalization of higher education according to some enters in a new "euphoria."

Before the Twentieth Century: Export of European Models and Individual Mobility to Europe

Higher education in the United States, often regarded today as the dominant model in international developments of higher education, was based on European influences and continued to reflect these for a long time. Oxford and Cambridge were the models for the first colleges established in the colony. Later, with the creation of Johns Hopkins University, the German model of research university was also imported. In addition to these external influences, in 1862 "land grant colleges" (now universities) were established to provide agricultural and applied engineering training for America's development, and to give access to higher education to other than the elite. As a side effect, many faculty and students sojourned to the universities in Europe, on which these institutions were modeled, to pursue further studies.

During colonial times there was an active movement of the children of rich planters to Europe, in particular the United Kingdom, for studies such as medicine and law. But as Halpern (1969) notes, opposition developed after the revolution: "Jefferson and Webster opposed sending young Americans to study abroad because they shared a common distrust of European ways and because they feared that American students would become denationalized" (p. 17). Although many American scholars and educators still went to Europe in the nineteenth century for further study and insight, these same people in their later careers became hostile to study abroad, in particular by undergraduate students.

Halpern (1969) provides several examples of political and educational leaders in the United States speaking out against foreign study. An example is Charles W. Eliot, written in 1873:

Prolonged residence abroad in youth, before the mental fibre is solidified and the mind has taken its tone, has a tendency to enfeeble the love of country, and to impair the foundations of public spirit in the individual citizen. This pernicious influence is indefinable, but none the less real. In a strong nation, the education of the young is indigenous and national. It is a sign of immaturity or decrepitude when a nation has to import its teachers, or send abroad its scholars. (p. 24)

According to Halpern, this attitude can be explained by a strong desire to break with the educational and cultural dependence on Europe (p. 25).

Nonetheless, American faculty and students continued to flow to Europe throughout the nineteenth century. Around the turn of the century one can see a shift. On the one hand, the emergence of American graduate schools presented American students with alternatives to study abroad at home. On the other hand, for the first time foreign students came in large numbers to the United States. "Foreigners, particularly non-Europeans, came to view America much as America viewed Germany in the nineteenth century" (Halpern 1969, 26–27). Halpern speaks of a new era in the history of travel for educational purposes.

The First Half of the Twentieth Century: Peace and Mutual Understanding

During the late nineteenth century, academic mobility from and to the United States became a regular phenomenon, but without a formal and institutional structure. This changed when private organizations, foundations, and universities began to recognize the educational value of study abroad. In 1890 the American Association of University Women created the first fellowship to enable a college professor to pursue research abroad. In 1902 the Rhodes Scholarships were founded to promote understanding between English-speaking people. In 1905 the American Academy in Rome established research fellowships for study in Italy, and in 1911 the Kahn Foundation started to offer fellowships for secondary school teachers to travel abroad.

Another organization that dates from this period is the American–Scandinavian Foundation (1910). In 1911 the Committee on Friendly Relations Among Foreign Students was established with the objective of counseling foreign students and gathering statistics on foreign students in the United States. Between 1905 and 1912, Harvard, Columbia, Chicago, and Wisconsin universities established exchange agreements with German and French universities (Halpern 1969, 27–28).

One example of international exchange and cooperation at the start of the twentieth century was the use by the Chinese government of $12 million in indemnity funds, owing to the massacre of Americans during the Boxer Rebellion, to send selected scholars to the United States for further training. A second example was the creation of the Belgian–American Educational Foundation in 1920, the result of the liquidation of World War I relief funds in Belgium. Thanks to this foundation, over 700 Belgian and American students were exchanged between the two countries.[2] These two examples from before World War II can be compared to the first and most known example of internationalization from after World War II, the Fulbright Program, in that its funds similarly did not come from the national budget, but from relief sources. However, there were also more regular bilateral exchanges between countries; for instance, with Germany via the DAAD and the IIE.[3]

Institutions were less active than foundations. Before World War II, it was mainly women's colleges that were involved in setting up junior year abroad programs in Europe: Marymount College in 1924 (Paris), Smith College in 1925 (Paris) and 1931 (Florence), Rosary College in 1925 (Fribourg).[4] Taylor (1977, 1518) argues that this arose because women needed more chaperoning when studying abroad, and that while female students went abroad for cultural enrichment, the men remained in the United States to work on their careers.

As Goodwin and Nacht (1991) make clear, what happened with exchange and cooperation also applies to the curriculum:

The demonstrated unpreparedness of the United States to comprehend the process of which it was part, both during World War I and at the Peace Conference afterward, suggested to many young Americans the need both to understand other countries better and to reflect on different ways to arrange relations among states. The study of international relations increased in the United States between the wars, with practitioners lodged both in universities and in nongovernmental research institutions like the Council on Foreign Relations, the Carnegie Endowment for International Peace, and the Brookings Institution. (p. 3)

A strong rationale for the internationalization of higher education has traditionally been the promotion of peace and mutual understanding. According to Halpern (1969, 28–29), this had its roots in the growth of the American peace movement after 1900.

The dark cloud of the upcoming World War I made this rationale for study abroad even more urgent. At the same time, the war itself provided, according to Halpern (1969, 29), a new impetus to study abroad. American soldiers serving in Europe on the one hand and the immigration of Europeans to the United States on the other acted as a catalyst. Although Halpern (pp. 88–89) calls the strong belief between the two world wars that people, simply by educating themselves, would develop views conducive to promoting peace and understanding "naive optimism" and "utopian," resulting from the fear of World War I and the hope inspired by the League of Nations, after World War II this optimism continued to be a driving rationale for international education.

In Europe, as we will see, similar trends can be observed, but in Europe the pursuit of peace and mutual understanding has influenced the international dimension of higher education less and for a shorter period than in the United States.[5]

In the United States this argument continued to be used during the Cold War, both by politicians and academics. In 1994, Senator William Fulbright, consistent with his views during his entire career and with the views expressed by many other American politicians and educators, called "the most important objective of transnational education the civilising and humanising of relations between nations in ways that are within the limits of human capacity." He spoke of educational exchange as, "from the standpoint of future world peace and order, probably the most important and potentially rewarding of our foreign policy activities" (p. 9).

Chambers (1950) assumes that "if men of good will in all corners of the world can come to know more of each other at first hand on an increasing scale, likelihood of wars will be lessened" (p. 8), though he also makes reference to academics being critical to these sentiments, citing an anonymous scholar: "Education for international understanding is a subject on which woolliness has positively run riot during the last thirty years" (p. 9). There are few fields other then this, the scholar added, "on which it has been possible to talk more nonsense and to get away with it in a smokescreen of sentimentalism" (p. 9). Gayner (1996) observes on the Fulbright Program that "it requires a leap of faith to conclude that the Fulbright program will create a more peaceful globe" (p. 7). However, even among academics this optimist view is still present, as the title of an essay by the former director of the Education Abroad Program of the University of California, William H. Allaway (1994), shows: "Peace: The Real Power of Educational Exchange."

Therefore, the first two decades of the twentieth century show a growth of mobility, in particular to the United States; more attention from private organizations and foundations for study abroad; and the start of institutional exchange and study abroad programs. Peace and mutual understanding became a driving rationale. What is striking in all this is the nearly exclusive focus on Europe.

The foundation of the Institute of International Education in 1919 was supposed to give the nation a center to promote and coordinate international education. The original idea came from Professor Stephen Pierce Duggan of the School of Education at the College of the City of New York (CCNY), who was joined by the president of Columbia University, Nicholas Murray Butler, and former U.S. secretary of state and chairman of the Carnegie Endowment, Elihu Root. Together they founded the IIE on February 1, 1919, in New York, with a grant of $30,000. Duggan became its first director, a post he held for twenty-seven years.

The IIE's first activities were also directed to Europe. After the end of World War I it soon became clear that exchanges with Europe were not yet possible, given the devastating situation in Europe. However, between 1920 and 1923, forty-four professors were supported financially with Carnegie grants to spend their sabbatical leaves teaching abroad, mainly in Europe but also elsewhere; for instance, Japan. In addition, the IIE began to promote exchanges and visits of faculty, and study abroad and exchanges for students. Foundations such as the Rockefeller Foundation also provided scholarships for foreign academics to visit the United States.[6]

Funding, though, was a problem. Where in Europe institutions such as the IIE and its activities would have been created or at least supported by national governments, in the United States both the creation and the financial support relied on private funding by foundations and sponsors. That this has not always been easy is demonstrated by Duggan's failure in the 1920s to get a Foreign Student's Revolving Scholarship Fund off the ground. He had more success with fellowships for the IIE's junior year abroad program in that period (Halpern 1969, 55–56).

In the 1930s the political clouds of Nazism forced American higher education and the IIE to change their plans. Europe became mainly a place from which to rescue refugee scholars. Institutions such as the New School of Social Research in New York were shaped by this influx of refugee scholars who had been helped to escape.[7]

The international situation forced American higher education to look for other regions, closer to home, for international cooperation and exchange: Latin America. The Convention for the Promotion of Inter-American Cultural Relations established opportunities for educational exchanges. American business interests, but in particular the anti-American propaganda of the Axis powers in Latin America (including the offering of fellowships to Latin Americans for study in Germany and Italy), created a public–private partnership in stimulating cultural relations between the United States and Latin America (IIE 1994b, 7–9). During the war the State Department asked the IIE to administer an exchange program for scholarships to more than 1,000 Latin American students between 1941 and 1943. The involvement of the U.S. government in cultural and educational diplomacy thus dates from the 1930s, in response to external threats. As Rupp (1999) states, "Intellectual imperialism, the imperialism of ideas, was at that moment just as serious a threat to the security and defense of the hemisphere as the possibility of a military invasion" (p. 58).

After World War II: Foreign Policy and National Security

World War II, as Goodwin and Nacht (1991) observe, added far more to the international experience of American scholars than its predecessor. In military service, but also in intelligence, planning, and, after the war, occupation and recovery, they traveled not only to Europe, but also to Asia and the Middle East. "For the first time many of these scholars were faced squarely with the necessity to understand the languages and cultures of both friend and foe and to comprehend the nature of past and potential global systems" (p. 3). Area studies (for instance, Japan Studies) also had a new impetus as a result of the war, because knowledge of the enemy and the countries where Americans had to fight became important.

While the early development of international education between the two wars was strongly driven by private initiative and by the rationale of peace and understanding, as well as being focused on Europe, World War II caused a radical change. Although peace and mutual understanding continued to be a driving rationale in theory, national security and foreign policy were the real forces behind its expansion and with it came government funding and regulations. In addition, although Europe continued to be an important point of orientation, the world outside the United States became broader than the traditional orientation on the European continent. With the new responsibilities of the United States in this new world order, "It was," as Goodwin and Nacht (1991) note, "no longer a luxury, but a necessity, to travel the globe to master all of its intricacies" (p. 4). American higher education as a whole was transformed by the war even more from periphery into center than had already been the case in the previous decades of the twentieth century.

Most clearly identified with the immediate postwar period and federal government involvement in international education was the creation of the Fulbright Program in 1946, "a trailblazer and catalyst" (Gayner 1996, 6) for academic exchanges within the United States but also beyond. The program's principal goals were, in the words of Senator Fulbright at the celebration of its fortieth anniversary, "To increase mutual understanding between the people of the United States and the people of other countries by means of educational and cultural exchange . . . and thus to assist in the development of friendly, sympathetic, and peaceful relations between the United States and the other countries of the world" (quoted in Gayner 1996, 1). In this quote the prewar idealism of peace and mutual understanding and the postwar foreign policy and national security rationales are brought together. However, the emphasis came to be placed more on the second rationale than the first. As Rupp (1999) writes,

After WWII, American leaders primarily directed US foreign policy towards forming a strong and stable Atlantic Alliance with Europe. In that sense, the Fulbright Program was to legitimize America's leading role in this alliance. Americans found among Europe's public elite—and among leftist intellectuals in particular "much misunderstanding and an appalling lack of knowledge and vision" about their country; in Europe, on the other hand, the question was raised as to whether the US would be capable of leading the Free World, a situation from which the Soviet Union might easily profit. European countries needed 're-orientation'. Germany and Japan . . . needed 're-education'. A better understanding of America had to be formed. (p. 59)

The administration of the Fulbright Program was put in the hands of the IIE, and as both Halpern (1969) and Rupp (1997, 207) describe, this decision was part of a debate on how strong the relationship should be between foreign policy and exchanges, or to be more precise, how strict the division between information services and educational and cultural exchanges should be within cultural diplomacy.

The Sargeant Report of 1946, "United States Program for the Exchange of Students and Industrial Trainees," according to Halpern (1996), recommended the assignment of the IIE as the agency to administer the placement of foreign students. But there were also references to the effect that student exchanges should implement U.S. foreign policy, and this generated concern in the IIE and in the sector of higher education. Laurence Duggan, who had succeeded his father as director of the IIE in 1946, wrote to Assistant Secretary of State William Benton on December 2, 1946, that granting fellowships to foreign students "is not and must not be a means whereby our Government hopes to influence foreign students in the United States in favor of particular policies and programs" (quoted in Halpern 1969, 189). In the end the IIE accepted the administration of the Fulbright Program and other government-sponsored programs, but on condition that this would be done free of government control and political motivation (p. 204). A Board of Foreign Scholarships would guarantee this. Halpern notes that, nonetheless, the IIE, by accepting the administration, "relinquished sufficient autonomy to make it vulnerable to governmental pressures" (p. 205).

Halpern's (1969) main argument is that the board is appointed by the government and has the final say over the program, whereas the IIE only administers the program. His second argument is the acceptance by the IIE of contracts with the U.S. Army. However, as he has to acknowledge, the board has always been closer to the IIE than to the government, even in the 1950s, when President Truman started his "Campaign of Truth" against the Communist threat of the Soviet Union and China and wanted to bring the program under governmental control. Originally, the board endorsed the statement by the State Department that the Information and Educational Exchange Program, since its establishment in 1953, had become coordinated by the U.S. Information Agency (USIA) and was "an arm of American foreign policy" (p. 206). However, later, under pressure from the higher education sector, the board distanced itself from this position. The Council on Student Travel (CST) also managed to make the State Department back down in 1958, with support from the academic community, when the State Department tried to block the creation of a Leningrad study program and other CST activities in the Soviet Union.[8]

Although Halpern (1969, 210–211) is right in his conclusion that by accepting the responsibility for government sponsored programs during and after World War II, the IIE moved away from its original role of an autonomous, private organization devoted to promoting academic exchange, he overstates the threats it posed to the original ideals of the organization.

The Impetus of the Cold War

However, as Holzner and Greenwood (1995) observe, "The arenas of defense and foreign policy have played an important role on several occasions" (p. 38) in international education, in particular during the Cold War. That period has influenced international education in the United States perhaps more than any other period. The National Defense Education Act (NDEA) of 1958, according to Vestal (1994), was a direct reaction to the launch the year before of Sputnik I by the Soviet Union and an effort by the United States to regain international leadership.

Internationalization of the curriculum was stimulated by the federal government by way of Title VI of the Higher Education Act of 1960. Title VI helped to develop multidisciplinary area study and foreign language centers, as well as programs for international studies and international affairs. As Goodwin and Nacht (1991) state, the reason for the involvement of the federal government was based on the United States's newfound role as "leader of the free world."

Area studies received a further big push as a result of the Cold War, in particular via the National Defense Education Act and the linked Title VI of the Higher Education Act, even though, as Wallerstein (1997) says, it did not always deliver the results the military had hoped. Wallerstein refers to this push of area studies for geopolitical reasons as a top-down enterprise, while other interdisciplinary studies, such as ethnic studies and women studies, although closely linked to area studies, were a bottom-up response. Area studies in Europe lacked this outside impulse. They emerged earlier in the context of colonialization and were developed further in a more academic than political setting. Both Wallerstein and Bender (1997) emphasize the political motivations for the development of area studies during the postwar and Cold War period and its strong orientation on Soviet and Chinese studies for that reason. At the same time, they mention a scholarly and intellectual agenda for the development of area studies and the role of foundations in funding, alongside foreign affairs and defense funding.

Foreign development assistance in the United States finds its rationale in President Truman's inaugural address of 1949, where he introduced his four-points policy for peace and freedom in the world, of which the fourth point became the basis for technical assistance programs, also in education (Smuckler 1999). Administered since 1961 by USAID, technical assistance programs, as Holzner and Greenwood (1995) remark, also came to be seen "almost exclusively in the light of Cold War conceptions of the national interest" (p. 39).

The failure of the International Education Act (IEA) of 1966 makes this perhaps even more clear than the implementation of the NDEA. The IEA was a major attempt by the government to stimulate international education. It was proposed by President Johnson and passed Congress, but was never funded by the new Congress elected shortly after it was passed. The Vietnam War and internal tensions in American society during that period meant that attention to international education and the IEA drifted away. As Vestal (1994) observes, "Federal funding for international education has been passed most successfully when brigaded with practical and strategic concerns: national defense (NDEA); public diplomacy . . . ; and intelligence (NSEA). . . . Funding for IEA-like programs then will depend upon the recognition of policy makers of the importance and relevance of international education to the national interest of the United States" (pp. 32–33). The case for international education on its own was clearly not strong enough and the relevance of the IEA for the national interest not manifest enough to make the act work. At the same time, both Vestal and Holzner and Greenwood (1995, 40) observe that the IEA did not get enough support from the academic community either. The failure of the IEA was the start of a period, lasting until the beginning of the 1980s, in which both the federal government and foundations shifted their attention from international education to domestic issues.

In summary, the post–World War II period and the Cold War—with an interval between 1965 and 1980 in which support to international education was reduced as a consequence of the Vietnam War and a related focus on national issues—drove the American government, for reasons of defense, public diplomacy, and security, to stimulate international exchange and cooperation. Even after the end of the Cold War, as the NSEA illustrates, these continued to be the main rationales for federal support.

The 1980s: Competitiveness

In the 1980s, at the same time as the European Union was launching its programs for research and education and the collapse of the Communist Bloc had begun, a revival in federal support can be observed. After the end of the Cold War the United States had found it exceedingly difficult to define its "national interest," offering at the same time new strategic opportunities (Rice 2000). The National Security Education Act (NSEA) of 1991 was a response to the collapse of the Soviet Union and the end of the Cold War, and a mechanism for maintaining its now less-disputed international leadership.[9] The program was, as with the NDEA, funded from the defense budget, which, in 1991, caused concern among institutions of higher education, who feared for the safety of their students and potential damage to individual and institutional relations with institutions and governments in those countries if sponsorship and supervision came from the Department of Defense and national security budgets (Holzner and Greewood 1995, 45). The fact that the head of the Central Intelligence Agency (CIA) had a seat on the board of the program was seen as an indication. The obligation for participants to perform a period of national service on their return was seen by the critics of the program as a recruiting device for the CIA. A "school of spies" and "sending students with a CIA-tag on their backs" were phrases used by these critics. But those concerns gradually faded away once the programs were implemented. Only in certain area studies associations (Africa studies, Middle East studies) is there still opposition to the program. Indeed, the national service obligation is seen by students these days as one of the more attractive aspects of the program (Desruisseaux 2000b). So, foreign policy and national security continue to be a factor, but are less dominant than in the past.

In the new area of globalization, the argument of "competitiveness" enters the international education vocabulary of the federal government, still closely linked to that of foreign policy and national security.

The creation of the Centers for International Business Education and Research under Part B of Title VI of the Higher Education Act is an illustration that "national interest came to be supplemented (but certainly not replaced) by the competitiveness paradigm" (Holzner and Greenwood 1995, 40). As an internal document of the Education Abroad Program of the University of California (1995) states, "With the demise of the Soviet Empire, definitions of national interest shifted from such goals as influencing the 'non-aligned' and studying 'the enemy' to learning how to compete and prosper in a far-flung global economy" (p. 6). Holzner (1994) states that "no longer only acquainting young people with the ways of foreign cultures" (p. 5), but also demands for high competence in a more competitive global market place became dominant. Mestenhauser (2000, 34) also refers to the change of rationale from international understanding and avoiding wars and conflicts to global competitiveness in American international education.

A memorandum for the heads of executive departments and agencies on "International Education Policy" by President Clinton, dated April 19, 2000 (White House 2000), underlines this supplementarity but also the shift in priority:

To continue to compete successfully in the global economy and to maintain our role as a world leader, the United States needs to ensure that its citizens develop a broad understanding of the world, proficiency in other languages, and knowledge of other cultures. America's leadership also depends on building ties with those who will guide the political, cultural, and economic development of their countries in the future. A coherent and coordinated international education strategy will help us meet the twin challenges of preparing our citizens for a global environment while continuing to attract and educate future leaders from abroad.

The memorandum also makes reference to the fact that the nearly 500,000 international students in the United States contribute some $9 billion annually to its economy, and recommends action for coordinated marketing and recruitment, the first time that this issue has been presented in economic instead of political terms.

Only time will tell if this memorandum will follow the same path as the IEA, or if it will get the strong political and financial commitment of the NDEA and NSEA. The absence of a strong foreign enemy and the pressure to focus on domestic issues are likely to receive more weight in the political arena than the argument of economic competition in the global economy.

EU–U.S. Cooperation

A specific aspect of the new emphasis on competitiveness in international education in the United States can be found in the pursuit of linkages with the European Union. Both at the federal level and the level of academic institutions, the fear of a "Fortress Europe" as a result of inner European cooperation and exchange was enormous. The European mobility schemes, in particular ERASMUS, were considered as a seclusive attempt to strengthen the Union's competitive edge. For that reason, President George Bush convinced the president of the European Commission, Jacques Delors, of the need for transatlantic cooperation between the EC and the United States, supplementary to the bilateral links of member states of the EU with the United States.

On November 22, 1990, the EU, its member states, and the United States agreed on a Transatlantic Declaration on EU/US Relations, which included cooperation in the field of higher education. The activities in the field of higher and vocational training are part of the New Transatlantic Agenda, launched at the Madrid Summit in 1995 to give new focus and direction to the economic and political cooperation between the EU and the United States, and which resulted from the contact between Bush and Delors. The New Transatlantic Agenda sets four main goals:

- promoting peace, development, and democracy.
- responding to global challenges by cooperation.
- contributing to the expansion of world trade and closer economic ties.
- building bridges across the Atlantic: people-to-people links (Davidson and Andrews 1998).

The declaration was followed by a pilot program in 1993–1994 based on an agreement in principle signed in Washington on May 20, 1993. The creation of an exploratory-phase pilot program, instead of immediately starting with a formal scheme, was caused by political delays on both sides of the Atlantic. In the United States, budgetary debates frustrated its start. Within the EU, discussions on subsidiarity and complementarity of the program caused delays (Haug 1998, 28).

The objectives of the EU/U.S. programs are as follows:

- to promote mutual understanding between the peoples of the EU and the United States, including broader knowledge of their languages, cultures, and institutions.
- to improve the quality of human resource development.
- to improve the quality of transatlantic student mobility, including the promotion of mutual understanding, recognition, and portability of academic credits.
- to encourage exchange of expertise in new development in higher education and vocational training.
- to form or enhance partnerships among higher education, vocational education or training institutions, professional associations, public authorities, business, and other associations as appropriate.
- to introduce an added-value dimension to transatlantic cooperation which complements bilateral cooperation between Union member states and states of the United States, as well as other programs and initiatives (Englesson 1995).

In the programs, the emphasis is on the development of joint curricula, recognition of credits and diplomas, and mobility of students, teachers, and administrators. In addition, the European Commission stimulated the development of European integration studies by funding, as of 1998, ten European Union Centers in the United States, intended to provide a framework for nurturing and developing existing knowledge of the EU and the transatlantic relationship in the United States. The main mechanisms to develop these activities are "joint consortia projects," including a minimum of three partners on each side of the Atlantic. The United States and the EU, in addition to existing bilateral agreements with member states, also include as part of the EU–U.S. scheme a small number of Fulbright fellowships for the study of EU–U.S. relations (two research and teaching awards for EU academics, and advanced doctoral study and postdoctoral research grants for U.S. citizens to study in the EU).

Regional Cooperation in NAFTA

A second political initiative was the inclusion of trilateral cooperation in higher education in the NAFTA treaty of 1994 between Canada, Mexico, and the United States of America. This regional higher education cooperation was discussed in two preparatory conferences, on September 12–15, 1992, in Wingspread, Wisconsin, and September 10–13, 1993, in Vancouver, British Columbia.

The Wingspread conference set the following objectives:

- Develop a North American dimension in higher education.
- Encourage an exchange of information on themes of mutual interest.
- Promote collaboration among institutions of higher education.
- Facilitate student and faculty mobility.
- Promote the strengthening of relations between higher education institutions and the public and private sectors in areas linked to the quality of higher education.
- Use the potential of the new technologies of communication and information to help implement these objectives.

The Vancouver conference proposed nine actions: the creation of a North American Network of Distance Education and Research; the introduction of a trilateral mechanism for education and business on mobility, transfers, and professional certification; the enhancement of relations between teachers and administrators; the establishment of an electronic data bank; the development of a trilateral program of exchange, research, and training for students; the founding of a North American Corporate Higher Education Association; the elaboration of a plan for distance graduate training; and the increase of financial support by agencies and foundations.

The plans faced several obstacles, however, as became clear at the third and last trilateral meeting, on April 28–30, 1996, in Guadalajara. Some of the most important challenges mentioned were promoting collaboration in spite of diminishing public resources, widening participation to involve more sectors, supporting specific partnership projects rather than "general frames of reference," including academic collaboration in North American foreign policy, establishing academic networks of excellence, and maintaining government support as facilitator and provider of funds without bureaucratic structures (Crespo 2000, 24–25; see also Barrow 2000).

These challenges, according to Altbach (1994), are a result of the variations and inequalities in educational, cultural, and technological power among the three countries; the concern about U.S. dominance of the other two partners; the ignorance in the United States on the cultures of the two other countries; and the lack of interest of American academics, in particular, in links with colleagues in the two other countries. If one compares this to the regional cooperation in the European Union (Chapter 3), the variations and inequalities there, although certainly present, are not as large as in the NAFTA case. In combination with the substantially lower amount of public funding for the cooperation, the impact is less than in the EU case. Although both Crespo (2000), Barrow (2000), and León García, Matthews, and Smith (2000) are generally positive about the development of academic linkages as a result of NAFTA, they stress the limitations. Crespo (2000, 34) mentions the forced focus on trilateral links and the lack of funding as the main reasons; Barrow (2000, 118) notes the lack of support from nongovernmental associations and organizations to supplement the limited role of the three governments. León García, Matthews, and Smith (2000, 47–51) mention funding, language, the different needs in the three countries, migration and visa problems, and sustainability as the major problems. Barrow's argument on nongovernment funding is more in line with the tradition of American higher education than the arguments of Crespo and León García, Matthews, and Smith who stress the technical obstacles more. But the experiences in the EU indicate that only substantial financial support at the government level and a facilitating government role in overcoming obstacles can make the difference between marginal projects and programs and the emergence of an open education space.

OTHER STAKEHOLDERS IN INTERNATIONAL EDUCATION

Until now attention has been given mainly to the role of the national government and agencies such as the IIE that administer programs for the federal government. But these were and are not the only bodies active in international education. In addition, governments of several states, such as Massachusetts, Oregon, Pennsylvania, Texas, and Virginia; philanthropic foundations, such as the Carnegie Corporation, Ford Foundation, Rockefeller Foundation, and Kellogg Foundation; scholarly and professional associations; and foreign-funded and/or foreign-based foundations, such as the U.S. Japan Foundation, stimulated international education during this period and continue to do so. Holzner and Greenwood (1995, 50–53) give an informative overview of all these national and international organizations and support structures, by activity. In absolute terms, private associations, foundations, and (consortia of) institutions moved and are still moving far more faculty and, in particular, students around the world than the federal government, and contribute to the development of international activities in higher education.

After World War II, the number of study abroad programs grew rapidly, owing to economic opportunities (lower transport costs to and living costs in Europe) and political reasons (the importance of international understanding). The number of study abroad programs sponsored by American colleges grew between 1950 and 1976 from 6 to 669, mainly in Europe (479). England (114), France (98), Germany (54), Spain (53), and Italy (33) were the main destinations. The same is true for summer programs (313 out of 410) (Taylor 1977, 1520).

One organization of many involved in this movement is the Council on Student Travel, later the Council on International Educational Exchange, that from 1949 onward has moved thousands of students each year to Europe and later also to other parts of the world, first mainly by ship and from the end of the 1960s by air. The CST was created with the goal of sending

American students to Europe to live and work, either as volunteers in reconstruction efforts or for worthwhile educational experiences. The Council grew into a large not-for-profit organization with a student travel company, a study abroad program, and programs for work placements, internships, and secondary school exchanges.

In addition to organizations such as the Council, and institutions such as Beaver College and Butler College, which operate extensive study abroad programs for American students, at the end of the 1950s one could see a growing awareness in institutions of higher education of the international dimension. The combination of incentives from the federal government, a shared concern for parochialism in American society and among students in particular, as well as the memory of the postwar idealism of peace and mutual understanding, drove American institutions of higher education in developing activities for the enhancement of the international dimension. External pressure by political and business leaders and internal pressure by students and faculty also played a role in this.

After World War II, the professionalization of international education administration became more and more important in institutions of higher education. At first the emphasis was on foreign student advising. In 1948, this resulted, on the initiative of the IIE, in the creation of the National Association of Foreign Student Advisors (NAFSA). Of the 218 persons participating in the founding conference at the University of Michigan, on May 10–12, 1948, 115 came from American universities and colleges, 3 came from institutions abroad, 75 came from agencies involved in international education, 17 were government observers, and 23 were observers from embassies in Washington (NAFSA 1998, 9). Ten years later, in 1958, membership had grown to 690 and conference participation to 443; in 1968, membership was 1,768 and conference participation 764; in 1978 the numbers were 2,607 and 1,010; in 1988, 5,591 and 3,018; and in 1998, 7,777 and 5,500. The development of NAFSA over the past fifty years is a clear indication of the growth of the professionalization of international education. Although in the beginning, as the name indicates, the emphasis was on foreign student advising, NAFSA soon covered other areas of international education as well, organized in several professional sections: study abroad advising, international admissions, English language teaching, community outreach, and so on. In line with this development, NAFSA first changed its name in 1964 to the National Association of Foreign Student Affairs. Its Section on U.S. Students Abroad (SECUSSA) was created only in 1971, giving special attention to outward mobility. In 1981 a second, smaller association was created, the Association of International Education Administrators (AIEA), bringing together the chief international education officers on campuses, who felt that their specific role and interests were no longer recognized within NAFSA. In the 1990s, NAFSA changed its name to the Association of International Educators, to recognize its broader coverage of international education and its international membership, even though it continued to be in the first place an American professional association.

The emerging professionalization of the field after the war and its gradual expansion in the past fifty years is an expression of the relative importance of international education in institutions of higher education, but has also contributed to the internal and external advocacy for its further expansion.

For longer, to a larger extent, and more professionally than anywhere else, American higher education has been developing a broad variety of activities, programs, and projects in international education: international curriculum development, area studies, foreign language training, study abroad, exchanges, foreign student recruitment and advising, and development cooperation and assistance, in particular at the undergraduate level. Groennings (1990) speaks of a "many-splendored chaos with momentum," and "a disorderly development, lacking clear definition, boundaries, and agreement" (p. 29). Greenwood (1993) correctly states that "the scope of activities included now under the rubric of international education administration is thus dizzying" (p. 16).

Ann Kelleher (1996), with reference to an article, "Internationalizing the University: The Arduous Road to Euphoria" by Humphrey Tonkin and Jane Edwards (1990), distinguishes between international education as a process and as a condition in her analysis of campus case studies in international program development. The condition model is one in which different programs stand side by side, without interrelation. The process model is a campuswide, dynamic overall process of international education. Kelleher states that many institutions and international educators adhere to the process model, but most cases of international education in the United States come closer to the condition model. Holzner and Greenwood (1995, 54) also state that most institutions of higher education do not have an international strategy for the whole of the institution. According to them, international education strategies are "component" strategies, relatively isolated from each other: development assistance and cooperation, area and language studies, international studies and international affairs, research and scholarly collaboration, international students and scholars on campus, study abroad and exchanges, ethnic and cultural diversity, internationalizing the professions, and public service and outreach.

The strategies for these different components are in most cases well defined and operationalized; they have also had a significant impact on the mission statements of many institutions, and their leaders speak in many cases with great enthusiasm and support about the importance of international education. But one will find very few attempts at comprehensive internationalization in American universities up to the 1990s. Rahman and Kopp (1992) describe how Pennsylvania State University is striving to create an institutional strategy based on commitment, centralization, and cooperation. Other examples of well-elaborated internationalization strategies can certainly be found, but they are exceptions. There is still a need for a conceptualization of international education as a "multifaceted package," instead of strands that are dealt with in isolation, as Harari (1992, 53) states. Alice Chandler (1999) is quite pessimistic about the current situation of international education in the United States. Foreign language studies enrollments are going down, international student enrollment growth is slowing down, sustainability of international curricula and area studies without federal funding is questionable. She makes a plea for a renewal of commitment and additional support by federal government and foundation funding. But in line with the autonomy of American higher education, one could say that it is primarily a responsibility of American universities and colleges to analyze their role in the new global environment and bring together the different isolated components of international education into an integral strategy for their institutions.

CONCLUSION

Characterizing the environment in which higher education operates in the United States in its effect on internationalization, Elaine El-Khawas (1994) mentions four important points:

1. There is no national, governmental policy that guides campus action.
2. The main sources of advice and guidance for campus action are private.
3. The actions of each college and university with respect to international activity depend, to a substantial extent, on the decisions of institutional leaders.
4. International activities, by and large, must depend on self-financing mechanisms (p. 90).

There is a direct relationship between the phenomena that El-Khawas (1994) describes, the unstructured approach to international education, the dominance of political rationales, and the overall character of American higher education. As Clark Kerr (1994b) states, "In America, colleges and universities have never inhabited the upper stories of that fabled Ivory Tower of the historic myth. They have always been subject to some pressures and constraints from their surrounding societies." At the same time, American higher education has been "a world of comparative institutional autonomy and comparative individual academic freedom" (p. 9).

In comparing American higher education, Burton Clark (1994, 365–376) comes to the conclusion that central bureaucracy cannot effectively coordinate mass higher education; that the greatest single danger in the control of higher education is a monopoly of power; that another great danger is domination by a single form of organization; that institutional differentiation is the name of the game in the coordination of mass higher education; and that planning and autonomous action are both needed as mechanisms of differentiation, coordination, and change. These are issues that are closely linked to the characteristics of El-Khawas (1994) for American international education.

In the twentieth century, American higher education has become dominant. The world of academia was turned upside down at the turn of the twentieth century, as Goodwin and Nacht (1991) describe, or as an American physicist explained that transformation to them: "In the 1920s we went to Göttingen; then we brought Göttingen here" (pp. 4–5). A sense of superiority is not absent in American higher education these days.

On the other hand, another aspect of American international education is its emphasis on overcoming parochialism. A feeling of cultural parochialism prevails. "Americans frequently tell themselves and are told by others that they are a parochial lot, ignorant of world geography, people, and events," according to Richard Lambert (1994, 12). Maurice Harari (1992) also points to the fact that "it is unfortunately clear that at the national level we remain somewhat parochial and monolingual, if not monocultural" (p. 56). This explains why international education in the United States, in particular study abroad, has been mainly an undergraduate issue, part of the general education that students have to receive in preparation for specialized education at the graduate level and for their future careers.

This phenomenon is linked to the generally insular character of American higher education. Burton Clark (1994, 365) explains the isolated and insular character of American postsecondary education in the following way: It is the largest national system, it is the most widely acclaimed system since the second quarter of the twentieth century, it is geographically separated from other major national models, it has many unique futures, and it is a hectic system, demanding a high level of attention. It is this combination of parochialism and arrogance that determined for most of the twentieth century, and still to a large extent today, the worldview of and the motivation for international education in the United States.

The fragmented development of a large number of not directly related activities, projects, and programs (study abroad, international students, international studies, area studies, technical assistance, in general brought together under the umbrella name of "international education"), and the prevalence of political rationales (foreign policy, national security, peace and mutual understanding) over other rationales determine the international dimension of higher education in the United States between the beginning of the twentieth century and the end of the Cold War.

In the context of marginal federal policy for postsecondary education, the drive for internationalization has to come from other factors, both outside higher education and from inside the institutions. If one looks at the development of international education, both trends are clear. Foreign policy and national security on the one hand and a strong emphasis on personal development, peace, and mutual understanding and multicultural exposure on the other dominate among the rationales. In that sense one can generalize what

Halpern (1969) says about the Institute of International Education to international education in general in the United States: "Confronted, as it was, with the demands of patriotism and internationalism it chose the former while espousing the latter" (p. 90). Economic rationales and academic rationales have only recently begun to get more attention.

Such a context explains the strong ethos approach in American international education, present at both the institutional level and the intermediate level between the federal government and the higher education sector, as well as the relatively strong presence of private foundations and organizations in international education and the strong advocacy culture.

Over the years a remarkable number of documents, studies, and agendas have been produced by a great variety of organizations, foundations, and associations to plead for the expansion of the international dimension of American higher education. Rahman and Kopp (1992) list in their references fifteen documents that appeared in the United States in the period between 1975 and 1990 making a plea for international education. Additional examples from the 1990s reconfirm this: National Task Force on Undergraduate Education Abroad (1990), *A National Mandate for Education Abroad: Getting on with the Tasks*; Carnegie Commission on Science, Technology and Government (1992), *Partnerships for Global Development: The Clearing Horizon*; National Association of State Universities and Land-Grant Colleges (1993), *Internationalizing Higher Education through the Faculty*; Institute of International Education (1994a), *Investing in Human Capital: Leadership for the Challenges of the 21st Century*; Association of International Education Administrators (1995), *A Research Agenda for the Internationalization of Higher Education in the United States*; Association of American Universities (1996), *To Strengthen the Nation's Investment in Foreign Languages and International Studies: A Legislative Proposal to Create a National Foundation for Foreign Language and International Studies*; American Council on Education (1998), *Educating for Global Competence: America's Passport for the Future*; and Alice Chandler (1999), on behalf of NAFSA and Educational Testing Service, *Paying the Bill for International Education*.

The Alliance for International Educational and Cultural Exchange is an association of not-for-profit organizations comprising the international exchange community in the United States that advocates in Washington, D.C. on their behalf. The Alliance has over fifty members and publishes together with the USIA an "International Exchange Locator" (Alliance for International Educational and Cultural Exchange 1998), a resource directory for educational and cultural exchange that lists in its 1998 edition over 130 organizations involved in international exchanges in the United States, another example of the strong presence of private foundations and organizations and the advocacy culture.

As Holzner and Greenwood (1995) state,

In a pluralistic, multicultural republic, governed within the framework of a federal constitution with strict limits on governmental authority, this national framework is not only governmental, even if the government's role is highly significant. It includes funding and service-providing organizations that link private as well as public efforts at the national level with various types of higher education institutions. It also includes a significant number of higher education lobbyists who are familiar with their state concerns and are known to all federalist representatives, and whose role it is to attempt to guide legislative outcomes which favor their constituents. . . . In other words, single institutions of higher education in the US tend to form their strategies in the context of a large, complex national system of institutions and agencies. (p. 35)[10]

In summary, the international dimension of higher education in the United States became more organized and structured between the two world wars and in particular immediately after World War II. This dimension was stimulated by a combination of a call for peace and mutual understanding and in particular by foreign policy. The post–World War II period and the Cold War drove American governments to stimulate international exchange and cooperation for reasons of defense, public diplomacy, and security. Even after the end of the Cold War these continue to be the main rationales for federal support, although competitiveness is increasingly entering the arguments for internationalization. It was a combination of parochialism and arrogance that determined for most of the twentieth century—and still to a large extent today—the worldview of and motivation for the international dimension commonly referred to as international education in the United States. For longer, to a larger extent and more professionally than anywhere else, American higher education has been developing a broad variety of activities, programs, and projects in international education, mainly at the undergraduate level: international curriculum development, area studies, foreign language training, study abroad, exchanges, foreign student recruitment and advising, and development cooperation and assistance. At the same time, however, most institutions of higher education do not have an internationalization strategy for the whole of the institution. As Mestenhauser (1998b, 10) notes, international education in the United States is unintegrated and fragmented. This can be explained through the specific characteristics of American higher education and the role of the federal government and private foundations with respect to higher education.

NOTES

1. It is important to note that the observation that the role of the U.S. Department of Education in international education is limited does not imply that it is

completely absent. Both the Center for International Education (CIE) and the Fund for the Improvement of Postsecondary Education (FIPSE) are responsible for administering several programs for international studies, area studies, foreign language studies (CIE), and the EU–U.S. mobility scheme (FIPSE). In particular, the Title VI programs under the Higher Education Act, administered by the CIE, are important for the development of the international dimension of American higher education. However, in these cases as well the impetus has come from outside higher education.

2. For an example from this period of the relationship between one Belgian university, the Université Libre de Bruxelles, and the United States, see Université Libre de Bruxelles (1996). For Belgian–American exchanges in this period, see Galpin (1943).

3. See, for instance, Littmann (1996), in particular Chapter 1, "New Beginnings after the End of the First World War, 1923–1933."

4. Even though the first junior year abroad program was, according to Halpern (1969, 110), established by the University of Delaware in 1923 in France.

5. Via the League of Nations Committee on Intellectual Cooperation, academics on both sides of the ocean met each other in their actions for peace and mutual understanding, an indication of the international character of the movement in that period (Halpern 1969, 30–31).

6. Many international scholars received Rockefeller fellowships to visit the United States, such as the Dutch historian Johan Huizinga in 1926, who was, in addition to being a respected academic and author on the United States, president of The Netherlands Commission for International Academic Relations and of The Netherlands–America Foundation (Huizinga 1993).

7. For an account of that period, see, for instance, Littman (1996), in particular Chapter 2, "Partnership in Conflict, 1933–1945."

8. Based on an unpublished personal account by Jack Eagle, the former CEO of the Council on International Educational Exchange, the successor of CST.

9. See, for instance, Vestal (1994), Holzner and Greenwood (1995), IIE (1997), and Heginbotham (1997).

10. This heterogenity expresses itself, for example, in the existence of six major national higher education associations: the American Council on Education (ACE), the American Association of Community Colleges (AACC), the American Association of State Colleges and Universities (AASCU), the Association of American Universities (AAU), the National Association of Independent Colleges and Universities (NAICU), and the National Association of State Universities and Land-Grant Colleges (NASULGC) (Holzner and Greenwood 1995, 48).

The International Dimension of Higher Education in Europe

In presenting Europe as a case study, we have to keep in mind that Europe is not a homogeneous region; still less is its education homogeneous, as the rationales behind the Bologna Declaration on the European space for higher education of 1999 make manifest.[1] This implies that when analyzing internationalization and globalization of higher education in Europe, one has to take account of several important issues, such as national and regional differences, diversity of language, different educational traditions and systems, diversity of stakeholders, and the coexistence of universities and a strong nonuniversity sector. In the previous chapter similar remarks were made for higher education in the United States. In Europe, the heterogeneity is even greater, with more systems than countries and little convergence. It would be difficult to make a classification for Europe such as the Carnegie Classification for the United States.[2]

It is also important to realize that international dimension of higher education in Europe is still in development. In comparison to the characterization by Elaine El-Khawas (1994, 90) of the environment in which higher education operates in the United States and its effect on internationalization as presented in Chapter 2, one has to be aware that for Europe, until recently, one could posit the opposite of these four characteristics to a large extent:

- Institutional strategies and actions have been initiated mainly by support provided by the European Commission and—although in a more limited way—by national governments.
- Private initiative and support for internationalization is almost negligible in Europe.
- The role of institutional leaders in the process of internationalization has been less proactive and more reactive than in the United States.
- The European Commission and national governments, on the basis of self-financing mechanisms that were and in many cases still are absent, have developed internationalization of higher education in Europe more on the basis of financial support, both at the institutional level and individually.

But a shift is taking place in the direction of

- More autonomous institutional strategies for internationalization, which are less dependent on governmental support.
- A growing involvement of private support in addition to public subsidies for internationalization.
- More active institutional leadership instead of reactive policies.
- The creation of more self-financing mechanisms at both the institutional and individual levels.

The shift in higher education and its internationalization, driven by market forces and privatization of higher education, goes hand in hand with attempts from governments and the EU to Europeanize higher education. Terms such as "Europeanization," the "European dimension," and creating a "European education space" are used.

Although reference will not be made exclusively to the EU policies for internationalization and Europeanization, the historical analysis presented coincides with the phases noted by Brouwer (1996):

- 1951–1972, the phase of incidental cooperation.
- 1972–1977, the preparatory phase of European cooperation in education.
- 1977–1986, the first phase of implementation of educational programs, mainly based on intergovernment cooperation.
- 1986–1993, the second phase of implementation, mainly based on action by the EU.
- 1993 onward, the first phase of implementation of the EU Treaty for EU cooperation (p. 515).

These phases are more or less the same as those presented by Field (1998, 25–26), who speaks of four stages: 1957–1973, when education and training received relatively little interest; 1974–1985, development of some interest but mainly in vocational training; 1986–1992, education becomes a significant area of policy for the EU; 1992 onward, development of a more radical approach seeking to promote the concept and practice of the learning society.

Brouwer (1996) stops in 1995, but one can extend his last phase until 1998. In 1999 a new phase started, in which cooperation and harmonization will meet in a more coherent European education policy, stimulated by the intergovernment declarations of Sorbonne and Bologna.

During the first three stages, between 1951 and 1992, the role of the European Commission in education was limited by claims of sovereignty of the member states, and the growth of its role was slow, although steady. After 1992, with the inclusion of education in the Maastricht Treaty, its role could become more proactive.

Here the historical development of the international dimension of higher education in Europe before 1950 will not be treated, given that in Chapter 1 Europe was the center of my historical analysis for that period. But it is important to note here that further study of the international dimension of higher education in different European countries is needed to make the picture complete. At present the overall picture is that in Europe this international dimension was marginal, mainly foreign-policy driven, and as far as there was a more active organized presence it was mainly in Germany (DAAD) and the United Kingdom (British Council). If we look into the membership of the Academic Co-operation Association (ACA), which brings together the major agencies in Europe responsible for the promotion of international academic cooperation, we note that, with the exception of the two agencies mentioned, all the other nine were founded after World War II, and, with the exception of NUFFIC in The Netherlands and the Swedish Institute in Sweden, which were founded in the postwar period, all are from the 1980s or 1990s (ACA 1999). Guy Haug (2000, 25) explains this on the basis of the catalyst role of the EU programs on the development of national agencies.

As mentioned in Chapter 2, bilateral links and exchanges between countries as Belgium and Germany with the United States did exist between the two world wars, as well as between certain European countries; for instance, France and Germany. The creation of the Confédération Internationale des Étudiants (CIE) in 1919 in Strassbourg, that had as its objective to strengthen ties of respect and to cultivate solidarity, is an indication of lively international student travel and contacts. These initiatives resulted in, for instance, the Student Identity Card and the development of student travel companies. These student travel companies, which emerged in most European countries and, after World War II, also in Australia, Canada, and the United States, and are organized worldwide in the International Student Travel Conference (ISTC), have played an active role in the mobility of students as well as faculty.[3] The International Committee on Intellectual Co-operation of the League of Nations is also an indication of active academic links in this period. Although the Committee, as with the CIE, was not exclusively European, it was European dominated, which resulted in a lively debate on the notion of "universal culture" in connection to this European dominance (see Kolasa 1962, 57–66).

It is clear that older comprehensive universities, in particular, have a long tradition of organized international linkages, such as the University of Tübingen in Germany, which was an international office dating from 1928 (Markert 1997, 62), but these are more the exception than the rule. Little is known about the size and impact of these activities or about the role of institutions of higher education in these activities. Of course, that does not mean that national governments, foundations, and/or institutions of higher education have not been active, as the Tübingen example indicates, but from the material available one gets the impression that their activities to stimulate the international dimension of higher education were marginal and ad hoc. Further research is needed to identify specific actions in different countries, agencies, foundations, and institutions.

THE 1950s AND 1960s: LAISSEZ FAIRE

To understand the present European situation, it is essential to place current developments in a historical perspective. As described in Chapter 1, macrohistorical changes affecting the international dimension of Europe's higher education were the emergence of nation-states in the nineteenth century and earlier; Europe's historical role in the world, in particular its role in colonization and in the process of decolonization; the impact of higher education in countries such as France, Germany, and the United Kingdom on higher education in the rest of the world; recent trends in European integration; the collapse of the former Soviet Union and associated East–West rapprochement; recession and financial constraints; "massification" of higher education; and the dissolution of some structures and blocs and the emergence of others.

Institutions, as they participate in these events, bring with them their own microhistories: their individual histories, which may stretch back many centuries or reflect a far more recent foundation. An institution's response to the "push" and "pull" factors for internationalization will always reflect the intersection of these micro- and macrolevel histories.

Confining discussion to the macrolevel and the post–World War II period, the 1950s and 1960s in Europe are not seen today as a period of internationalization, but it would be entirely wrong to believe that international student mobility was absent then. In general, the period from 1950 to 1970 was, according to Baron (1993), characterized by a "foreign policy" among receiving countries of "benevolent laisser-faire," of open doors to foreign students, who to a large extent came from the former and, at that time, still existing French and British colonies. Some elements of this are still seen in the pattern of student flow to these countries, although (in the British case especially) the impact of more recent policies has largely transformed the picture. According to Baron, in the period from 1950 to 1970, "Promoting academic mobility was predominantly seen as an element of foreign policy. From the point of view of the receiving countries, provision and care for foreign students were perceived as connected to foreign policy objectives, such as maintaining political influence with future elites in other countries and preparing useful contacts for international relations in commerce and industry" (p. 50).

As we have seen in Chapter 1, Guy Neave (1992a) sees massification of the student flow and its bipolar nature (i.e., the dominance of the United States in the Western Bloc and of the former Soviet Union in the Communist Bloc) as the main characteristics of the international dimension of higher education in the 1960s and 1970s. The open door and laissez-faire policy and the one-way dimension were the other characteristics of the process of internationalization of higher education at a global level and in Europe in particular. The universities themselves played a mainly passive role as receivers of foreign students.

Gisela Baumgratz-Gangl (1996) gives the following characteristics of internationalization in Europe before the introduction of the European programs: historical ties with former colonies (usually combined with cultural and linguistic ties); political considerations; presence of political refugees; economic considerations; educational demands; research cooperation in the natural sciences; top-level postgraduate study; migration of "guest workers"; increasing foreign language competence at the school level; traditional links between disciplines (mainly philology); traditional mobility of elites; improvement of transport and communication and expansion of tourism; cooperation at the postgraduate level between Western Europe and the United States; and mobility of Third World students and staff to Western Europe (brain drain).

Although this list looks impressive, the effects of these factors on higher education cooperation within Europe were marginal. International activity was mainly oriented toward the cooperation of European higher education with the United States (outward mobility) and with the Third World (inward mobility). A European policy for internationalization did not exist, and the same applies at the institutional level. At the national level, international cooperation and exchange was included in bilateral agreements between nations and in development cooperation programs, driven by political rationales. Institutions were passive partners in these programs.

THE 1970s: THE FIRST STEPS TO POLICIES OF
EUROPEANIZATION IN EDUCATION

In the1970s this changed. In 1972 Sweden set up a program emphasizing internationalization as a means to promote international understanding, cooperation, and peace, a program in which the universities would play an active role as change agents. The program included measures to internationalize the curriculum, credit transfers, and exchanges (Löwbeer 1977). Germany also shifted around that time from a foreign affairs policy of internationalization to a more regulative and differentiated approach. Outgoing mobility was given more emphasis than the previous open door policy for foreign students. The establishment of an Integrated Study Abroad Programme, administered by the DAAD, is an illustration of that change. A change in pattern from South–North mobility to North–North mobility accompanied these changes (Baron 1993; Kehm and Last 1997).

In 1976 the Council of the European Communities adopted an action program for education. This was the first such move, since the 1963 Treaty of Rome did not mention education as an area for community action. The Treaty of Rome (Belgium, France, Germany, Italy, Luxembourg, and The Netherlands) only included the principles of common vocational training, not other areas of education. Action was limited mainly to information exchange and exchange of young workers. Other initiatives, such as the creation of European schools, cultural and scientific cooperation, the creation of a European University, scientific and technological cooperation, and mutual recognition of diplomas, were—although linked to and inspired by the cooperation among the six countries that signed the treaty—not a formal part of the treaty, owing to political motives and related delays in decision making (Brouwer 1996).

The Commission therefore had to justify its action program by noneducational, mainly economic criteria. As Field (1998, 85) notes, the European Community and also its successor, the European Union, tends to use other areas of activities to pursue its plans when its policy thinking exceeds the limits of the competency of the treaty.

Brouwer (1996, 58) gives four reasons why the European Community was reluctant to give priority to actions in the field of education until 1972: its emphasis on economic integration, a legal dispute on the limitations of the EC for actions in the field of education, the political context that limited the role of the EC in areas that the member states saw as their own competency, and the differences in national educational systems and the national orientation of these systems.

The action program of 1976 was a result of the first meeting of ministers of education of the European Community, on November 16, 1971, in Brussels. The basis for that meeting was laid at the conference of heads of states of the European Community in December 1969 in The Hague, where cooperation in the area of education was advocated as part of further political integration. The 1971 meeting recognized the importance of broadening European action from vocational training to other areas of education, in particular higher education, because of its economic significance.

The extension of the EC from six to nine countries with the inclusion of Denmark, Ireland, and the United Kingdom as of January 1, 1973, coincided with a period of stagnation due to economic and political problems.[4] For education, though, new initiatives were taken as a follow-up to the 1971 meeting of ministers of education. In 1973 the creation of a Directorate for Education, Research and Science (DG XII) under the responsibility of the first commissioner for science and education, Ralf Dahrendorf, not only institutionalized education within the Commission structure but also linked EU policies for education and research. With this, the Commission was able to move away from having to base its rationales for an education and research policy on noneducational arguments—economic rationales primarily—to a proactive and integrated policy in these fields.[5]

Brouwer (1996) gives seven rationales for the legitimization of European cooperation in the area of education:

- The importance of training and education for the process of European cooperation and integration (both from the perspective of quality improvement of education and from the point of mutual understanding).
- The need for more harmonization between the different national systems.
- The need for the creation of solutions resulting from the free movement of persons (foreign languages, education for children of immigrants, and recognition of diplomas and qualifications).
- Closer cooperation between national policies for education and actions of the EC in other fields.
- More involvement of European youth in the building of Europe.
- The need for a systematic exchange of information.
- The need for linking European actions with other intergovernment bodies, such as UNESCO, OECD, and Council of Europe, as well as incorporation of education in development cooperation (p. 86).

In these rationales we recognize the first signs of issues that are still dominant in the European policy for education: harmonization, Europeanization, and globalization.

In 1974 the ministers of education of the European Community adopted the principles for an education action program that was launched in 1976. It was composed of three main categories: mobility in education, education for children of immigrant workers, and the intention to implement a European dimension in education. The action program included three measures for higher education: "Joint Study Programmes," Short Study Visits, and an educational administrators program.

Although important in itself, the impact of the action program was marginal (Field 1998, 32). In that sense, the period from 1972 to 1985 can be seen as a period of stagnation. In comparison to the Integrated Study Abroad Programme of Germany, the scope of the European programs was limited. But for other European countries who lacked a national policy and action program, at least it was something. The reasons for this stagnation, according to

Brouwer (1996, 121), were the financial crisis of 1971, the energy crisis of 1973, and the resulting global economic crisis of the 1970s that stagnated economic and political integration and focused attention on national solutions.

THE 1980s: THE GREAT LEAP FORWARD

The 1980s produced four distinct changes: first, in the open door mobility of individual students; second, in the development of a research and development policy for the EU; third, in student mobility as an integrated part of study; and fourth, in the widening of scope to other regions—third countries in Western, Central, and Eastern Europe, third countries outside Europe, and development cooperation.

Individual Mobility

With respect to the individual mobility of students, the European nations and universities began changing their benevolent laissez-faire policy to a more controlled reception and in some cases the active recruitment of fee-paying foreign students. Alice Chandler (1989) stated,

What has changed in recent years is the balance of motives. Humanitarianism and internationalism still exist as rationales for foreign student enrolments. But they have been overshadowed in both rhetoric and reality during the 1980s by the increased emphasis on pragmatics: by the monies to be derived from foreign student tuitions, by the purchases and expenditures made by foreign student tuitions, by the purchases and expenditures made by foreign students as tourists, and by the less measurable but ultimately even more important contribution to be made by foreign graduates as future financial and diplomatic allies. (p. viii)

At first, this applied nearly exclusively to the case of the United Kingdom: the British decision in 1979 to introduce full-cost fees for foreign students. Higher education as an export commodity quickly became dominant in the United Kingdom. For the United Kingdom this created a conflict with the development of the European mobility programs. Gribbon (1994, 24) refers in that respect to the dilemma of British institutions in reconciling their interest in these programs focused on European partners and their interest in export, mainly outside Europe.

For most people on the European continent, considering the education of foreign students as an export commodity was still anathema at that time. On the European continent, the reception of foreign students was and in most cases still is based more on foreign policy arguments than on considerations of export policy. Often it can be claimed in all fairness that foreign students cost more than they bring in, owing to the subsidization of higher education. This is also the case in the former Communist countries such as the Soviet Union, where students were received for ideological reasons but after the collapse of communism were no longer welcome for a number of years because of the high cost to their hosts' faltering economies.

At the end of the twentieth century, the international movement of students as an export commodity had spread over the European continent and became a more important element of higher education policy than it had been in the past, both at the national and institutional level. Examples of this new focus can be seen, for instance, in The Netherlands. Policy documents of the Dutch government declare the recruitment of foreign students to be a policy issue. This is a remarkable difference from the previous two decades, when national policy aimed at discouraging foreign students from study in The Netherlands.[6] Other examples can be seen in Germany, France, and also Central and Eastern Europe, where universities develop programs for foreign students in order to attract the foreign currency that is so important for their infrastructure because of lack of sufficient national support (see Bremer 1997). One market is the children of former emigrants to the United States, who see the relatively cheap training in their countries of origin as an alternative to the high costs of academic training in the United States.

Similar trends can be observed in France, Germany, and Scandinavia, although in these cases the rationale of status and indirect, long-term economic effects is more important than direct income, which is the driving rationale in the United Kingdom.[7] The shift to higher education as an export commodity over the European continent resulted in a reaction from the leading Anglo-Saxon countries in this market (the United States, Australia, the United Kingdom, and Canada). They realized that they had to defend their markets and more actively compete with each other and the continental Europeans, as well as some Asian countries, such as Singapore.[8]

The Research and Technological Development Programs

Internationalization of research is a phenomenon that is generally accepted. International joint ventures of research groups are not exceptional, and there is a long tradition of conferences, seminars, workshops, and congresses for academic exchange of ideas and findings. In addition, the technological needs of modern society demand very expensive research projects that individual research groups, institutions of higher education, companies, or even national governments cannot finance alone. Therefore, a logical role exists for the European Commission in stimulating international cooperation in science and research in the Union: those activities in which European cooperation offers major advantages and generates the maximum beneficial effects. Another rationale was the challenge posed by new technologies and related competition with the United States and Japan.

An R&D stimulation policy was in existence several years before the moves took place to establish a general education policy in the EU. In the period between the 1960s and 1983, cooperation in this field was mainly intergovernmental and the role of the EC was still marginal and concentrated on coal, nuclear energy, and steel. In 1974 it expanded to other areas. In 1974 a Committee for Scientific and Technical Research (CREST) was established, which formed the basis for the involvement of the EC in this area. In 1979 a stimulus toward an R&D policy was given with the establishment of the European Strategic Programme for Research and Development in Information Technology (ESPRIT), followed by programs such as RACE (communication technology), BRITE (industrial technology), SPRINT (innovation and technology transfer), and ECLAIR (linkages between agriculture and industry).

The objectives of the European R&D policy (Preston 1991) were

- to establish a European research and technology community.
- to increase the capacity of European industry to develop its own technological capability through research and innovation.
- to strengthen the international competitiveness of the European economy.
- to establish uniform rules and standards where these were needed.
- to improve the quality of life and living.

As is clear from these objectives, Europeanization, harmonization, and globalization are central elements in this policy.

Since 1984, most of the programs have taken place within so-called Framework Programs, the first running from 1984 to 1987, the second from 1987 to 1991, the third from 1990 to 1994, and the fourth from 1995 to 1999. In 1994 a program for Training and Mobility of Researchers was approved. Larédo (1997) sees the development of public–private networks of research institutes with industry, based on the public initiative of the European Union, as an extremely valuable result of the Framework Programs. These programs promoted a new structural arrangement whereby large European firms gained access to new technologies, stimulated industrial competitiveness, and were geared toward innovation in "collective goods."

R&D funding, though, is still seen by universities as just one additional resource for large research projects in an area that is already so global that individual, institutional, and even national research projects are more the exception than the rule. The complexity of procedures and the extremely low success rate of submitted proposals have reinforced the resistance to get involved. Gradually, though, one can observe a more active and systematic attention to EU tenders in R&D, following the experience of the more successful universities in the United Kingdom.

There is a remarkable difference in emphasis on the R&D programs and the educational programs between the United Kingdom and the continent. For reasons explained earlier, in the United Kingdom there is strong hesitation toward active involvement in educational programs, but the number of submissions and the success rate of these submissions are higher. Two possible and related explanations can be given for this phenomenon, based on personal observations of some U.K. universities. In the United Kingdom, national research funding is less than on the continent and more complex in procedures, so the need for EU funding is higher. Second, the investment in R&D liaison officers to guide the tender process is greater than on the continent. The opposite applies to educational programs.

Although the R&D programs are more substantial in terms of quality and funding than the educational programs of the European Commission, they are considered in most institutional policies—with the exception of the United Kingdom and some of the newly entered members, in particular in Scandinavia—to be less closely related to internationalization strategies than are the educational programs.

The EC Mobility Programs

In the late 1970s and early 1980s the notion of "study abroad," in the sense of sending students to foreign institutions of higher education as part of their home degree program, became an issue on the continent that overshadowed the developments in individual mobility of students. Since the 1980s, student mobility as a one-way, individual process stimulated by political and/or economic considerations has (with the exception of the United Kingdom) lost prominence as a policy issue. It has been marginalized by the greater attention given to student mobility in the framework of exchange programs, which have been among the top priorities in higher education policies of the 1980s and 1990s.

Before this period, organized programs for the exchange of students and staff did exist, such as the Fulbright Program in the United States and the bilateral cultural and academic agreements of European countries. But these programs were limited in both funding and scope, stimulating mainly unrelated exchanges at the postgraduate level. As we have seen, in the 1970s more structural exchange programs were established, first in Sweden and the Federal Republic of Germany. These programs were inspired by the development of study abroad programs at American universities in Europe in the same period, but the German and Swedish schemes distinguished themselves from their American examples by the fact that they were much more focused on integration of their own students into the foreign host universities, while the American programs were more isolated satellites of the American home institutions.

The 1976 Joint Study Programmes scheme of the EU aimed at the promotion of joint programs of study and research between institutions in several member states. The focus of this experimental program was primarily the stimulation of academic mobility within the EU. The program grew gradually from 32 projects in its first year, 1976–1977, to 200 in 1983–1984, with a budget of 700,000 ECU. In 1984, the Commission added a budget line for student grants into the Joint Study Programmes scheme. This scheme was replaced in 1987 by its successor, the European Action Scheme for the Mobility of University Students (ERASMUS).

The action program of 1976 was the basis for future activities in academic cooperation and exchange within the European Community. The member states limited the role of the European Community in the field of education, however, to complementary measures, decided only with the authorization of the Council of Ministers. Education would remain the exclusive task of the national governments, although from 1982 onward social and economic factors gave the Commission more room to extend its role in this area (Brouwer 1996, 202–205). The objectives of the EU policy for education in that period were a pluricultural Europe, a Europe of mobility, a Europe of education for all, a Europe of expertise, and a Europe open to the world (p. 252). One can observe in these objectives a more pragmatic and less ambitious approach. Pluralism and complementarity are more dominant than harmonization and Europeanization.

Ironically, the lack of a legal basis for action in the field of higher education gave the European Commission a great deal of freedom for creative programmatic action in the field of education in the period after 1982, a freedom and creativity that would have been less within a more formal legal structure. The launch of COMETT, a program for cooperation between higher education and industry, in 1986, and of ERASMUS, a program for cooperation within higher education, in 1987, took place in this period, followed by several other education programs: EURTECNET, a scheme for the development of professional education and information technology, in 1985; PETRA, a program to promote cooperation and exchange in further education, in 1987; DELTA, a scheme for learning technologies, in 1988; IRIS (later NOW), a scheme to promote professional education for women, in 1989; LINGUA, a scheme for the promotion of the learning of European languages, in 1989; and FORCE, a scheme for continuing education of workers, in 1990 (Brouwer 1996; Wächter, Ollihainen, and Hasewend 1999).

The development of the European mobility schemes influenced the creation of a new profession of international relations officer, both at the institutional, intermediate, and European levels. In 1988 this resulted in a plan to create a European professional organization of university staff involved in international affairs, forty years after the creation of their American sister association NAFSA. The letter of invitation for this new organization, dated July 6, 1988, makes the strong link with the mobility programs of the EU clear: "European action programmes like ERASMUS and similar schemes being developed make the foundation of a professional organisation mandatory" (EAIE 1999, 5). The creation in 1989 and further development of the European Association for International Education (EAIE) with a membership and conference participation of over 1,500, went hand in hand with the further expansion of the European mobility schemes and institutional responses to the internationalization of higher education in Europe. The European programs and, broader, the internationalization of European higher education, also became more dominant on the agenda of the European Rectors' Conference (CRE; later renamed Association of Universities in Europe). In 1993 the major national agencies in Europe responsible for the promotion of international academic cooperation, such as the British Council in the United Kingdom, DAAD in Germany, NUFFIC in The Netherlands, and CIMO in Finland, created the Academic Co-operation Association to support, improve, manage, and analyze academic cooperation in Europe and between Europe and other parts of the world (ACA 1997, 29).

Wächter, Ollihainen, and Hasewend (1999, 63) call ERASMUS "the Community's flagship programme," which, although it might be perceived as such in the higher education community, is an exaggeration of its importance. Since the implementation of the ERASMUS program in 1987, however, significant results have been achieved in cooperation and exchange within higher education in the European Union. To give an idea of the impact of the programs, the following is an overview of the results of the ERASMUS program, based on a number of sources.

Thanks to ERASMUS, in the period from 1987 to 1993, more than 200,000 students and 15,000 faculty were exchanged. This took place in the framework of 2,200 Joint Study Programmes, in which 14,000 departments of 1,300 institutions of higher education worked together. In addition, 700 intensive courses and 800 joint curricula were established, 20,000 short visits of faculty and administrators were supported, and 100 European faculty and 30 student organizations were given subsidies to stimulate their activities. In 1993–1994 almost 48,000 students were exchanged, and more than 8,000 lecturers participated in staff mobility programs, illustrating the rapid growth of this program. In 1991 the EFTA countries were allowed to take part in the ERASMUS program, and when Austria, Finland, and Sweden joined the EU in 1995, Norway, which stayed out of the EU, was allowed to continue its participation.[9] Switzerland, which had also decided not to join the EU, did not get that privilege because of disagreement on other issues. This country established a separate budget to continue participation in ERASMUS activities on a bilateral basis. In 1998–1999 the SOCRATES program was gradually opened to countries from Central and Eastern Europe: Bulgaria, the Czech Republic, Hungary, Poland, Romania, the Slovak Republic, and Slovenia, as well as the Baltic States (Estonia, Latvia, and Lithuania) and Cyprus.

In the 1990s the creative and informal period of educational policy of the European Community came to an end. The Maastricht Treaty, signed in 1992 and ratified on November 1, 1993, included education for the first time. This decision was, according to Brouwer (1996, 229), influenced by the following factors: the existing practice of cooperation in education, a recognition of the importance of the contribution of education to the realization of the objectives of the treaty and related policies, existing jurisprudence of the Court of Justice in Luxembourg since 1985 in the field of education, the need to expand the responsibilities of the community as a result of the decisions on European Monetary Union (EMU) and European Political Union (EPU), and changing opinions on the role of European institutions and national governments among the member states.

In preparation for the changing role of education under the Maastricht Treaty, the European Commission presented two memoranda, one on open distance education and one on higher education. The first one expanded the role of the Commission to a new important area of education; the second confirmed the new role of the Commission with respect to higher education.

In 1991, the EC published the *Memorandum on Higher Education in the European Community*. This document was the basis for an intensive debate on the role of the European Union in education and on the future of the educational programs. The "added value" of EU action in the sphere of education was, according to the Commission and in the words of its president, Jacques Delors (1994): "The mutual integration and opening up to each other of general education and professional training systems are an economic issue, in terms of maintaining competitiveness, and a political issue, in terms of defending democracy and human rights."

Although in general it was well received, critical comments were made by the educational sector on the one-sided focus by the EC on economic and political criteria at the expense of a broader cultural and academic approach. The European Association for International Education (1992), in a comment on the *Memorandum on Higher Education in the European Community*, acknowledges the positive role of the EC in stimulating internationalization of higher education within Europe, but also questions the confusion of internationalization with Europeanization:

For the European Commission, the main focus of internationalisation is Europeanisation: achievement of European excellence; strengthening of Europe's position in the global economy; safeguarding and strengthening Europe's cultural heritage; strengthening the basis for further political development and for European Political Union; a European Community dimension in higher education; the European dimension of curricula. (p. 11)

The EAIE points to the danger of a Eurocentric view of internationalization, and (citing Peter Scott 1992) sees a potential contradiction between Europeanization and internationalization: "Intra-European exchanges cannot be regarded as fully 'international.' Indeed, as the European Community deepens and widens, they will increasingly be seen as 'internal' rather than 'external' exchanges. Nor can they be regarded as a substitute for wider global relations" (p. 10). Others have a more optimistic view on the European programs, for instance, Rob Kroes (2000), who calls the ERASMUS program "a shining example of Europe producing Europeans" (p. 12).

The importance of strengthening the European dimension in education was placed high on the agenda. The programs should contribute to the realization of this dimension and its four objectives (Brouwer 1996, 262):

1. Preparation of young people for their involvement in the economic and social development of the European Union.

2. Improvement of their knowledge of the historical, cultural, economic, and social aspects of the union and its member states, the European integration process, daily life in other member states, and the relation of the union with Third World countries.

3. Improvement of their opinion in the advantages of the union, the challenges of its greater economic and social space, the European identity, the value of European civilization, and the foundations for its present development.

4. Strengthening of their image of Europe as a Europe of citizens and improvement of the knowledge of its languages.

For higher education, the EU was of the opinion that the existing programs (COMETT, ERASMUS, and LINGUA) were not sufficient to realize these objectives, and for that reason introduced in 1989 the action JEAN MONNET, to support initiatives for the development of research and education on European integration.

While the European Commission has played an active role in stimulating and supporting intra-Community educational mobility and cooperation for a number of years—recognized, as we have seen, as a part of a new Directorate for Education, Research, and Science, with Ralf Dahrendorf as its first commissioner—its legal competence in the educational field dates only from the adoption of the Treaty of Maastricht in 1993. The EC, confronted with the fast-growing interest in its educational programs, conscious of the new role for education under the Maastricht Treaty, and aware of a positive change of attitude in the institutions of higher education toward its educational programs, prepared for the follow-up to the mobility programs, as December 31, 1994, was the expiry date of the first phase.

In 1993 Antonio Ruberti, commissioner for education and research, published a new discussion paper in which he stressed the importance of a more coherent continuation of the existing programs (combining ERASMUS and LINGUA in one program) and a closer link between these and the research and development programs of the European Union. The Commission decided to consolidate the existing individual programs into two large framework programs:

1. LEONARDO DA VINCI in the area of vocational training and replacing COMETT, EUROTECNET, PETRA, FORCE, and a part of LINGUA.

2. SOCRATES in the area of general and higher education, with three chapters: ERASMUS for higher education, COMENIUS for secondary education, and a third chapter directed to transverse measures (promotion of linguistic skills, open and distance learning, information promotion education, and adult education).[10]

For higher education, ERASMUS continued as the program for promoting mobility of students and staff. Disciplinary and institutional networking are the basis of this phase of ERASMUS. An important element of the new ERASMUS scheme is that institutions, instead of departments as hitherto, are the main actors working together in curriculum development and staff and student exchange. Institutions are eligible to receive a contract from the Commission, based on concrete proposals for mobility of staff and students, joint curricula, intensive courses, credit transfer, distance education, and language preparation. Under the new scheme institutions have to prove that they have a well-defined policy before being awarded a contract: the European Policy Statement.

This shift of responsibility for the administration of the partnerships from the academic coordinator to the institutional administrator was intended to make it possible for the faculty to concentrate on the academic aspects of internationalization while the administrator handled the administrative part. This change recognized the new role of the institution, and its rights and obligations in internationalization. It can also be read as recognition of the growing professionalism of the institutional administrator in internationalization. At the same time, it has been criticized by both academics and administrators for its top-down approach (a shift from what was perceived as a bottom-up approach in the first phase), and the emphasis on the departmental joint study programs. Also new within SOCRATES was the possibility of the creation of "thematic networks," with the primary objective of creating platforms to analyze and study the status of development in the different fields of education in Europe, the promotion of the European dimension, and improvement of the quality of training.

According to Barbara Kehm (2000; Barblan et al. 1998, 10) the managerial change of the SOCRATES program challenged institutions of higher education to reflect and place a strong emphasis on the coherence of goals, to strengthen the responsibility of the central level of the higher education institutions, and to develop and reinforce strategic thinking. A study of the first round of applications and their policy statements (Barblan et al. 1998) does show indications of the success of this strategy, but also that the impact was still marginal and reactive and needed more time to become systematic and proactive (see also Teichler 1999, 15–17).

Related issues that were also given attention were the development of a European Credit Transfer System (ECTS) as part of ERASMUS-SOCRATES, recognition of diplomas, and the development of an open European space for cooperation in higher education. Together, these new measures redirected step by step the scope of the debate to harmonization, integration, and Europeanization, moving gradually away from the previous direction of pluralism and complementarity, but without stating that explicitly as such.

The Involvement of the EC with the Rest of the World

The role of the European Commission in higher education has not been limited to educational mobility and exchange within the European Union. Four other regions can also be mentioned. The first group, composed of the other European countries that were not hidden behind the Iron Curtain during the Cold War (the EFTA countries, Switzerland, Cyprus, Malta, and Turkey) were, with the exception of the last three, allowed to take part in the R&D and educational programs in preparation for their future membership of the EC. In the 1990s, Austria, Finland, and Sweden indeed became members of the EU. Norway and Switzerland decided not to become member states. Norway was allowed to continue to take part in EU programs, but Switzerland, because of disagreement on other matters, was excluded and had to establish separate bilateral relationships with their former partners in SOCRATES. Cyprus was allowed participation in 1998; Malta and Turkey have to await further decisions in relation to their negotiations on future membership in the EU. As we will also see for Central and Eastern Europe, this is a clear example of a foreign policy rationale: using education as a test case to prepare for strengthening political relations.

The relationships with these countries can be seen as a natural process of widening European integration. Although this is also true for Central and Eastern Europe, this took more time and a transition period was created to make that integration process possible.

Cooperation with Central and Eastern Europe

The opening up of Central and Eastern Europe has had an enormous impact on higher education in this region and on cooperation between institutions of higher education in Western, Central, and Eastern Europe. As Dennis Kallen (1991a) makes clear, academic cooperation and exchange already existed before this opening up and was developing rapidly in the 1980s, in particular with Poland and Hungary. Cooperation concentrated mainly on staff exchanges and far less on student exchanges. From the point of view of the regimes in these countries, academic cooperation was mainly a political issue and little institutional or personal autonomy was possible.

Although, as Ladislav Cerych (1996) states, the opening up of Central and Eastern Europe had a global effect, the increase in academic mobility with Western Europe was quantitatively greater than with any other area. Regional proximity and the political push by national governments and the

European Commission formed the basis for this strong inner-European academic cooperation. The EC, through its Poland and Hungary: Assistance for Restructuring of the Economy (PHARE) program, opened the way in 1989 for several forms of cooperation, both in R&D and in education. An example is the Trans European Mobility Programme for University Studies (TEMPUS) scheme. Its general objective was to contribute, as part of the overall PHARE program, to the general economic, social, and humanitarian reforms in Central and Eastern Europe, and to their transition to a market economy and multiparty system. Its specific objectives (Brouwer 1996, 300) were

- to simplify the coordination of support in the area of exchange and mobility of students and staff.
- contribution to the improvement of the quality of higher education.
- to stimulate cooperation with EU partners.
- extending opportunities for foreign language study.
- extending opportunities for study and internships.

In summary, the program provides support for the development of education by way of mobility grants for students and faculty and infrastructural support. In the second phase, from 1993 to 1996, the specific objectives were more oriented to national needs and strengthening of the development of higher education systems than to mobility and economic aid.

In 1994 TEMPUS covered most countries in Central and Eastern Europe: It was originally in Hungary and Poland (July 1, 1990), but on September 1, 1990, it was directly expanded to Bulgaria, Czechoslovakia, Yugoslavia, and Romania. In January 1993 Czechoslovakia was split into the Czech Republic and the Slovak Republic. In January 1994 the program was extended to Albania, Latvia, Lithuania, Estonia, and Slovenia (Brouwer 1996, 301). Owing to the split in the former Yugoslavian Republic and the political conflicts that followed that split, other members of that republic stayed out of the program. Also excluded were the republics of the former Soviet Union, for whom a new scheme, TEMPUS–TACIS, was established in 1991.[11]

Thanks to TEMPUS and other programs supported by national governments and other international private and public organizations, a rapid improvement in the educational infrastructure and the quality of education in Central and Eastern Europe has been achieved. One of the main problems still to be solved is the brain drain of qualified faculty and students. But although this and many other important problems remain, an important step forward in bridging the gap between higher education in Western, Central, and Eastern Europe has been made. In the field of R&D also, the situation in Central and Eastern Europe is better than it was fifteen years ago, thanks to the support of the EC and national governments.

It is important to add that other OECD countries can also join PHARE and TEMPUS activities, but their involvement has been minor. With the exception of Russia, most Central and Eastern European countries were more EU-oriented (Bremer 1997, 215), and for institutions of other countries it was also difficult to get access to the TEMPUS structure, which was so closely related to experiences with ERASMUS and COMETT.

It is also important to add that, in addition to the European programs, many national governments had their own educational programs for Central and Eastern Europe, such as the CEEPUS program of Austria with six neighboring countries: Bulgaria, Croatia, Hungary, Poland, Slovakia, and Slovenia.

Based on this successful development, most countries taking part in TEMPUS have been given access to the regular R&D and educational programs of the European Union in preparation for future full membership. There is still ground, however, for some concern in the lack of cooperation between the institutions of higher education in the Central and Eastern European countries themselves, and, related to that problem, a tendency to national instead of regional approaches. Another cause of concern is a tendency to give almost exclusive priority to the natural sciences, economics, and law in programs for Central and Eastern Europe, seen as directly related to economic development, at the expense of the "vulnerable sector" and disciplines in higher education. Further concern lies in the one-way direction of mobility and cooperation. Only recently has a small but growing stream of students begun to move from West to East. If higher education in Central and Eastern Europe is to escape from its dependence on support from Western Europe, then a relationship of two-way exchange and cooperation must prevail. Although countries from Central and Eastern Europe have gradually been allowed to participate in European R&D and education programs since 1998, a move from aid to cooperation, it will still take quite some time to get on equal terms (see Barblan and Teichler 2000, 9).

Cooperation with Third Countries

Timothy Light (1993, 263), questioning the American supremacy in higher education, argues that there is a shift from a one-way relationship of higher education in the United States to the rest of the world to a two-way, "twinning" relationship. He, like many other authors, considers the European programs to be important contributors to this development. The ERASMUS program has been the example for similar projects between the European Community and the rest of the world.

These include the already discussed extension of the Framework Programs for R&D, and the ERASMUS, LINGUA, and COMETT programs to the EFTA countries (Norway, Sweden, Finland, and Austria, the last three now member states of the European Union) and Switzerland (later withdrawn), and the cooperation between higher education in Western, Central, and Eastern Europe through the PHARE and more specifically the TEMPUS and TEMPUS–TACIS programs. But the extension goes beyond Europe. In 1990, a program was started to promote cooperation in higher education with the Maghreb countries around the Mediterranean Sea (MEDCAMPUS).[12]

In 1994 a program called ALFA was set up to stimulate cooperation with Latin American universities. The activities funded by this program include the development of academic and administrative management, measures to facilitate recognition, development and adaptation of curricula, cooperation between institutions of higher education and companies, innovation and systematization of education, institutional assessment, joint research projects, and the mobility of students (Wächter, Ollihainen, and Hasewend 1999), 65).[13]

In Asia, the EU started several bilateral projects and programs, of which the most important are the EU–China Higher Education Co-operation Program of 1996 and the EU–India Cross-Cultural Program of 1997, which were intended to stimulate the development of European studies degrees and centers and to provide professorships, fellowships, and grants for study and training.

In North America the introduction of a program for cooperation in higher and vocational education between the European Union and the United States in 1993 (exploratory phase, formalized in 1995), and a similar program for cooperation with Canada in 1995, were intended to confirm to the transatlantic partners that the process of "Europeanization" is not intended to create a "Fortress Europe." In October 1995 the official EC–U.S. scheme for cooperation in higher education started. The counterpart of the EC for the pilot phase and the final program is the Fund for the Improvement of Post Secondary Education. One month later a similar EC–Canada program was launched. The Canadian counterparts of the European Commission DG XXII are Human Resources Development Canada (HRDC) and the Department of Foreign Affairs and International Trade (DFAIT). Both schemes were approved for a period of five years (see Chapter 2).

The early fear on the part of some governments and academics outside Europe of the emergence of a Fortress Europe in international education has been proved to be unfounded by a booming number of exchange agreements and programs of cooperation linking institutions of higher education in Europe with counterpart institutions all over the world. Guy Haug (2000, 28) predicts that, in the future, when the European internal market is more or less established, there will be an even stronger emphasis on exchange and cooperation between Europe and the rest of the world.

These initiatives may have been launched by EC or national governments, but in most cases have developed independently of such funding, and are based rather on the growing awareness in higher education that the world of science is not limited to Europe.[14]

Development Aid Programs

Support to the Third World in general, and to higher education in the South in particular, has received much attention in Western Europe. In the Netherlands, for example, internationalization of higher education in the 1970s and 1980s was almost exclusively oriented to cooperation with higher education in developing countries, with financial support from both the national government and the institutions themselves.

This situation changed in the course of the 1980s. As Alan Smith states in an unpublished report to the 11th General Assembly of the CRE in Budapest, "When it comes to the role of the academic community in the context of providing development aid, however, the current situation appears to be much less encouraging. In so far as figures are available, it would appear that support for such activities has tended to stagnate or even recede, and even in the more positive cases growth-rates have tended not to keep pace with those in the area of co-operation between industrialised countries" (p. 5).

The orientation toward support for higher education in Central and Eastern Europe, and the policy shift of major education funders such as the World Bank away from higher education and toward the primary education sector, are among the factors that explain this development. For some parts of the developing world, notably countries of sub-Saharan Africa, the displacement effect of the transformations in the former Soviet Union and the consequent loss of formerly available study opportunities there exacerbate the picture.

But in the 1990s, development aid to higher education in the Third World received new attention. Ismail Serageldin (1994), vice president of the World Bank, states,

Europe, which has given so much to the world, both good and bad, must remain engaged with the rest of the world at this time when the end of the Cold War brings both crises and opportunities. It is important that the next generation of Europeans should continue to look beyond their own frontiers, not motivated by dreams of empire or domination, but by the individual and collective enrichment that will come to Europe and the Europeans in recognising our common humanity in the billions of the poor beyond their borders as well as in the peoples of the competing industrial economies across the world. (p. 12)

The European universities have an important role in this process, "as the defender of core values of humanism, tolerance, rationality and reason" (p. 12).

The European Commission in the 1990s became one of the international funding organizations for development cooperation in the educational field, alongside national governments, international organizations such as the World Bank, foundations, and institutions of higher education themselves. One fact becoming clear is that institutions of higher education in Europe wishing to be active in development cooperation will increasingly need to work together in European consortia—a requirement of the European Commission—instead of acting alone.

Although cooperation in education with the developing world was already mentioned in the early 1970s as a potential area for the EC, the role of the EC remained marginal, as development cooperation was seen as a national responsibility. In the so-called Janne report of 1973 on an EU policy for training, cooperation with developing countries is mentioned as one area. In the same year Commissioner Dahrendorf confirmed this in his work program (Brouwer 1996, 76–78). Activities in this area took place mainly in the scope of R&D action programs (such as life sciences and technologies for developing countries).

Complementarity is one of the main objectives of the EC in this area, together with the strengthening and development of democracy, durable economic and social development, integration in the world economy, and the fight against poverty. In 1994 the role of the EC in education and development cooperation was recognized, but given the sensitive relationship between national and EC responsibilities, the activities of the Commission in this area are developing only gradually (Brouwer 1996, 475–477).

THE PRESENT DECADE: TOWARD HARMONIZATION OF SYSTEMS AND STRUCTURES

At the turn of the century, Europe is preparing for a big step forward in Europeanization. It manifests itself in the Bologna Declaration on the European Higher Education Area. On June 19, 1999, in Bologna, Italy, the ministers of education of twenty-nine European countries signed the Declaration on the European Higher Education Area. The joint declaration was based on the understanding that

A Europe of Knowledge is now widely recognised as an irreplaceable factor for social and human growth and as an indispensable component to consolidate and enrich the European citizenship, capable of giving its citizens the necessary competences to face the challenges of the new millennium, together with an awareness of shared values and belonging to a common social and cultural space. The importance of education and educational co-operation in the development and strengthening of stable, peaceful and democratic societies is universally acknowledged as paramount, the more so in view of the situation in South East Europe.

The wide support for this declaration beyond the member states of the European Union is unique and has attracted broad international attention. In the declaration, the ministers aim to reach the following objectives:

• Adoption of a system of easily understandable and comparable degrees, including the adoption of a Diploma Supplement.

- Adoption of a system essentially based on two main cycles, undergraduate and graduate.
- Establishment of a system of credits—such as the European Credit Transfer System (ECTS)—as a means of promoting student mobility.
- Promotion of mobility by overcoming obstacles to the effective exercise of free movement.
- Promotion of European cooperation in quality assurance.
- Promotion of the European dimension in higher education.

The groundwork for what is already widely known in higher education as the Bologna Declaration was laid by the Sorbonne Declaration, signed on May 25, 1998, in Paris by the ministers of education of France, Germany, Italy, and the United Kingdom on the occasion of the anniversary of the University of Paris. In this "joint declaration on harmonisation of the architecture of the European higher education system," the ministers of the four dominant countries of the European Union foresee that Europe is

Heading for a period of major change in education and working conditions, to a diversification of courses of professional careers, with education and training throughout life becoming a clear obligation. We owe our students and our society at large, a higher education system in which they are given the best opportunities to seek and find their own area of excellence. An open European area for higher learning carries a wealth of positive perspectives, of course respecting our diversities, but requires on the other hand continuous efforts to remove barriers and to develop a framework for teaching and learning, which would enhance mobility and an ever closer cooperation.

The Sorbonne Declaration was a French initiative based on the Attali report, "Pour un modèle Européen d'enseignement supérieur," which compares the French system with other European systems of higher education as the basis for a reform of the French system. The declaration came as a surprise, not only to the higher education community but also to the European Commission and the ministers of education of the other member states. It seemed rather unlikely that four countries with fundamentally different higher education traditions would be willing to lead the way to harmonization. In 1993, in the Maastricht Treaty, education did become an area in which the European Commission could take action, but only as a subsidiary focus. Thus, joint European action on higher education was not high on the agenda of the European Council of ministers.

It appears that the ministers of education of the four countries acted deliberately as representatives of their national governments, outside the context of the European Commission. Perhaps they saw this as a way to maintain control over the necessary process of harmonization. Such a proposal would have been far more difficult to sell if presented by the Commission, by one of each of the four larger countries, or by the smaller countries.[15] Thus, the United Kingdom needed France, Italy, and Germany to convince the British public of the advantages of a joint initiative to harmonize European higher education with the British system. The Germans, for their part, needed the support of the other countries to sell a plan at home to introduce the bachelor's and master's degree structure.[16] And the French and Italians needed the others to convince their peoples of the need for reform of their higher education systems, something that had previously been blocked by massive protests.

Of course, intensive debates followed, complicated by discrepancies between the French and British versions of the declaration. However, the Sorbonne Declaration was surprisingly well received, both in the political arena and in the higher education community of the four countries and in the rest of Europe. Andris Barblan (1999), secretary general of the CRE, gives the following explanations for this positive reception:

- The process was initiated from unexpected quarters, the European role of the Commission being taken over at the national level by ministers of education. "Four Ministers were calling the European tune."

- Political decision makers were urging the development of a process they had entrusted earlier to those people first responsible for higher education, academics. "As if there was no time left for further university hair-splitting."

- The discussion at the Sorbonne was an extremely rare constellation of users, providers, and political leaders. "The declaration was itself part of a learning process aiming at a long-term goal, the European space of higher education—still to be defined."

This positive reception of the Sorbonne Declaration set the stage for a broader initiative. On the invitation of the Italian minister of education, a meeting took place in Bologna, Italy. The debate was based on the Sorbonne Declaration and on a study prepared by the Association of European Universities and the Confederation of European Union Rectors' Conferences on "Trends in European Learning Structures" (Haug, Kirstein, and Knudsen 1999). The study showed the extreme complexity and diversity of curricular and degree structures in European countries. Whereas the Sorbonne Declaration spoke of harmonization, both the study and the resulting Bologna Declaration avoided this word, owing largely to the potential negative interpretations. Instead, the study by Haug, Kirstein, and Knudsen speaks of "actions which may foster the desired convergence and transparency in qualification structures in Europe."

What effect will the two declarations have on higher education in Europe? First of all, they reconfirm trends underway in Germany, Austria, and Denmark to introduce a bachelor's and master's degree structure. Second, they have stimulated similar movements in countries such as The Netherlands, where several universities had already started to develop bachelor's and master's degrees and where the minister of education has now paved the way for allowing them to do so. But most of all, a strong incentive has been given to the realization of an open European higher education environment. The declarations, in themselves an attempt to keep a political grip on developments in the higher education sector, will work as a catalyst for reform of higher education throughout Europe. There is still a long way to go, in particular in countries such as Germany, France, and Italy, three out of the four countries that initiated the declaration. The reason is that radical reforms in higher education in these countries traditionally spark massive protests, and even more so when such a reform is perceived as an import from the United States of America, even though the reform can be seen also as an adaptation to the British model of higher education.

The creation of a European space for higher education, the prime objective of the Bologna Declaration, should be completed in 2010. A set of specific objectives has been formulated to make this possible:

- a common framework of understandable and comparable degrees.
- undergraduate and postgraduate levels in all countries.
- ECTS-compatible credit systems.
- a European dimension in quality assurance.
- the elimination of remaining obstacles to mobility.

The Bologna Declaration not only looks at the internal implications for higher education, but also explicitly refers to the need to increase the international competitiveness of European higher education and to make it more attractive to students from other continents (van der Wende 2000). In that sense, the declaration follows the pattern visible everywhere, with competitiveness becoming a driving rationale for the internationalization of higher education. The fact that the Bologna Declaration was signed not only by the ministers of education of the member states of the European Union but also of other European countries is also a sign that education is at the forefront of Europeanization beyond the Union.

THE IMPACT OF THE PROGRAMS ON THE INTERNATIONALIZATION OF HIGHER EDUCATION

The European programs for exchange and cooperation have transformed international mobility from a purely one-way flow involving very small numbers of unrelated movers to managed flows involving large numbers within directly related multilateral exchanges at all levels of higher education. With the ERASMUS program, the international dimension, already present in research, also entered education in a systematic way (Laureys

1992, 109). One could call this development the external democratization of the international mobility of students, giving students from the lower and middle classes and of middle-level qualifications access to study abroad that had once been restricted to the upper classes and a limited number of highly qualified students.

Gisela Baumgratz-Gangl (1993) stresses the different road internationalization has taken thanks to the European programs: "Compared with traditional mobility patterns in Europe and the United States, the programmes have introduced a new pattern: limited periods of study abroad forming part of the study course at undergraduate level; educational co-operation and staff exchange alongside the traditional research co-operation; and highly selective postgraduate programmes for free movers" (p. 250).

The response of the institutions of higher education to the EC initiatives was positive but at first rather reactive: "As long as Brussels is giving us money, why should we oppose the idea." As Ladislav Cerych (1989) has said, "Community funds are not and never will be a manna available to European higher education to solve its financial problems; they will never cover more than a very small proportion of needs. Misunderstandings and overexpectations in this respect have been and probably remain common among European universities, their staff and their students" (p. 327).

Soon it became clear that participation in the European programs did not generate income but demanded active involvement and investment on the part of the institutions and departments. This involvement has in turn created, however, a shift from passive response to active involvement. Institutions of higher education, departments, faculty, and students have had to decide what would be the positive effects of participation in ERASMUS and other schemes and what price they were prepared to pay. Such decisions were traditionally made from the point of view of academic and personal experience. Now, under the schemes, instead of being something extra and exceptional, a study abroad experience had to be an integral part of the curriculum. For that reason, exchange of information on the courses being offered and levels of study became crucial, as was the development of mechanisms of recognition of courses taken abroad through systems of credit transfer.

For varying reasons and to differing extents, the sending of students and faculty abroad was generally seen as the most important aspect of the exchange programs. That this also entailed the reception of foreign students and faculty was at first seen by many institutions as more a drawback than an advantage. The reception of foreign students in large numbers confronted institutions of higher education with unforeseen problems in both classrooms and support facilities. Language barriers, different academic backgrounds and academic calendars, housing, and insurance were among the many problems to be solved. The problems that face institutions of higher education differ by country and type of institution. An example are the problems of institutions of higher education in the United Kingdom. This country is confronted with a high demand from students wishing to spend their study abroad period in the United Kingdom, mainly for language reasons. Students of the different countries of the European Union, when asked for their first preference for study abroad mentioned the United Kingdom as their first choice, with the exception of U.K. and Irish students (first preference France) and students from Luxembourg (first preference Germany). At the same time, for financial reasons higher education in the United Kingdom is less keen to receive large numbers of non-fee-paying students from the continent and also has problems stimulating its own students to participate in the exchange programs with the continent.

Despite these problems, we can say that ERASMUS and the other EC programs have placed internationalization high on the priority lists of national, institutional, and departmental strategic plans. Several national governments, private funds, and regional entities have established funds alongside the European programs to stimulate international cooperation and exchange. Since the creation of ERASMUS in 1987, institutions of higher education in Europe have largely learned to cope with its demands and those of the other European programs. In many institutions of higher education offices of international relations, small or large, have been established at institutional, and frequently also at departmental, levels.

The European Commission, despite its crucial and dominant role, is not the only stakeholder influencing the development of internationalization in Europe. In general, any common view among stakeholders about the "what," the "why," and the "how" of internationalization is lacking. Within Europe, a great diversity of arguments—social, economic, and educational—are deployed to support the internationalization of education. Some of these arguments have their origin in the needs of society and/or the economy, some in the needs of education itself. Together they constitute a set of overlapping rationales for the process and activities of internationalization. In turn, they form the basis of the incentives for internationalization that are perceived by stakeholders, and the justifications that are made internally and externally. And there is potential overlap, but also conflict, between the interests of the different stakeholders: (inter)national governments, the private sector, institutions, departments, faculty and students.[17]

Teichler (1999, 18) identifies four different types of approaches toward internationalization of higher education in Europe:

1. "Would-be internationalization." This applies to academics and institutions that want to be involved in internationalization but face problems in being considered on equal terms. Southern European academics and institutions (in particular in Greece and Portugal) face this, as do Central and Eastern European institutions now that they are entering the European programs.

2. "Life or death internationalization." This applies to countries and their academics and institutions, which view international cooperation as indispensable for

their status and role in Europe and beyond. Teichler gives the example of Sweden and Israel. Perhaps better examples are countries such as Finland and Cyprus.

3. "Two areas." In these cases, academics and institutions have the option of striving for either more national or more international status and orientation. Teichler gives the example of Germany, but one could say that this still applies to all European countries and beyond, and will vary by academic field.

4. "Internationalization by import." This refers to countries and institutions that treat internationalization only as coming from outside, by hosting foreign students and considering research only if published in English. Teichler gives the example of the United Kingdom.

This typification of national approaches toward internationalization of higher education is too simple, and mixes rationales, approaches, and historical developments into a structure that does not contribute to explaining the diversity in European approaches to internationalization. But it clearly illustrates its diversity.

With due regard to variation and exceptions, the trend is for institutions to give internationalization a central place in their mission statements, strategic plans, and budgets. From a move imposed by the outside world, internationalization is becoming an integral part of higher education policy, though still as a separate strategy. Institutions of higher education, faculty, and students are increasingly placing international education at the center of their strategies.

For the beginning of the 1990s, Karl Roeloffs (1994) describes the impact in the following way: "The intra-Community programmes sponsored from Brussels did not, as was feared, exhaust the potential of systems and institutions for international co-operation on the level of individual member states and their higher education system. One can rather say that initiatives and financial support from Brussels have stimulated motivation and have provided experience and infrastructure for increased activities on the national level and outside the scope of the Community programmes" (p. 31). It is, however, important not to overstate the uniformity of this trend. To quote Peter Scott (1992), international education is "regarded as an optional activity, an add-on at the periphery of higher education and research [where it should be] at the core of the curriculum" (p. 14).

At the end of the decade the situation is seen as slightly more positive. An analysis of European policy statements (Barblan et al. 1998, 133; see also Kehm 2000) concludes that the majority of higher education institutions state clear goals for Europeanization and for internationalization, although only a few can be identified as consistent and many others as not more than an enumeration of extremely varied activities. The fact, however, that most statements did not distinguish between Europeanization and internationalization and referred to linkages beyond Europe is an indication that institutions have moved away from a reactive approach to initiatives from the European Commission to a more proactive internationalization strategy.

Ulrich Teichler (1999, 5) calls internationalization, together with institutionalization, one of the two major changes in higher education in Europe in the last two decades. He identifies three quantum leaps in internationalization of higher education in Europe:

- "from a predominantly 'vertical' pattern of co-operation and mobility, towards the dominance of international relationships on equal terms,
- from casuistic action towards systematic policies of internationalisation, and
- from a disconnection of specific international activities on the one hand, and (on the other) internationalisation of the core activities, towards an integrated internationalisation of higher education." (pp. 9–10)

Comparing these three leaps with my account, moving from North–South orientation in individual mobility and emphasis on development cooperation from the 1960s into the 1980s to cooperation and mobility on equal terms (individual mobility, EU programs for R&D, and ERASMUS) in the 1980s coincides with the first leap. The second leap takes place in the 1990s, when institutions of higher education move from a reactive and casuistic approach to internationalization to a more proactive, systematic, and strategic approach, clearly marked at the EC level by the change from ERASMUS to SOCRATES. At the turn of the century, we are facing a third leap toward connecting the specific international activities with the core functions of higher education, teaching and learning, and research. It is important to repeat that these leaps do not take place equally and at the same time among all countries and institutions of higher education in Europe. Some countries and institutions are still in the first leap, others in the second. There are countries and institutions that have bypassed the first and/or second leaps and made a direct leap from a local–national orientation to a more systematic and strategic approach to internationalization.

The third leap is the most complex and substantial one. Ulrich Teichler (1999) might have been too optimistic in his judgment that this third leap is already taking place. A CRE study, *Implementing European Strategies in Universities: The SOCRATES Experience* (Barblan and Teichler 2000), does not show a snowball effect in internationalization, but rather a sustainment and, in reaction to globalization, a shift to commercial recruitment of students. As Machado dos Santos (2000) shows, as a consequence of the need for continuing and lifelong learning and related expansion of education markets, there is also a move to more transnational education in Europe— higher education activities in which the learners are located in a host country different from the one where the awarding institution is based—in particular in southern European countries such as Greece, Italy, and Spain, but certainly not only there.[18] It is more realistic to state that where most European institutions have developed a more targeted approach to internationalization as a result of SOCRATES (Kehm 2000), the vast majority of institutions of higher education have not yet moved beyond the second leap.

The third leap implies a move away from internationalization as a separate strategy toward internationalization as a natural element of the overall strategy of the institution. The role of national governments—already diminished by deregulation and privatization of higher education—is becoming more concentrated on removing barriers and obstacles and creating facilities. The same applies to the European Commission. This does not imply that the role of the European Union is completely disappearing. Guy Neave (1997) states, "The loosening of ties between State and university and the paradoxical creation of new bodies to recouple market and higher education should not cause us to lose sight of the fact that there is now a super ordinate level of operation which has its own legal, administrative and revenue-raising powers above the Nation-State" (p. 113). The involvement of the European Union in higher education via its research and education programs and the resulting program and organizational strategies have had an impact on and continue to affect higher education institutions in all facets, forging a higher education space in Europe. The Bologna Declaration can be interpreted as part of this changing role of the national governments and the Commission. Although issues such as exchange of students and staff and curriculum development will continue to play important roles in European policies for higher education, the European Commission and national governments will increasingly shift their attention to issues such as harmonization of structures, accreditation of degree programs, and equivalency of degrees and diplomas, in order to create a European higher education area.

It is still too early to assess the speed and impact of this third leap. Again, there will be regional and institutional differences. It is not difficult to predict that only a small number of institutions will be able to make that third leap in the coming decade and by doing so will not only become major players in Europe but in the global arena.

In summary, the internationalization of higher education in Europe in the 1980s can be described as "piecemeal and limited" (Callan 2000) and "on equal terms" (Teichler 1999), and in the 1990s as "striving for strategy" (Callan 2000) and "systematic" (Teichler 1999).

CONCLUSIONS

Because of the complexity and diversity of the European situation with regard to higher education and the systemic changes in progress at all levels, some of whose long-term effects are hard to predict, it is not possible to draw a simple model of uniform progress toward internationalization for

Europe in the last two decades of the twentieth century. Some broad trends, however, can be discerned with respect to internationalization of higher education in Europe in the 1990s.

1. A broad tendency for strategies for internationalization that used to be tacit, fragmented, and ad hoc to become explicit, managed, and coordinated. This tendency is more marked in Northern than in Southern Europe. In Central and Eastern Europe, this process manifests itself more in a reform of the old highly centralized and controlled central policies, and their transformation into a more open and autonomous structure.
2. The gradual development of a more interactive model of internationalization, with policy decisions, support systems, and organizational structures located both at central and decentralized levels, and with flexible connections between these levels.
3. A gradual change from a reactive response to EC and national programs and funds for internationalization to a more autonomous, proactive policy of internationalization, both at the institutional and departmental levels.
4. A gradual diversification of resources for internationalization, combining EC and national funds with institutional and private funds.
5. More attention to networking on a multilateral and structural basis in research, curriculum development, and delivery.
6. An increasing professionalization of those with responsibility for international activities in institutions. This is again more marked in the North than the South of Europe, and may have negative as well as positive results, since there is a danger that international activity may become "ghettoized" rather than integral to the life of the institution.
7. An increasing priority being given by European institutions to strategies for cooperation with the rest of the world: globalization of international cooperation in response and in addition to the process of Europeanization as stimulated by the European Commission.
8. A growing awareness of the importance of the academic aspects of internationalization, such as curriculum development, credit transfer, and research training.
9. A growing recognition of the value of effective procedures for evaluation, monitoring, and quality assurance with respect to international activity.

Set against these trends, certain counterpressures and tensions should also be noted:

1. The tension between incentives to internationalize and the rationales for cultivating a distinctive institutional and national identity; resistance to what may be called the "denationalizing" effect of internationalization.
2. The emergence within Europe of a new "localism": an assertion of local and regional identities in other spheres as well as education. Cross-border cooperation at the institutional level, which is an emerging pattern in some areas, combines elements of internationalism and regionalism. At present it is impossible

to predict what accommodations there will be between these new groupings and the centralizing forces in Europe, such as the competencies of the EU.[19]

3. The cost–benefit balance of international activity, with regard both to the institution and the individual.

4. The proliferation of different types of institutions, the expansion of new sectors and specialties, and the growth in numbers of private-sector institutions seeking an international presence in Europe. These developments present challenges to the more established institutions, authorities, and policy-making structures, whose outcome cannot be clearly foreseen.

5. The emergence of competitiveness as a more decisive factor, both at the institutional and national levels and in the policy of the European Commission.

It is important to emphasize that it is extremely difficult to make generalizations in the analysis of internationalization that are valid for Europe as a whole. General overviews of developments in Europe do not give sufficient credit to the complexity of Europe, in particular its regional and national differences. This analysis itself has a certain Western European, even Northwestern European bias, giving insufficient attention to the specific conditions in Southern, Central, and Eastern Europe. There is still a long way to go before studies on internationalization of higher education are truly able to reflect the diversity and cultural pluralism in Europe.

Second, any analysis of internationalization is faced with the lack of a research tradition in this area in Europe, in particular with respect to the institutional aspects and to the effects of internationalization. Many reports have been published about the programs for internationalization in the European Union, but few about the processes of internationalization as institutional and national strategies.[20]

NOTES

Elements of de Wit (1995a) and Callan and de Wit (1995) were used for this chapter.

1. Although reference will be made to countries outside the present European Union, the emphasis of my analysis is on the European Union and its member states.

2. For an overview and analysis of European higher education systems and structures, see Haug, Kirstein, and Knudsen (1999), *Trends in Learning Structures in Higher Education*.

3. For a short history of the Dutch Student Travel Company (NBBS) and its relationship with the Dutch Student Council, the Confédération Internationale des Étudiants, the International Union of Students, and the International Student Travel Conference, see NBBS (1982).

4. In 1981, Greece would become the tenth member. In 1986, Spain and Portugal were included; in 1990, the former DDR, as part of Germany; and in 1995, Sweden, Finland, and Austria.

5. See, for instance, Wächter, Ollihainen, and Hasewend (1999, 62) and Brouwer (1996, 74).

6. With the exception of students from developing countries, provided with fellowships to be trained at specialized International Education Institutes.

7. The change from political to economic rationale as the dominant rationale in Northern European internationalization strategies is clear from the reports in Kälvermark and van der Wende (1997), although less for Southern European countries, as the Greek report illustrates.

8. The government of Tony Blair, based on market shares of 63 percent for the United States, 17 percent for the United Kingdom, 10 percent for Australia, and 5 percent for Canada and a trend to sliding shares for the United Kingdom, has recently presented a plan to raise its share from 17 percent to 25 percent in 2005 by streamlining immigration procedures, fewer regulations for work permits, 5,000 extra scholarships, and better marketing at a cost of £5 million (*The Times*, Higher Education Supplement, 11 February 2000).

9. In 1989 the Nordic countries (Norway, Sweden, Finland, and Denmark) created their own program for cooperation and exchange in education: Nordplus. This program continues to be active, even after the inclusion of Sweden, Finland, and Norway in the European programs in 1991.

10. Adult education in the second phase of SOCRATES became a separate chapter, called GRUNDTVIG.

11. Originally in the Commonwealth of Independent States and Georgia. Later, in 1993, in White Russia, the Russian Federation, and Ukraine (Brouwer 1996, 305).

12. In 1996 this program was frozen, but it is in the process of a restart.

13. The Association of European Universities, which already had a program, Columbus, with its counterpart in Latin America, played an important role in getting the ALFA program approved.

14. See, for instance, Laureys (1992, 110). ERASMUS has also been the inspiration for similar regional plans without involvement of the European Union; for instance, in Asia and the Program for North American Mobility in Higher Education between the United States, Mexico, and Canada in the framework of NAFTA. See also Chapter 2.

15. In reality, some smaller countries, such as Denmark, were already further on their way toward accomplishing what the Sorbonne Declaration intended.

16. A structure that was introduced into Germany in 1998, parallel to the present structure.

17. For an overview of these arguments, see Callan and de Wit (1995).

18. For further analysis of transnational education, see Chapter 8.

19. This relates to interregional cooperation, a fast-growing trend in higher education in Europe.

20. Exceptions are Kälvermark and van der Wende (1997) on national policies, and Barblan et al. (1998) on institutional strategies.

Chapter 4

The Development of Internationalization of Higher Education in the United States of America and Europe: A Comparison

The active role of the European Commission, national governments, and institutions of higher education in Europe with respect to the internationalization of higher education as of 1985 has received a lot of attention in the higher education community in the United States. In a book review on the American view of international education, the following explanation for this phenomenon was given:

One can feel a sense of envy of internationalization of higher education in Europe. Envy that probably has a great deal to do with a feeling of frustration about European global "superiority" compared to American cultural parochialism, whether right or wrong. In their "envy," several authors overestimate the efforts in Europe with respect to internationalization, maybe also out of "sheer frustration" with the limited federal support to internationalization. Not only is ample reference made to ERASMUS and other European programs, but there is also a tendency to paint too rosy a picture. In many cases the description of these programmes is incomplete. (de Wit 1993, 6)

The new views on internationalization seem to come from Europe.[1] But it is important to note that what Ulrich Teichler (1996c) has said about research on international education and academic mobility is still to a large extent true for Europe as much as for the United States; namely, that it is "occasional, coincidental, sporadic, or episodic" (p. 341).

There are several reasons why passion, ethos, parochialism, and the call for a national agenda are more strongly present in international education in the United States than in Europe. The main reason is that international education in the United States saw its growth in reaction to World War II and, even more, the Cold War: the period between the 1950s and the 1980s. Although this international education was motivated mainly by political interests, it has resulted in a great variety of national, private, and institutional programs for international education, far more than in Europe at that time.

Those who still dominate American thinking on international education (Burn, Groennings, Harari, Lambert, and Mestenhauser) wrote their work in that period. They tried to design a kind of conceptual framework for international education in the United States. It is not surprising that the length of that period, four decades, and the great tradition developed during that period—combined with the conceptual thinking to place it in perspective—makes it difficult for U.S. international education to move in new directions. That is something that became manifest in the second part of the 1980s and 1990s, when in Europe, under the impetus of the European Commission, strategies to Europeanize and internationalize higher education were placed high on the agenda of the Commission, national governments, and institutions of higher education. These are strategies that are more integral and profound than the fragmented and isolated approaches that characterize most of American higher education.

The differences in developments in internationalization of higher education in Europe and the United States in general terms can be described as follows:

- Immediately after World War II the international dimension of higher education was more dominant in the United States, and founded on arguments of foreign policy and national security. In Europe the tradition is still rather young, only became more important as part of the European economic and political integration process, and was primarily motivated by arguments of economic competition. At the same time, many older European universities regard themselves as belonging to a deep-rooted tradition of international institutions.

- For that reason, the international dimension of higher education has a longer tradition of organization and higher level of professionalization in the United States than in Europe.

- In the United States, the objective of international education, both at the governmental and institutional levels, is more directed to global and intercultural awareness in response to cultural parochialism, while in Europe the accent is more on the extension and diversification of academic performance.

- In the United States, for that reason, the emphasis in study abroad activities is on undergraduate mobility, while in Europe exchanges at the graduate level have more priority.

- The focus of international education in the United States is more directed to globalization of the curriculum, area studies, and foreign language study, while in Europe the focus is more on networking and mobility.

- In the United States, study abroad and foreign student advising have a tendency to be seen more as different, unrelated activities, while in Europe they are seen as related parts of mobility schemes, with the emphasis on exchanges.
- In the United States, study abroad has the tendency to take the form of faculty-supervised group mobility, while in Europe mobility is based more on mutual trust and is individual oriented.
- In the United States, the push for internationalization comes more from the Departments of Foreign Affairs and Defense, from private foundations and professional associations, and from institutions of higher education and their representative bodies than from state governments and the Department of Education. This has contributed to an active lobbying and advocacy tradition. Given the top-down development of internationalization of higher education from the European Commission via national governments to institutions of higher education, in Europe such an active advocacy and lobbying tradition only recently has emerged and still has more the character of lobbying for national than for European interests.[2] The lack of an active national policy for postsecondary education and the more autonomous character of American higher education are the main reasons for this active advocacy culture in international education in the United States in comparison to Europe.
- In the United States, at both the policy and professional levels, there is a lack of strategic approach and a tendency toward fragmentation. In Europe, the different programs and organizational aspects are more integrated into an overall strategy, and at the professional level one can see a higher level of integration.

Explanations for these differences are as follows:

- In the United States, internationalization is seen as part of general education, while in Europe it is seen more as an activity within academic specialization.
- In the United States, undergraduate education has to compensate for the lack of global and intercultural education and foreign language training in primary and secondary education. In higher education, this takes the form of international education. In Europe, general education, including global and intercultural education and, at least in some countries, active foreign language training, are an integral part of primary and secondary education. Higher education can undergo internationalization more as an integrated part of academic specialization.
- In the United States, area studies, foreign language training, the study of international relations, and development studies are externally added and sponsored programs, while in Europe they have developed as regular disciplines, no different from others, such as law, economics, and medicine.
- In the United States, internationalization is more driven by political rationales of national security and foreign policy, while in Europe economic competition and academic quality are the main rationales for the internationalization of higher education (see de Wit 1995a, 49–50).

If we look to the future, in spite of all the differences mentioned, we are moving in each other's direction. America and Europe, although having the same higher education roots, come from different starting points in international education:

- Different cultures and structures in primary, secondary, and undergraduate education.
- Different emphases in foreign policy after World War II.

Related to these, we see

- a lack of national policy for higher education and its internationalization in the United States.
- a lack of private initiative in higher education and its internationalization in Europe.
- different leadership traditions.
- different funding mechanisms.

These differences have influenced to a large extent our perceptions and our strategies for internationalization. But in recent years both our political and educational systems have moved toward each other. Globalization, competitiveness, and new forms of education are important factors influencing this development.

The implications in Europe are clear: less importance of national policies in higher education, more emphasis on private initiative and funding, and growing importance of individual leadership in higher education. For the internationalization of higher education in Europe this will mean a period of uncertainty and change after the booming decade of the recent past. The "flavor of the month" no longer exists. In that sense, Europeans have a comparative disadvantage to their American colleagues, who are experienced in situations where funding is not guaranteed and strategies are designed in a proactive instead of a reactive way. As Rob Kroes (1996) states,

Europeans have never stopped laughing at America, yet their collective imagination has filled with a repertoire of Americana. They may have reacted vehemently to it, producing a litany of Anti-Americanism that has been one long attempt at exorcism, driving out the devil of a pernicious American culture. Nevertheless, the devil was not simply to be wished away. If cultural guardians were watching the front door, American culture slipped in through the rear entrance. (p. ix)

This applies to culture, but also to higher education. Now it is time for the Europeans to become jealous again. They should learn again to be "fascinated by the history of higher education in America and attracted to the good American University . . . infused with a vitality and a social and educational commitment," and move away from "displays of arrogance and self importance" (Flatin 1998, p. 5) typical of so many European universities. At the same time, some top-ranked American universities will have to abolish their arrogance and superiority and isolation, which they have developed in the twentieth century with respect to higher education in Europe and the rest of the world.

NOTES

1. One should add that Europe is not alone in this. In particular in Canada and Australia, international educators and researchers play a leading role in the present discussion on internationalization of higher education.

2. National governments, the Association of European Universities, the European Association for International Education, and the Academic Co-operation Association do fulfill at the EU level the role that the Alliance plays at the federal level in the United States, but in Europe, private foundations and organizations are not involved in this advocacy. That does not mean there are no private foundations and organizations active in international education in Europe. At the national level in particular, one may find a great variety, but they are not as organized and active in advocacy as in the United States.

Part II

The Internationalization of Higher Education: A Conceptual Framework

Chapter 5

Rationales for the Internationalization of Higher Education

In Part I, a comparative overview of the historical development of the internationalization of higher education in the United States of America and Europe was presented. The concept of the internationalization of higher education will be the subject of this second part. A better understanding of the rationales for and the meaning of the internationalization of higher education will help to contribute to the improvement of the theoretical basis of analysis and research methods of internationalization of higher education. This chapter will deal with the "why," the rationales for internationalization of higher education.

Why in the words of Ulrich Teichler (1999), is internationalization a rising phenomenon? Why are institutions of higher education, national governments, international bodies, and increasingly the private sector so actively involved in international education activities? There is not one single answer to that question. According to Ollikainen (1996), "There are very few attempts at exploring the rationales and processes of international educational co-operation in the microcosms of academic working communities. . . . The prevailing motives and means of universities and various organizations promoting internationalization of higher education have not been questioned" (p. 83).

The question "why" and attempts to answer it are present in a lot of studies, but only in general and not in an explicit and structured way. An example of answering the question is a publication by Goodwin and Nacht (1988), who, in *Abroad & Beyond*, dedicate a chapter to "the point of it all," giving an overview of educational and social goals of education abroad. Another example is Platt (1977, 1539–1541), who mentions "aid to and co-operation with developing countries," "foreign policy," "educational and cultural enrichment," "prestige," and "profit."

This fundamental question received more structured attention only in the 1990s. In 1991 de Wit (1991, 62–69) presented an overview of social and academic rationales for internationalization and indicated that social rationales, in particular economic rationales, are more dominant than academic rationales for internationalization. Aigner, Nelson, and Stimpfl (1992) mention three major reasons for the internationalization of higher education: security, economic competitiveness, and international understanding. Robert Scott (1992) mentions seven reasons, which can be grouped into economic competitiveness, labor market, national security, and mutual understanding. Warner (1992) also writes that there are different reasons and motivations for internationalization. Jane Knight (1994) states that "there is no single motivation for internationalizing. Instead there are a variety of imperatives, which are not necessarily mutually exclusive, but which may be viewed as such" (p. 5).

In "Strategies for Internationalisation of Higher Education: Historical and Conceptual Dimensions," Knight and de Wit (1995) have developed a conceptual structure for rationales and introduced stakeholders as an important factor linked to rationales. They wrote (p. 9) that the rationales and incentives for internationalization are influenced and to a large extent constructed by the role and viewpoint of the various stakeholders: international, national, and regional governments; the private sector; institutions; faculty; and students. While each of the stakeholder groups has a distinctive perception and set of priorities with respect to internationalization, there is also substantial overlap.

In policy documents and statements, a great diversity of arguments—social, economic, and educational—are deployed to support the internationalization of education. Some of these arguments have their origin in the needs of society and/or the economy; some in the needs of education itself. Together (Knight and de Wit 1995, 10) they constitute a set of overlapping rationales for the process and activities of internationalization. In turn, they form the basis of the incentives for internationalization that are perceived by stakeholders, and the justifications that are made internally and externally. And there is potential overlap, but also conflict, between the interests of the different stakeholders.

Rationales can be described as motivations for integrating an international dimension into higher education. They address the "why" of internationalization. Different rationales imply different means and ends to internationalization (see de Wit 1998e, 1999).

Knight and de Wit (1995) identify two groups of rationales: economic and political, and cultural and educational. In later studies Knight (1997a, 1999a) separates them into four: political, economic, social–cultural, and academic.

Others (van der Wende 1996, 1998; Ollikainen 1996, 1998; Gacel-Avila 1999; Callan 2000; among others) follow this division in four groups of rationales. Blumenthal and colleagues (1996) also refer to four dimensions of "explicit or latent objectives underlying many programmes and actions in the academic mobility and co-operation field" (p. 4): economic; political; sociocultural; and academic, scientific, and technological. Some make other subdivisions; for instance, Wächter, Ollikainen, and Hasewend (1999), who divide rationales into educational motives (referring only to quality); economic considerations (referring only to fees from international students); foreign cultural policy; and promotion of peace and global responsibility, regional integration, and development. In this division the social arguments are missing and the other arguments are rather narrowly defined.

This division into four categories of rationales will also be the basis for this study, and to each of them will be added different subcategories: political (foreign policy, national security, technical assistance, peace and mutual understanding, national identity, and regional identity), economic (economic growth and competitiveness, the labor market, national educational demand, and financial incentives for institutions and governments), social–cultural, and academic rationales (providing an international dimension to research and teaching, extension of the academic horizon, institution-building, profile–status, enhancement of quality, and international academic standards).

POLITICAL RATIONALES

Foreign Policy

The political rationale links education in the first place to foreign policy, or, as Alladin (1992) says, education is seen as "the 'fourth dimension of foreign policy', to improve the 'image' of a country, to cast its policies in a favourable light" (p. 12).[1]

This argument considers educational cooperation as a form of diplomatic investment in future political relations. In the first place, the provision of scholarships to those likely to become future leaders is considered to be a way of endowing them with knowledge of the host country and sympathy with its political system, culture, and values. In addition, cultural and academic agreements between countries can be vehicles for the development or preservation of economic and political relations. In extreme cases, for example, they can be a way of keeping communication going between governments when formal diplomatic relations have been broken, and form a "stepping stone" for their reestablishment. As the U.S. Advisory Commission on Public Diplomacy (1995) states in *Public Diplomacy for the 21st Century*, "Exchanges and training have direct and multiplier effects that make them among the most valuable instruments of America's foreign relations."

The twin arguments of economic and diplomatic investment were the traditional rationales in the United Kingdom for welcoming foreign students and educating them on generous terms, in the years before fee revenue became the dominant incentive (see, for instance, Kogan, cited in Humphrey 1999, 7). In the case of Germany, Roeloffs (1994, 29) states that the policy in Franco–German relations—aiming at reconciliation in the first postwar phase, then cooperation, then integration—has been the motive for academic cooperation between France and Germany.[2] For Europe and The Netherlands, Rupp (1997, 1999) has analyzed the political aspects of the Fulbright Program and the exchange programs of the British Council. Rupp (1997) states, for instance,

De Nederlandse wetenschappelijke wereld is gericht geraakt op de wetenschap van de Engelssprekende wereld, vooral op de Verenigde Staten en in iets mindere mate op Engeland. De Amerikaanse (Fulbright) en de Britse (British Council) wetenschappelijke uitwisselingsprogramma's hebben in deze veranderingen een beslissende rol gespeeld [The Dutch academic world has become oriented toward the English speaking academic world, in particular the United States and to a somewhat lesser extent England. The American (Fulbright) and British (British Council) academic exchange programs have played a decisive role in these changes]. (p. 263)

One can also say that the opening of the educational and research programs of the European Commission to the EFTA countries and later Central and Eastern Europe was intended to prepare the climate for the future incorporation of these countries into the European Union. The decision on the withdrawal of Switzerland from these programs was based on a political conflict with regard to its relations to the European Union.

National Security

Closely related to the foreign-policy argument is the argument of national security, which is rather dominant in American international education, in particular in the period between the 1960s and the 1980s, as we have seen in Chapter 2. NATO is also active in providing international scholarships on the basis of security considerations.

Apart from the United States and NATO, no other examples of such explicit links between national security and internationalization have been encountered, but this argument probably applies to the former Soviet Union and other countries as well. The Cold War period is a clear example of how political rationales have set the agenda for the internationalization of higher education. It is important to note that the donor and/or the receiver do not always meet the aims of the foreign policy and national security arguments for internationalization with the intended results.[3]

Technical Assistance

A third political rationale for internationalization is technical assistance or development cooperation. After World War II, and in particular in the period after decolonization in combination with the intensification of the Cold War, technical assistance to developing countries became an important part of foreign policy in most industrialized countries. Assistance to higher education in these countries has always been one element. Institution-building projects, the sending of experts, training programs, and scholarships were funded by national governments, international organizations such as the World Bank, and private foundations. Institutions also contribute to development cooperation from their own budgets. In particular, in countries such as Australia, Canada, and The Netherlands, international cooperation and technical assistance to higher education in developing countries were one and the same until the 1980s. At that time, in Australia, as Back, Davis, and Olsen (1996, 7) put it, "educational aid" became "educational trade," and in The Netherlands internationalization became at least as important as technical assistance. In Canada it took longer for educational trade and internationalization to overshadow educational aid, but its exclusive dominance has also disappeared.

Peace and Mutual Understanding

Sometimes coinciding with but frequently also in conflict with foreign-policy rationales of national governments, internationalization is promoted for ideological reasons as an instrument to realize the aspiration of peace and mutual understanding. In many publications and policy documents, this rationale is present as a driving force for internationalization. The use of the term "internationalism" is closely related to this argument, as Dennis Kallen (1991a, 26) observes in linking "internationalism in education" with idealistic and political roots.

Political rationales, such as providing peace and mutual understanding, have been more dominant in international education in the United States than in other parts of the world, and date back to the period between the two world wars, as we have seen in Chapter 2. It can be related to the first element of the definition of Maurice Harari (1989) for internationalization of higher education, the "international ethos."

In American studies, documents, and political statements, you can find many examples of this peace-driven rationale. de Wit (1998e), states that, although seen in the rest of the world by many as a sign of American imperialism (matched by a similar trend in the former Soviet Union) internationalization is presented by politicians in the United States as a stimulus for peace and mutual understanding.

This optimistic view of international education as a peacemaking force has been dominant in American politics and higher education for the past fifty years, and is still rather widespread there and has found supporters elsewhere. For instance, the *Policy Statement on Internationalization of Higher Education in the World* of the International Association for University Presidents (IAUP 1995) speaks of "promoting vigorously the internationalisation of their institutions and the global competence and literacy of their students as being essential to the long term pursuit of a more peaceful world where international understanding and co-operation in solving problems will be increasingly critical for the quality of life and sustained economic, social and cultural development."[4]

This argument is mostly used hand in hand with that of technical assistance. As remarked elsewhere (de Wit 1998b, 15), although it is quite tempting to sympathize with such a view of internationalization of higher education, one should be careful with such a purely political rationale for internationalization. Whose peace is it and who's understanding of the world? Was and is higher education in the rest of the world in the position to place its understanding on equal terms with that of the American and European academic world? Does such a view provide space for one's own national identity?

National Identity

In a comparative study of internationalization strategies in Asia-Pacific countries, Knight and de Wit (1997, 23–27) found that enhancement of national identity was given as a rationale for internationalization of higher education. By becoming part of a global environment, higher education and society can move away from dependency on and dominance of Western technology, Western means, and Western languages of instruction. Not the expansion of English as the language of instruction—an issue in several continental Europe higher education institutions—but the option of the introduction of local languages of instruction in addition to the use of the colonial, mainly English, language, a heritage from the past, is part of the internationalization strategy in several Asian countries and universities (see Welch and Denman 1997, 26). This is not pursued as a nationalist reaction to globalization, but to neocolonialism.

There is a link between foreign-policy arguments and national-identity arguments for internationalization in their consequences. Many national leaders have had their education abroad as a result of the foreign policy of industrialized countries such as the United States and the United Kingdom, and, in that other cultural environment, became even more attached to their own national identity than before. In 1952, the Czech-born political scientist Karl Wolfgang Deutsch (1997), wrote, at Harvard, "There is an excellent chance that among the hundreds and thousands of foreign students at the universities today there may be a considerable number of young men and women who may go back one day to their countries with a deeper emotional attachment to their own nation and often with a deeper nationalism than the one with which they came" (p. 34). There is also a link between cultural rationales and national identity, which is closely related to preservation of cultural identity.

Regional Identity

As with globalization in relation to nationalization and regionalization, one can also identify, in addition to the global-identity and national-identity arguments, regional identity as an argument for internationalization. This rationale is strongly present in the aspiration of a European dimension and Europeanization in the European Union programs. The creation of a "European citizenship" is a crucial rationale in its education programs.[5] It also is present, for instance, in the Japanese orientation on Asia in its international programs (IIE 1997, 65). Pratt and Poole (1998a, 15) see some evidence that Australian universities are evolving toward regional strategies focused on Asia.[6]

ECONOMIC RATIONALES

Economic rationales are becoming more dominant, and there is a direct link with the globalization of our economies. That does not mean that certain economic rationales have not always existed.

Economic Growth and Competitiveness

According to this argument, the internationalization of education will have a positive effect on technological development and thus on economic growth. This argument is for both the public and the private sectors, perhaps the most important reason for investment in international cooperation in higher education, in particular since the end of the Cold War. For Europe, a study on national policies for internationalization of higher education showed that, increasingly, "concerns related to international competence and competitiveness, and thus economic rationales" became more important (van der Wende 1997a, 227).[7] For the United States, Lyman (1995) observes a similar trend: "Today, internationalizing education in the US is proposed as a way to help restore our economic competitiveness in the world" (p. 4). According to Joseph Johnston and Richard Edelstein (1993), "Today, the dominant argument for internationalizing higher education is that it will ensure the nation's economic competitiveness." And Groennings (1997, 105) speaks of a reframing of rationales from Cold War foreign policy to a global knowledge economy.

One consequence of the economic-growth rationale is the investment by national governments in future economic relations. For many national governments this is the reason for the creation of scholarship programs for foreign students, in the hope that they will become the future decision makers in the private and public sectors of their home countries and by then will remember with gratitude the host country that gave them the opportunity to become what they are now. Such investment will, it is hoped, bear fruit in the form of favored treatment of the former host country when large orders are placed and contracts negotiated against international competition. This is true for many scholarship programs for Third World students and recently also for students in Central and Eastern Europe.

Another consequence is the investment in international programs for research and development. The Framework Programs of the European Commission since 1984 and their predecessors since 1979, created with the intention of stimulating European research and development, are clear examples of such investments, motivated by competition with the United States and Japan.

The Labor Market

Closely related to the economic-growth argument is the labor-market argument. The more international the labor market becomes as a result of the globalization of our economies, the more a graduate has to compete with people from other countries and the more he or she has to work in an international environment.

The demand of the labor market in a global economy is used very frequently by politicians and international educators as a reason for the internationalization of higher education, but little research has been done on the effect of internationalization on the labor market.[8] Although Dick Krasno and others at an ACA meeting in 1996 (ACA 1997, 5) mentioned market-driven human resource requirements as an important external factor, the views of employers and the labor market itself may be less clear on the need for "international" graduates. There is some evidence that representatives of the private sector, in particular the multinationals, are less outspoken on this matter than politicians and educators. A study by Hubert B. van Hoof (1999) among job recruiters in the United States confirms this view. Huebner (1994) found that international education is at best a fifth concern for a company looking for staff for an international assignment: "What most corporations do not seem to be looking for, however, is some standardized 'global' man or woman" (p. 74).

National Educational Demand

In some European countries the lack of sufficient higher education provision at home has stimulated the mobility of students and faculty. For instance, in Norway the government deliberately stimulates study abroad instead of creating new facilities at home. In other countries also, such as Greece and Portugal, the academic infrastructure has not been adequate in the past to absorb national demand for higher education and research, thereby generating a high net outward mobility. The same pattern is true for developing countries and their external mobility to the industrialized world. Asia is a relevant example that also illustrates the dynamics of this rationale. Certain countries, such as Singapore, are moving from import of knowledge by sending their students for training abroad, to exporters of knowledge by receiving students from other parts of Asia and even beyond (Knight and de Wit 1997).

Financial Incentives for Institutions and Governments

Internationalization activities, such as contract education, recruitment of foreign students, and international education advisory services, can be initiated for reasons of income generation. University entrepreneurialism is becoming more dominant these days as a consequence of globalization, as Slaughter and Leslie (1997) argue. This also affects internationalization strategies.

"International education marketing is now big business for Australian universities," observe Pratt and Poole (1998a, 8), and this is becoming true in more and more countries. On the other hand, one should not exaggerate this development. As other studies show (for instance, on Australia, Back, Davis, and Olsen 1996), there are also counterbalancing measures for internationalization, such as exchanges and programs to stimulate outward mobility of students and faculty.

Higher education as an export commodity is becoming a dominant rationale for internationalization, not only for national governments, but also for institutions and the private sector. The more foreign students there are paying high tuition fees, the higher the economic return and the less the national government needs to invest in higher education. In 1979 the U.K. government adopted a full-fee policy (i.e., the requirement that students pay a tuition fee equivalent to the "real cost" of their education) with regard to students from outside the European Community. As a consequence, the internationalization of higher education in the United Kingdom has been mainly concentrated on attracting high-tuition-paying foreign degree students, and has been understood in that manner. Indeed, many administrators in British higher education institutions have seen the exchange of students, where there is no net income gain, as an expensive burden rather than as something to stimulate.

One can see the same trend in other English-speaking countries in the 1980s and 1990s, in particular in Australia and New Zealand and to a lesser extent Canada.[9] The United States, the leading country in receiving international students, has until now been able to maintain that position without active investment in recruitment campaigns, based mainly on status and reputation, but more recently has become concerned by the competition, not only from the other English-speaking countries, but also from the European continent (France, Germany, and The Netherlands in particular) and from newly industrialized countries in Asia such as Malaysia and Singapore, which are becoming both sending and receiving countries.[10]

There is an institutional argument based on finance, as indicated by Callan (1993) for the United Kingdom: "The full-cost fees policy was resisted at first, but later became, ironically, a financial lifeline to institutions in the face of progressive restraints of public expenditure through the 1980s" (p. 9). And there is a national economic argument, as indicated for the United States by Lambert (1992), who states that "the US has come to realize that even financially, the import of foreign students is a major asset on our international balance sheet" (p. 1). Export of knowledge and recruitment of international students have become the number-one export product of Australia.

As Carnestedt (1997) concludes from a comparison of internationalization strategies of Swedish and Australian universities, for Swedish and other Scandinavian and European continental universities it is not so much the financial motive that is the incentive for recruitment—through lack of or rather low fees—but status. Status (and similar qualifications as reputation, profile, prestige) is seen as an indirect economic rationale of perhaps greater importance than the direct financial incentives by Van Rooijen (1998) and Knight (2000).[11]

The different positions became clear in statements in the *Chronicle of Higher Education* by the rector of the University of Bonn, Germany, Klaus Bochard, and the chief of the Committee of Vice Chancellors and Principals of the Universities of the United Kingdom, Baroness Diana Warwick. Bochard, noting that state universities in Germany do not charge tuition, stated that "the only currency we value is brain," while Warwick states that recruitment is "for the sake of our country's prosperity" (Desruisseaux, 2000a).

CULTURAL AND SOCIAL RATIONALES

Alongside these economic and political rationales there are arguments that have a more cultural and social character. John Davies (1992) explains why international activities have been expanding in the past decade on the basis of a combination of economic and cultural rationales. He states that internationalization is "closely linked with financial reduction, the rise of academic entrepreneurialism and genuine philosophical commitment to close cultural perspectives in the advancement and dissemination of knowledge" (p. 177).

Cultural Rationales

The first of these is the "cultural function" of internationalization. This function is stressed as important in many studies on the internationalization of education. In some cases, in particular in French and American policy, this cultural function constitutes a nationalist argument, one which emphasizes the export of national and cultural and moral values. It thus merges with the foreign-policy and national-identity arguments already described. Heginbotham (1997) observes on this that "it is not inappropriate to consider American cultural and educational activities, including the notion of 'exchanges,' a third sphere of American rules" (p. 86). This attitude is not only found among politicians. Burkart Holzner (1994) makes reference to an Ivy League professor who insisted that international education "really meant the education of the people of the world about the achievements of American civilisation" (p. 6).

Davies (1997) observes, on the basis of case studies of twenty European universities, that for these institutions there is confusion about the term "European values," but that they see "an essential role of the university in propagating civilizing and cultural values" (p. 83). This can be interpreted as a strong hesitation by the higher education sector with respect to attempts to impose ideological values from outside versus the autonomous role of higher education with respect to the spread of cultural values.

The cultural rationale, as related to foreign policy and national identity, is present in cultural and scientific agreements and programs between governments. Intermediary agencies such as the British Council and DAAD in Germany are an expression of this in the same way as institutes such as the Goethe Institute for Germany, Maison Descartes for France, and again the British Council for the United Kingdom are for the arts. The support given by national governments and universities to the promotion of their national languages and country studies is also linked to this rationale.

Such a nationalist case stands in contrast to the cultural function of internationalization as described by the director of UNESCO, Federico Mayor (1989): "The university is an institution in which the production, transmission and reproduction of culture meet harmoniously and in which the latter are completed by reflection on the role and the function of culture in the life of nations and individuals." It is for this reason, as Mayor continues, that "the cultural function of the European university goes hand in hand not only with its humanistic search, but also with its international dimension. To develop an awareness of the interdependence of peoples and of societies in today's world must be one of the basic functions of the universities" (pp. 5, 13).

The Liaison Committee (1992), in a comment on the European Commission's "Memorandum on Higher Education in the European Community," also stresses the cultural function of the university: "The direct usefulness of universities for their community is not limited to their economic function; they are also, or primarily, cultural centres or 'think-tanks,' offering a forum for learning, research and social debate" (p. 3). Davies (1998, 79) refers to the role of the universities in "transmission of cultural values."

These views on the cultural function of the university are more related to the notion of "universalism" of knowledge and its institutions, the universities. Such universalism is frequently used as a rationale for internationalization.

Social Rationales

These rationales emphasize the relevance of internationalization for the individual, in particular the student. Kallen (1991b) has called this "social learning," others refer to it as "personal development." It stresses the importance of the individual development of the student and the academic through a confrontation with other cultures, but also, and perhaps even more, with the home culture. In the context of fieldwork training in social anthropology, this has been called "the daily experience of not knowing." For this confrontation Mark Twain's comments about travel are true, namely "that it is fatal to prejudice, bigotry, and narrow mindedness," and also as Paul Theroux wrote, "Being mistaken is the essence of the traveler's tale." Most studies indicate that studying abroad does not change much in the student's attitude to their host country, but there are clear indications that overcoming mistakes and the prejudices of their own culture are equally important effects as overcoming those of other cultures.

It is frequently argued that international academic exchange is more important for the individual's development than for academic or cultural reasons. American universities, in particular, focus on individual development as an important argument for internationalization. On this issue, in a study by the Institute of International Education, an interesting observation is made about the different rationales for international education in Japan and the United States: "The prevailing Japanese ryugakusei rationale stresses long-term commitment to gain knowledge and insight from a foreign expert. In contrast, the dominant American rationale of 'mutual understanding' stresses moderate overseas exposure as a stimulus for expanding personal awareness" (p. 10). Chambers described it already in 1950 in the following way: "Young students or industrial apprentices can be greatly enlightened by the experience away from the homeland, even though their individual motives may be scarcely more than a dilettante wish to 'see the world' or a vague feeling that 'travel is broadening.' These attitudes, characteristic of youth, may be trite, but they hold vast possibilities for good" (p. 32).

American universities fear parochial orientation of their students and the American population in general and for that reason encourage study abroad at the undergraduate level. Elsewhere (de Wit 1998b) it is written that reading publications on international education in the United States one gets the impression that a central drive for internationalization is the feeling among academics that the population in general and the youth in particular are ignorant of global issues. Briggs and Burn (1985, 42) quote a report for the Rockefeller Foundation on "persistent American parochialism" as an argument for study abroad for American undergraduate students. Richard Lambert (1994) observes that "Americans frequently tell themselves and are told by others that they are a parochial lot, ignorant of world geography, people, and events" (pp. 12–13). Richard Lyman (1995) stresses cultural parochialism and arrogance as main factors in policies for internationalization. He provides an interesting explanation for the view that Americans are "monoglot and widely ignorant." He states that a lot of it has to do with "self-serving testimony from international studies scholars" and "sheer frustration" by the lack of global awareness, and their actions should mainly be considered as "cries of alarm, which are proverbially a wasting asset" (pp. 11–12).

This is further underlined by Lambert (1989a), who made an evaluation of American study abroad programs and discovered that "all of the evaluative studies, almost without exception, were concerned with what I would call the characterological benefits which a foreign sojourn provided. There is almost no evaluative literature on the academic, as distinct from the characterological, benefits of study abroad" (p. 162). The strong emphasis in the United States on global–transnational–intercultural–international competencies is also linked to this view.

It has been observed elsewhere (de Wit 1998b, 16) that the concern for global awareness is also an important issue in Europe, but the focus for solutions is directed at primary and secondary education, rather than at the postsecondary level.[12] It is surprising that few American authors see a role for the internationalization of education at any level before higher education.[13]

Parochialism is less of a concern in the call for international education in Europe than in the United States. But it is not so clear anymore that one should continue to underestimate social learning and global awareness as a force in the internationalization of higher education in Europe, and the policy of the European Commission to stimulate the European dimension and the development of a European citizenship by way of mobility schemes and support to curriculum development is a specific interpretation of this rationale.[14]

ACADEMIC RATIONALES

Providing an International Dimension to Research and Teaching

It can be said, and has been said by many, that the internationalization of education is inevitable, as the advancement of knowledge and understanding is a global enterprise that has no borders. It can also be said, and has been said by maybe even more people, that universities by nature are international. That being said, it is important that a thoughtful approach be taken to why and how higher education institutions are giving more importance and priority to integrating an international dimension into their teaching and learning, research, and service mandates.

In terms of academic study, an international approach attempts to avoid parochialism in scholarship and research and to stimulate critical thinking and inquiry about the complexity of issues and interests that bear on the relations among nations, regions, and interest groups. Often introducing or emphasizing the international and intercultural aspects leads to more inter-disciplinary cooperation in research endeavors.

Internationalization efforts are intended to enable the academic community to have the ability to understand, appreciate, and articulate the reality of interdependence among nations (environmental, economic, cultural, and social), and to prepare faculty, staff, and students to function in an international and intercultural context. Even students who never leave their own country are affected by the impact of our globalized society and economy. Institutions of higher education have the opportunity and responsibility through teaching and research to increase awareness and understanding of the new and changing phenomena that affect the political, economic, and cultural–multicultural developments within and among nations.

Internationalization strategies such as curriculum innovation, study abroad programs, faculty–student exchanges, area studies and centers, foreign language study, joint international research initiatives, and cross-cultural training are important activities that require serious review and reflection as to their greatest impact on the student and faculty experience.

As far as research is concerned, the international dimension has been less discussed and more assumed as a natural and implicit element. Studies on internationalization of research are limited in number, compared to those on the internationalization of education. Gingras, Godin, and Foisy (1999) distinguish two components: the training of researchers and the production of knowledge. Studies on the internationalization of research tend to focus on citation indexes, technology transfer, funding issues, networking, training of researchers, dissemination of research, licensing and patents, the academic profession, and so on. Internationalization is already integrated and mainstream in research, although the global knowledge economy gives it a new dimension.[15]

That is certainly not still the case with the internationalization of education. Most studies are directed to this sector of higher education, and then in particular to the internationalization of the curriculum (van der Wende 1996) and to student mobility (Blumenthal et al. 1996) and the organizational aspects of these two. Less attention is given international staff mobility and development (Bunt-Kokhuis 1996). But all in all, one can say that this rationale is the main theme of studies on the internationalization of higher education.

Extension of the Academic Horizon

This argument is part of the previous one, but given the dominance of study abroad as an instrument for the internationalization of higher education, it is also relevant to treat it here separately.

As stated, internationalization in the sense of mobility of students and faculty is seen in the United States mainly as a form of social learning by means of a multicultural experience. In Europe, on the other hand, the importance attached to study abroad, faculty mobility, and research cooperation tends to be measured more from the academic point of view: Can one learn something at a foreign institution that one cannot learn at the home institution? This has a negative side in that in some cases opportunities have been reduced for cooperation between institutions in Northern and Southern Europe owing to prejudices on the Northern side with respect to the quality of research and education in Southern Europe. It also applies to the continuing dominance of Europe as the destination of study abroad for the United States. Recently in the United States the academic rationale for study abroad has been gaining importance, and in Europe the added social and cultural value of study abroad is becoming more recognized.

Institution-Building

Closely related is the argument that internationalization can strengthen the core structures and activities of an institution, and may enable initiatives to be taken that would not otherwise be possible on the basis of local resources and/or expertise. The pursuit of knowledge in the modern world requires vast resources that are not all available in any one university; international cooperation between higher education institutions, in many cases, then becomes a necessity. Electronic communication is facilitating this cooperation in a significant way.

North American educators have long been aware of the resource value of graduate students from abroad in staffing research programs and in undergraduate teaching. In some countries of Europe, resource constraints have led to a situation in which the "catchment area" for recruitment of both faculty and students in some subjects needs to be international if the departments themselves are to be viable. In the United States already, but in the near future also in European countries, mainly Asian faculty and students will occupy science faculties. The negative side of this case is, obviously, the brain-drain problem. It is important, therefore, to acknowledge the necessity of mutual benefits for partner institutions–countries in international cooperation activities.

Profile and Status

A related and at first glance contradictory issue is the growing tendency to competitiveness among institutions of higher education across national borders. For research institutions and professional schools in particular, international ranking is increasingly becoming more important than competition with neighbor institutions within national borders. Participation in international research, teaching, service, and institutional networks is an important aspect of this competition.

This argument refers to the aspiration on the part of institutions to increase their international profiles for status and marketing purposes, based on an assumed perception that the more international a university is, the better it is. This is a perception that Rudzki (1998, 227–229) seems to adhere to in describing three scenarios: the international institution, the opportunistic nationalists, and the parochial institution, in which the first scenario is linked to status and presumed excellence. Callan (2000) uses the term "negative rationale," "the fear of falling behind competitively when an entire system or sector is moving in the direction of greater international involvement" (p. 17). This also falls under the profile and status argument.

Linking this rationale to the economic rationale of financial incentive is one way of positioning, but it is also an element that belongs to the educational rationale. For instance, the recruitment of Ph.D. students in Asia by the faculty of science of the Universiteit van Amsterdam is not in the first place based on financial incentives—although certainly also part of its motivation—but on maintaining its profile as a high-class research faculty.

Enhancement of Quality

Quality assurance of education and research is receiving more and more attention, and its assessment instruments are widely debated (Woodhouse 1999). This is also true for the quality of internationalization and transnational education (Knight 1999c). As Alan Smith (1994b) has pointed out, there are two aspects to the link between internationalization and quality of education: "The first is quality of the delivery of international education, but just as important is the question of how the international dimension of higher education can actually enhance the quality of higher education provision. . . . The two are linked in the sense that the international dimension of higher education can make the best contribution to enhancing quality in higher education if it is itself of high quality" (p. 17).

van der Wende (1999c) also emphasizes the relation, with both tensions and coherence, between the two. In Chapter 9, the issue of and relationship between quality and the internationalization of higher education will be handled.

As a rationale for internationalization of higher education, the issue of enhancement of the quality of higher education is relevant. This rationale is used frequently, although mostly in a very general way, without providing clear indicators of the way internationalization enhances the quality of higher education.

International Academic Standards

Related to the arguments of profile and status and quality assurance and assessment is the argument of international academic standards. Two studies by Jane Knight (1995, 1997b) for Canada, a study by CHEMS (1996) on the Commonwealth, and the comparative study by Jane Knight and de Wit (1997) on internationalization of higher education in Asia-Pacific countries mention the achievement of international academic standards as important motivations. Meeting international academic standards is a way for institutions of higher education to match others and receive recognition in the international arena. As Jane Knight (1999b, 225) points out, there is also a fear that standardization implies uniformity and Westernization.

SHIFTS IN RATIONALES

When analyzing rationales, we have to take into account the diversity of stakeholder groups in higher education and within each stakeholder group: the government, the private sector, and the educational sector. Within the first group we see a trend away from national governments towards regional bodies (the EU) and international entities (the United Nations). In the second group there is a difference between multinational companies and foundations and smaller national or local companies. Within the last group we have to distinguish between several subgroups: the institutional level, the academics and their departments, and the students. Jenkins (1977) writes, "International educational interchange is, almost by definition, a partnership that involves at least two parties, the student applicant and the admitting institution, and often a third, the governmental or private agency or organization that is providing all or part of the funds for the educational programme. Each of these partners will have different and sometimes conflicting purposes" (p. 1513).

In a study of national policies for the internationalization of higher education in Europe, Marijk van der Wende (1997b, 36) has brought the four rationales together in a figure in which each rationale is represented by a separate line and in which the position on the line in relation to the center of the model indicates the relevant importance (minimum in the center, maximum at the edge) of the rationale (Figure 5.1). This model can be used not only for national policies but also for other stakeholders and can in addition be used to compare the relative importance of rationales at a certain moment between stakeholders, as well as the change in importance of rationales in time within one group of stakeholders.[16]

In Part I, the shift in rationales was already referred to in the historical analysis of the international dimension in higher education. There, one clear example was the shift in the United States from the political rationale (which dominated until the end of the Cold War) to the economic (competitiveness), as well as a shift within the political rationale from "peace and mutual understanding" (between the two world wars) to "foreign policy" (after World War II) to "national security" (during the Cold War). Another shift we have seen, for instance, in Australia, is from the rationale of "technical assistance" to "trade," higher education as an export commodity.

Figure 5.1
Rationales for the Internationalization Policy

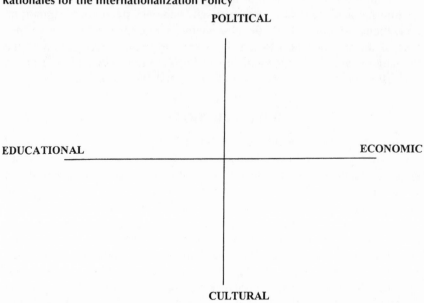

Source: Marijk G. van der Wend, Missing Links: The Relationship between National Policies for Internationalisation and Those for Higher Education in General, in *National Policies for the Internationalisation of Higher Education in Europe*, ed. T. Kälvermark and M. van der Wende (Stockholm: Högskoleverket Studies, National Agency for Higher Education, 1997), 36.

At the same time, we have seen that the rationale for one stakeholder does not necessarily have to coincide with the rationale of another stakeholder. For instance, the rationale of personal development for a student can be different from the rationale of national security for a government or the labor market argument for a private company. The effect can still be the same. On the other hand, as illustrated in the Peruvian case (see note 3 of this chapter), the outcome can be different than that intended—the rationale—by the initiator.

It is important to keep in mind (de Wit 1998e) the following:

- There is a strong overlap in rationales within and between different stakeholders' groups; the main differences are in the hierarchy of priorities, as Jane Knight (1997b) has illustrated for Canada.

- In general, stakeholders do not have one exclusive rationale but a combination of rationales for internationalization with a hierarchy in priorities (see also Knight, 1997b).

- Rationales may differ between stakeholder groups and within stakeholder groups, as, for instance, Davies (1997, 83) illustrates for Europe.

- Priorities in rationales may change over time and may change by country and region. A clear example is the change in time of the rationale from development assistance to export in Australia, and the difference in rationales between the United Kingdom (export) and the rest of the European Union (cooperation and exchange).

- Rationales have a strong influence on the internationalization of higher education, but, as has been indicated, the question "why" is in many cases not explicitly formulated. Or, as Overbeek (1997) explains for the Dutch case, they are described in very general terms, such as "improving the quality of education" or "enhancing the chances on the labor market," and cannot be measured.

NOTES

1. See also Tierney (1977, 1509–1510), who gives examples of political rationales from the 1960s.

2. See also the frequent accounts by Littmann (1997) and Markert (1998) on academic mobility between Germany and the United States, and on the foreign-policy aspects of this mobility. See also Heginbotham (1997) for Japan and the United States.

3. I remember from my own time as a student in Lima, Peru, that Peruvian students from lower-income groups who had studied with a scholarship in the former Soviet Union were said to have returned as convinced capitalists, while students from rich families who had studied in the United States came back as leaders of the radical left. They were affected in quite the opposite way to that intended by their host countries, and returned with a different impression than that for which their sponsors—the (at that time left-wing) military regime and the conservative oligarchy, respectively—had hoped.

4. It is also present in UNESCO (1998). Wächter, Ollikainen, and Hasewend (1999, 20–22) give several examples of this argument from organizations such as the IAUP, UNESCO, and the CRE.

5. Wächter, Ollikainen, and Hasewend (1999, 22) give some examples of this argument. See also Chapter 3.

6. Back, Davis, and Olsen (1996) disagree. They see a global focus in the internationalization strategies of Australian universities. Successful or not, there are certainly enough indications that Australian universities are working in the direction of tapping markets that according to Pratt and Poole (1998a, 22) are still largely untouched, such as South Africa, the Gulf States, and South America, but also Europe and the United States.

7. As remarked elsewhere (de Wit, 1998d, 88), it would be better to read, for Europe, "Northern Europe," because the case studies are, with one exception on Greece, limited to that region.

8. See Maiworm and Teichler (1996) and Bremer (1998) on the impact of exchanges on the career of students.

9. For Australia, see, for instance, Pratt and Poole (1998a, 1999b), and Back and Davis (1995). For New Zealand, see I. Smith and Parata (1997).

10. For the United States, see Dunnett (1998). For The Netherlands, see de Wit (1998c). For Asia, see de Wit (1997a).

11. On foreign students flows, policies, and industries, see Altbach (1997a, 1997b) and Cummings (1993), who gives a useful overview of push and pull factors in international student flows.

12. Dronkers (1993, 298), however, observes that the growth of international education in The Netherlands—in particular in primary and secondary education—is primarily the result of the development of a cosmopolitan culture by part of the Dutch elite.

13. An exception is, for instance, the Institute of International Education (1997, 55-57).

14. Knight and de Wit (1995, 13) wrote that while more research analyzing the benefits of international experience to the development of the individual is welcomed, for such analyses to be useful one must clearly distinguish between benefits accruing from the educational content of the experience and those that might be more loosely characterized as "academic tourism."

15. Few studies have been done on the internationalization of research. A positive example is the article by Gingras, Godin, and Foisy (1999). For a study on doctoral students, see Blume (1995) and Kyvik and colleagues (1999). On the global knowledge economy, licensing, and patents, see, for instance, Etzkowitz and Leydesdorff (1997). On the international aspects of academic publishing, see Altbach (1988), and on the academic profession, see Altbach (1996) and Welch (1997).

16. For an example of the use of this model on Finnish SOCRATES European Policy Statements, see Ollikainen (1998). Jane Knight (1997b) has made a study of rationales and stakeholders' perspectives in Canada. In a study on transnational competence (IIE 1997, 46-56), an analysis is given of the changes in rationales of international education in the United States and Japan. These studies and one on national policies for internationalization of higher education in Europe are among the few case studies on the rationales for internationalization of higher education.

Chapter 6

Meanings of and Approaches to International Education and the Internationalization of Higher Education

One of the fundamental problems we face when dealing with the internationalization of higher education is the diversity of related terms. Terms frequently used, both in the literature and in practice, are international education, international studies, internationalism, transnational education, and globalization of higher education. There are also regional variants, such as regionalization of higher education—best known through the use of Europeanization of education—and more concrete subdivisions of the field: academic mobility, international cooperation, study abroad, and international exchange. More curriculum-focused terms include area studies in education, multicultural education, intercultural education, cross-cultural education, education for international understanding, peace education, global education, international studies, transnational studies, and global studies. And there are more competence-related terms, such as global competence and transnational competence. Sometimes they are used to describe a concrete element of the broad field of internationalization, but in other cases these terms are used as *pars pro toto* and as a synonym for the overall term internationalization.

Each of these terms has a different emphasis and reflects a different approach, and are used by different authors in different ways. For a better understanding of the internationalization of higher education it is important to place that term in perspective to approaches and other terms used, and to provide a working definition of its meaning, which is the purpose of this chapter.

MEANING OF INTERNATIONAL EDUCATION AND THE INTERNATIONALIZATION OF HIGHER EDUCATION

Over the past ten years a lively debate has taken place on the definition and meaning of the internationalization of higher education and the related term, international education, reflecting the growing relevance of this area. Several publications, seminars, and symposia have dealt with this fundamental question: "What exactly does it mean to internationalize?" as one symposium and related book (Hanson and Meyerson 1995) phrases it. Usually the answers are given only in vague and implicit terms, by providing an overview of related aspects. Others attempt to come to a definition of its meaning.[1] In doing so, the terms international education and internationalization of education are used interchangeably. As will be demonstrated later, international education is strongly related to activity approaches, as well as rationale, competency, and ethos approaches. American authors tend to use the term international education more frequently, while the internationalization of (higher) education is used more in the non-American literature. This can be explained through historical developments, as described in Part I. For that reason it is relevant to return first to the original use of the term international education.

The Origins of International Education

The purpose of this section is to place international education within the broader context of comparative and international education. In most literature the basic overall term within which most of the other terms are placed as a kind of subdivision is international education, in itself a term directly related to comparative education. International education is most frequently used in place of the internationalization of higher education.

Historically, writes Epstein (1994), "Comparative education grew out of, and was inspired by, international education" (pp. 918–919). The origin of international education lies, according to him, in the call by César Auguste Basset in 1808 for the appointment of a scholar free from national and methodological prejudices to observe education outside of France. According to Epstein, comparative education found its origin in the publication of a series of five articles in 1816–1817 by the French scholar Marc-Antoine Jullien, in which he set out a method for the comparative study of education. Other scholars generally accept this historical description of the two terms. There is disagreement on the further development of the two related fields.

Altbach, Arnove, and Kelly (1982) state that in essence comparative education is a post–World War II field of study. Although its intellectual roots lie in the nineteenth century, "the field's legitimacy was established only after World War II. Since that time, comparative education has sought to delineate itself as a distinct area of inquiry in educational studies that reaches beyond education for theoretical perspectives and methodology" (p. 505). The same might be said about international education, which also became more important after World War II, in particular in the 1960s and 1970s.

Epstein (1994) states that comparative education and international education are often confused. He describes comparative education as "a field of study that applies historical, philosophical, and social theories and methods to international problems in education." According to him, "Comparative education is primarily an academic and interdisciplinary pursuit." By comparison, he describes international education as fostering "an international orientation in knowledge and attitudes and, among other initiatives, brings together students, teachers, and scholars from different nations to learn about and from each other" (p. 918). In this way, Epstein, similar to many other comparative educators, makes a distinction between comparativists, being primarily scholars "interested in explaining why educational systems and processes vary and how education relates to wider social factors and forces," and international educators, focusing "more directly on descriptive information about nations and societies and their educational systems and structures. International educators use findings derived from comparative education to understand better the educational processes they examine, and thus to enhance their ability to make policy relating to programs such as those associated with international exchange and understanding" (p. 918). Elsewhere, Epstein (1968) even more clearly distinguished comparative education from international education by stating that the latter "is concerned more with practice and implementing policy" (p. 377).

D. N. Wilson (1994) also states that "the apparent dividing line between international and comparative education is the distinction between **researchers** (either descriptive or analytic) and **practitioners** directly concerned with policy and practice" (pp. 453–454). D. Adams and Theisen (1990, 286) differentiate not between scholar and practitioner, but between basic and applied research, where basic research is knowledge driven and applied research solution driven.[2]

It is true that much work in international education, whichever description one gives to this term, seems to be practically oriented, while much comparative educational work seems to be more scholarly oriented. The same might be said about the distinction between basic and applied research. However, as Altbach, Arnove, and Kelly (1982, 506) and D. N. Wilson (1994, 484) make clear, one can find both practitioners and scholars among comparative and international educators. D. N. Wilson synthesizes them in the term academic-practitioner: "The confusion between comparative and international educators is compounded by the dual roles played by academics who occasionally consult for these [UNESCO, ILO, World Bank, etc.]

agencies and by agency personnel who continue to undertake 'academic' research and publication, even though not based in academia" (p. 453). This synthesis is also true for the area of internationalization of higher education, although with a different emphasis: primarily practitioners who do academic work, instead of academics doing consultancy and/or practical work.[3] One might say that both the distinction and the synthesis between basic and applied and between scholarly and practical is relevant to all fields of study, and so does not help us much in clarifying the distinction between comparative and international education.

Paulston (1994) sees international education as a result of the late 1960s, a new branch of comparative education as he calls it, that "addressed problems of educational planning, development, and theory construction in macrostudies of educational and social change in largely poor, newly independent countries" (p. 925). Willis Griffin and Ralph Spence, cited by Anweiler (1977), note that "the term international education has been used to refer variously to curriculum content that deals with other countries and societies, with international relations among countries, exchange of students between countries, assistance to other countries' educational development, training of specialists for diplomatic and other international work, cultural relations programs between nations and the general informing of the public of world affairs" (p. 110). According to D. N. Wilson (1994, 481), this broad and vague definition is a reflection of their inclusion of topics such as development education, cross-cultural education, and international cooperation and exchange.

More authors have a tendency to create subdivisions within comparative and/or international education, in particular as far as it concerns the more practitioner-oriented aspect of the term. One group of subdivision terms mentioned frequently in the literature relates to development education, peace education, education for international understanding, multicultural education, and cross-cultural education. These terms have a strong common basis in the post–World War II efforts to promote peace and international understanding, and later development cooperation. Another group of subdivision terms relates to study abroad, academic mobility, international exchange, and international cooperation (see, e.g., D. N. Wilson 1994, 461). This subdivision reflects more what we refer to in this study as international education.

Harari (1977) refers to Freeman Butts in 1969, who described international education as "embracing the programs of activity which identifiable educational organizations deliberately plan and carry out for their members (students, teachers, and closely related clientele), with one of (possibly both) two major purposes in mind: (a) the study of the thought, institutions, techniques, or ways of life of other peoples and of their interrelationships, and (b) the transfer of educational institutions, ideas, or materials from [one] society to another" (p. 2293). Harari identifies on the basis of that definition three strands: "the international content of the curricula, the international movement of scholars and students concerned with training and research, and the arrangements that engage a system of education co-operation programs beyond its national boundaries" (p. 2293). As will be explained later, this way of looking at international education and the internationalization of higher education—terms used interchangeably by Harari—has been rather influential in the American literature on the internationalization of higher education.

Halls (1990) arrives at the following typology for comparative education:

- "Comparative studies," subdivided in comparative pedagogy, that is, the study of teaching and the classroom process in different countries; and intraeducational and intracultural analysis.
- "Education abroad," the study of aspects of an educational system or systems other than one's own, including area studies.
- "International education," subdivided in international pedagogy, that is, the study of teaching multinational, multicultural and multiracial groups, or the education of linguistic or ethnic minorities, but also the study of subjects such as peace education; and the study of the work of international education institutions, closely related to international pedagogy, but more concerned with policy matters, such as the establishment of international acceptability of qualifications, the promotion of educational exchanges and the initiation of cultural agreements.
- "Development education," the production of information and plans to assist policy makers, particularly in "new nations," the development of appropriate educational methods and techniques, and the training of personnel to implement programs (pp. 23–24).

Hall's (1990) typology does not help much in clarifying the concept of comparative and international education; in fact, it causes more confusion. He uses the term education abroad to describe something different to what is described by study abroad. He also uses the term international education in a different way to most other authors. Halls himself admits that there is "no agreement among comparative educationists as to the use of terms," giving as an example the confusion between the use of the terms international education and development education (p. 23). Vestal (1994, 13) also makes reference to the diversity in meanings of international education and the multiplicity of definitions. He, like other American authors on international education, such as Lambert (1989a) and Harari (1977), tends to make a subdivision between curriculum—using international studies as an alternate term—and organization—using study abroad or international exchanges as synonyms for international education.

Two European authors have made an attempt to give the "international" in comparative and international education a clearer and, as far as the internationalization of higher education is concerned, more relevant place. Anweiler (1977) writes that "in the current American usage," comparative education is "comparing and contrasting different national systems of education," and international education is "many different theoretical studies or practical activities, which are held together by the term 'internationism.'" As an alternative, he emphasizes internationalization as "a characteristic feature of comparative education." He answers the question, What is the meaning of international in comparative education? as follows: "Comparative education is concerned with problems at the different levels of internationalization, which, as such, it is able to determine from the historical analysis of the internationalization process, and from contemporary review" (pp. 109, 113).

Husén (1994) describes international education as "a cross-disciplinary study of international and intercultural problems in education. As such, it overlaps to some extent with comparative education but goes beyond it in its international orientation." According to him, "International education refers both to the objectives and content of certain educational pursuits and to the internationalization of such activities." Like others, he makes a distinction between the scholar, "the academic pursuit," and the practitioner, "efforts that aim to foster an international orientation in knowledge and attitudes" (p. 2972). He sees links with multicultural education, peace education, as well as new forms, such as education for development and for a new international economic order. UNESCO is mentioned as its main promoter. He refers to a meeting of UNESCO in 1991 in Tunis on the integration of international education into higher education.

Husén (1994) states that international education can be studied from the following perspectives: historical development, goals and objectives (typically to increase the awareness of students and to promote reflection and research on global issues, and in this way to promote international understanding, cooperation, human rights, peace, and so on), implementation and institutional arrangements (national and international agencies and units to dispense educational programs in the field), and means (curricular provisions, teaching material, publications, and research programs, as well as the use of media in dispensing international education).

According to Husén (1994), global interdependence and global education[4] demanded

internationalising education, with two major objectives, one more idealistic and elusive and one more tangible and pragmatic. In the first place, by means of certain programs in the formal educational system, a heightened awareness is sought among young people of global interdependence by presenting them with, among other things, certain basic facts. This could be regarded as sensitivity training in international thinking with the purpose of fostering certain attitudes that lead to international solidarity, rejection of racial prejudices, and understanding of other cultures. The other overriding objective is to impart certain skills and competencies that will enable young people to function in an international setting, such as mastery of foreign languages, knowledge and insights into foreign cultures, and the history and geography of other nations. (p. 2974)[5]

Anweiler and Husén bring into the debate two related elements that are relevant for the study of the internationalization of higher education: the historical factor, and the term internationalization, emphasizing that it is a process and not something static, as the term international education suggests. These two elements are essential in the analysis of international education and the internationalization of higher education, the subject of the next section.

Meanings of International Education and the Internationalization of Higher Education

Sven Groenings (1987a) commented as early as 1987 that, even though it is moving along a massive front, "like the early scientific revolution, internationalization lacks orderly process or agreed upon definitions" (p. 2). The Association of Universities and Colleges of Canada (AUCC) concluded in 1993 that "there is no simple, unique or all encompassing definition of internationalization of the university. It is a multitude of activities aimed at providing an educational experience within an environment that truly integrates a global perspective." Grünzweig and Rinehart (1998) comment: "The field of international academic exchange and study abroad has become a curious hybrid between an academic discipline and a professional practice whose discourse is often characterised by the repetition of unquestioned dogmas and the use of inadequately defined terms." Teichler (1996c) concludes, "There is no unanimously agreed definition among experts" (p. 344). Mestenhauser (1998a) paraphrases it as follows: "Everything that quacks must be international education" (p. 70). And Halliday (1999) speaks of this "fetish" covering a variety of issues and meanings: "It is at once a spur and a sales gimmick, an appeal that issues as easily from the mouth of the financial manager as from the lips of the cosmopolitan scholar" (p. 99).

The comment, "There is no simple, unique, or all encompassing definition," may very well summarize the current sentiment and situation in several countries regarding the meaning of internationalization and parallels the observation of D. N. Wilson (1994, 480) on the term international education, which was referred to in the previous section.

Originally, in the research field the term international education covered several elements of the internationalization of higher education, such as study abroad, but gradually during the last two decades this has diminished. In the field of internationalization practitioners, however, the term international education is still used as an equivalent of the internationalization of higher education. Organizations such as the IIE, NAFSA, and AIEA in the United States; the CBIE (Canadian Bureau for International Education) in Canada; and the EAIE in Europe, all use the term international education. The same is true for the *Journal of Studies in International Education*.

One possible explanation for the use of the term international education by these organizations is that in the 1960s and 1970s there was a close link between technical assistance, development education, and internationalization. Organizations such as the CBIE in Canada and NUFFIC (Netherlands Foundation for International Co-operation in Higher Education) were primarily oriented to technical assistance and development education at that time. This correlates with the close similarity in much literature of international education and development education. Another explanation may be found in the strong link seen by several researchers between international education and practice. The organizations mentioned all have a strong focus on administration; they are mainly organizations of practitioners. Both arguments are relevant, but more important in my view is that the term international education, as described earlier in the historical part, covers the fragmented but organized state of development in the international dimension of higher education as it emerged in the United States and to a lesser extent in Europe after the two world wars, and in particular during the Cold War.

The term international education, however, creates confusion when used as an equivalent to, or shorthand for, the internationalization of higher education. As has been remarked, researchers of comparative and international education have used the term international education in recent years to refer more to issues such as development education and country studies than to the internationalization of higher education. The *Comparative Education Review*, the academic journal of the CIES, for instance, has seldom if ever dealt with issues related to the internationalization of higher education. The cumulative index from 1957 to 1998 of the *Comparative Education Review* (Parker and Epstein 1998) mentions six articles on internationalization, none of which deals with the internationalization of higher education as such. Sixteen articles deal with study abroad, of which eight were published in a special issue on foreign students in comparative perspective in May 1984. In February 1998 an article on academic staff mobility in the European Community was published. This is the result of the forty years of existence of the review on this area of study.

Others, in particular American authors, use the term international education more in relation to activity, competency, rationale, and ethos approaches than to process approaches to internationalization (see section two of this chapter), and for that reason may be considered as covering a different stage of development closer to the meanings as presented in the field of comparative and international education research.

However, we have to recognize the general acceptance of the term international education as covering and even being an abbreviation for the term internationalization of higher education. General acceptance of the limitation of the use of the term international education as an abbreviation of the internationalization of education would help in solving the confusing mix of terminologies in the study of comparative and international education. At the same time, the use of international education as an alternative term for the internationalization of higher education disregards the crucial aspects of history and process.

In addition, given the different interpretation of international education within the Comparative and International Education Society, it is unlikely that this terminology will be accepted there easily. For that reason, the confusion between the two terms and the two worlds should be recognized as a fact of life, with internationalization of higher education related to the process approach and international education related more to one or several of the other approaches.

This is not the case for another term that is sometimes used in place of international education and the internationalization of higher education: internationalism (Altbach 1998; P. Scott 1999). Authors such as Altbach and Scott use the term in particular to describe the generic international character of universities, such as "the long tradition of internationalism in higher education" (Altbach 1998, 347) and "internationalism has always been part of the life-world of the university" (P. Scott 1999, 37). Used in this way, the term is rather superficial. As an alternative for the two other terms, as for instance in the title of an article by Barbara Burn (1996, 19) and by Altbach (1997c), it is confusing and unclear, because internationalism is identified more with ideological than conceptual meanings (see also Knight 1999d). Zoltán Abádi-Nagy (1999) gives an interesting critique on the use of internationalism, writing on internationalism and national identity in Eastern Europe: "For eastern Europeans, 'internationalism' can stir unpleasant memories" (p. 10).

The following overview of meanings of international education and internationalization of higher education illustrates the different perceptions behind the use and meaning of these terms.

Maurice Harari (1989) suggests that international education must encompass not only the curriculum, international exchanges of scholars and students, cooperative programs with the community, training, and a wide array of administrative services, but also "distinct commitment, attitudes, global awareness, an orientation and dimension which transcends the entire institution and shapes its ethos" (p. 2). His work in the 1970s and 1980s reflects the development of the internationalization of higher education in the United States and the acceptance in the United States of the term international education for that, although other terms are also used, such as international studies (see, for instance, Lambert 1996).[6]

Stephen Arum and Jack Van de Water (1992) identify the need for a clearer and more focused definition of international education. They base their search for a definition on an analysis of concepts and definitions used in the United States during the past thirty years. The definition they favor is one proposed by Harari in 1972. It combines three main elements: (1) international content of the curriculum, (2) international movement of scholars and students concerned with training and research, and (3) international technical assistance and cooperation programs. They built on this perspective and developed their own tripartite definition, which refers to "the multiple activities, programs and services that fall within international studies, international educational exchange and technical co-operation" (p. 202).

Mestenhauser (1998a, 70–71) questions the possibility of fitting international education into a single definition, given the genuine conceptual confusion surrounding the term. He proposes a "contingency concept" of international education, a collage of nine different pictures: target groups, the levels of education, the defining disciplines, theories about the nature of knowledge, structure and goals, "meta-knowing" perspectives, the dramatically changing nature of changing international relations, the geography of international education, and the nature of change. Elsewhere (Mestenhauser 2000) he describes international education as a complex, multidimensional, and interdisciplinary phenomenon, with several levels of analysis. Although he raises several relevant and important points in his descriptions of these nine pictures, his contingency concept of international education is even more confusing with regard to understanding its meaning than the confusion surrounding international education itself.

Schoorman (1999) defines internationalization as "an ongoing, counter-hegemonic educational process that occurs in an international context of knowledge and practice where societies are viewed as subsystems of a larger, inclusive world. The process of internationalization at an educational institution entails a comprehensive, multifaceted program of action that is integrated into all aspects of education" (p. 21). This definition, which includes several aspects that are explicitly or implicitly present in the definition by Jane Knight (such as process, integration, and international dimension [see pp. 113–114]), limits itself to the teaching function of the institution and is too abstract and too complex to be useful.

Kerr (1994b, 12–13) describes internationalization of learning as being divided into four components: the flow of new knowledge, the flow of scholars, the flow of students, and the content of the curriculum. According to P. Scott (1998, 116–117), the international dimensions of higher education are also concentrated in four aspects: student flows, flow of academic staff, collaboration between institutions, and the flow of ideas. Elements of this description of internationalization are to be found in van der Wende (1996), Rudzki (1998), and others. Halliday (1999, 104), for instance, gives the following four elements: students, staff, income, and location.

What is remarkable about these definitions, which come mainly from American authors, is that they sum up or emphasize activities, rationales, competencies, and/or ethos, and that they use the term international education rather than internationalization of higher education. This will be illustrated by comparing these definitions with those by non-American authors and organizations over the past decade.

The European Association for International Education (1992) states that the internationalization of higher education covers a broad range of activities and can only be defined in a general way as meaning all the activities dealing with the internationalization of higher education, "internationalization being the whole range of processes by which higher education becomes less national and more internationally oriented."

One of the recommendations from a British Columbia Centre for International Education (BCCIE) Task Force (Francis 1993) addresses the "need for clarification of the definition of internationalization, both in the context of the post-secondary system as a whole, and at the individual institutional level." This results from the Task Force finding that "not only did the meaning attributed to the term vary between individuals, but so too did the comfort level with using the word." The Task Force suggests the following as a working definition for the province of British Columbia: "Internationalization is a process that prepares the community for successful participation in an increasingly interdependent world. In Canada, our multicultural reality is the stage for internationalization. The process should infuse all facets of the post-secondary education system, fostering global understanding and developing skills for effective living and working in a diverse world."

Kazuhiro Ebuchi (1990) gives the following definition: "Internationalisation is a process by which the teaching, research and service functions of a higher education system become internationally and cross-culturally compatible." The problem with this definition is that it implies a greater homogeneity of outcome than is necessarily the case.

The Programme on Institutional Management in Higher Education (IMHE) of the OECD (1994) uses a formulation of the internationalization of higher education in the following general terms: "The complex of processes whose combined effect, whether planned or not, is to enhance the international dimension of the experience of higher education in universities and similar educational institutions" (see also Knight and de Wit 1995, 2, 16).

Rudzki (1998), observing that "one of the major problems . . . has been the lack of an accepted definition of 'internationalization' within the context of education," defines it for the purpose of his work as "a process of organizational change, curriculum innovation, staff development and student mobility for the purpose of attaining excellence in teaching, research and the other activities which universities undertake as part of their function" (p. 16).

Jane Knight (1993) adopts a process view of internationalization. An international dimension is described as "a perspective, activity or programme, which introduces or integrates an international/intercultural/global outlook into the major functions of a university or college" (p. 6). In later publications she presented a slightly adapted version of her original definition. She adds to the definition the intercultural dimension: "Internationalisation of higher education is the process of integrating an international/intercultural dimension into the teaching, research and service functions of the institution" (Knight 1997a, 8, 1999a, 16).

Comparing the American definitions of Harari, Arum, and van der Water and Mestenhauser—Schoorman is an exception on the American side, from a younger generation and influenced by the new literature from outside the United States[7]—and the non-American definitions of the EAIE, the BCCIE, Ebuchi, Rudzki, the IMHE, and Knight, one notes that the last emphasize internationalization as a process, while the first sum up programs and activities relevant to the American study abroad tradition. This is also reflected in the use of the term international education by most American authors and internationalization of (higher) education in most non-American literature. Halpern (1969) illustrates the American position clearly with the case of the Institute of International Education:

The Institute failed to give international education real definition. Its goals were vague, its programs eclectic and its work with foreign exchange projects excessively administrative. There was a tendency to regard almost any kind of transnational academic contact as part of international education, a tendency which was intellectually lazy and misleading. Years after international education was fully accepted in America it was unclear to many what it actually meant and whether it had proven accomplishments. (p. 123)

As we saw in Chapter 1, from a historical point of view, international education reflects the period between World War II and the end of the Cold War and is more strongly observed in the United States than elsewhere, and the internationalization of higher education reflects the period starting with the end of the Cold War and is more predominant in Europe, as well as Australia and Canada. The differences in the meanings of American authors and others can be explained by the fact that most practice and analysis in the period before the end of the Cold War was done by Americans and still dominates American practice, whereas most practice and analysis of the international dimension of higher education now takes place outside of the United States, in particular in Europe, Canada, and Australia.

As Knight and de Wit (1995, 16) have observed, the conclusion "there is no simple, unique or all encompassing definition of internationalization of the university" itself can be seen as an accomplishment, given the fact that until recently both the formulation and the implementation of internationalization was predominantly American based, the debate relatively new, and the research tradition young. As the international dimension of higher education gains more attention and recognition, people tend to use it in the way that best suits their purpose. While one can easily understand this happening, it is not helpful for internationalization to become a catchall phrase for everything and anything international. A more focused definition is necessary if it is to be understood and treated with the importance that it deserves. Even if there is no agreement on a precise definition, internationalization needs to have parameters if it is to be assessed and to advance higher education. This is why the use of a working definition in combination with a conceptual framework for internationalization of higher education is relevant.

The working definition of Jane Knight (1999a) ("Internationalisation of higher education is the process of integrating an international/intercultural dimension into the teaching, research and service functions of the institution") and the related conceptual framework as designed by Knight and de Wit (1995) now seem to be increasingly accepted as a useful working definition and framework. Callan (2000) qualifies it as "a now classic formulation of internationalization at institutional level in terms of its desired or intended effects" (p. 16).[8]

However, van der Wende (1997b, 18–19) notes that this definition limits the focus to institutional strategies and policies and excludes national governments. This could be solved by changing "of the institution" into "higher education" in Jane Knight's definition, but would ignore the fact that national policies, as well as those of other stakeholders, are only relevant if they are directed to or at least channeled by institutions of higher education. She also comments that internationalization defined in this way suggests that it is an aim in itself, lacking a wider goal. But as we will see later, these wider goals, which are part of the rationales for internationalization, are explicitly left out of the definition in order to give it a more workable and general meaning.

In the context of the same study on national policies for internationalization, van der Wende (1997b) presents an alternative definition of internationalization, including "any systematic effort aimed at making higher education (more) responsive to the requirements and challenges related to the globalisation of societies, economy and labour markets" (pp. 18–19). With the lack of a generally accepted definition, there seems to be a general trend in studies on the internationalization of higher education to define it "in the context of" or "for the purpose of" specific studies. This is a correct way of defining an approach to internationalization, as long as an explicit reference to the domain itself is made, such as in the definition used by van der Wende in her study of national policies, or the one used in her study on the internationalization of the curriculum: "the process of curriculum development or curriculum change which is aimed at integrating an international dimension into the content of the curriculum, and, if relevant, also into the method of instruction" (van der Wende 1996, 18).

However, in many cases no definition is given at all, and terms are used in parallel without any distinction. As indicated already and on other occasions (de Wit 1998b), several American definitions have a tendency toward an implicit national approach to and description of international education as a synonym for internationalization of higher education. Examples of such national American approaches are to be found in the work of Richard D. Lambert (1993a, 189, 1993b, 298) and Ann Kelleher (1996).

The various definitions for international education and the internationalization of higher education reflect different approaches to the role of the international dimension in higher education: activity, rationale, competency, ethos, and process approaches.

APPROACHES TO INTERNATIONALIZATION

If we look at the literature and practice of the internationalization of higher education, in many cases its meaning is linked to its rationales, its means, its content, and/or its activities. This has contributed to the confusing overlap in terms used to describe (elements of) internationalization. As long as the limitation is made explicit and the author does not claim general use of the term, this is no problem, but there is a trend to be rather superficial in the use of these terms. Sometimes three or more terms are used to describe the same phenomenon in a single article.

Four different approaches to internationalization of higher education are identified here: activity, rationale, competency, and process.[9] While each approach has a key aspect that distinguishes it from the others, it is important to recognize that they are not mutually exclusive. It may be more appropriate to think of them as different strands in a cord that integrates the different aspects of internationalization. A brief description of each approach follows.

Activity Approach

The activity approach describes internationalization in terms of categories or types of activities. These include academic and extracurricular activities, such as curricular development and innovation; scholar, student, and faculty exchange; area studies; technical assistance; intercultural training; international students; and joint research activities. This approach focuses exclusively on the content of the activities and does not necessarily include any of the organizational issues needed to initiate, develop, and sustain the activities. It is this approach, however, that is most widely used in the description of internationalization, and terms related to this approach are frequently used as being equivalent to the internationalization of higher education.

Curricular development and innovation or internationalization of the curriculum might be considered a crucial—perhaps the most crucial—activity in internationalization. Terms used frequently in relation to curriculum as an activity approach are international education, area studies, multicultural education, intercultural education, cross-cultural education, education for international understanding, peace education, global education, development education, international studies, transnational studies, and global studies.

As we will see, most definitions relate to this approach, and most studies on the internationalization of higher education fall under it. The next two, rationale and competency, are more specific and narrow approaches. Jane Knight (1999a, 15) mentions that the activity approach is seen by some as synonymous with the term international education. This, in my view, is also true for the rationale and competency approaches.

Rationale Approach

The rationale approach defines internationalization in terms of its purposes or intended outcomes. In Chapter 5, the rationales for internationalization were extensively dealt with. Here it is important to note that the rationale approach analyzes and defines internationalization from the perspective of its purpose. This is true in particular for several American studies on internationalization and its aspirations for peace and mutual understanding (de Wit 1998b), but also for recent studies on internationalization, in which it is seen as a mechanism for income generation through foreign student recruitment, in particular in Australia and the United Kingdom (Pratt and Poole 1998a, 1998b; Humpfrey 1999). Terms frequently used in relation to this approach—referring to a specific rationale—are peace education, education for international understanding, development education, and technical assistance.

Knight (1994) mentions the ethos approach, which focuses on developing an ethos or culture that values and supports intercultural and international perspectives and initiatives. This approach is most frequently addressed in American studies on international education, such as Harari (1989), Pickert (1992), Klasek (1992), and Kelleher (1996), as was demonstrated in Chapter 2. As a separate approach it is too narrow and should be seen in the context of the broader rationale approach as presented here.

Competency Approach

The competency approach looks at internationalization in terms of developing new skills, attitudes, and knowledge in students, faculty, and staff. The focus is clearly on the human dimension, not on academic activities or organizational issues. In the literature one can identify use of the following competency terms: learning competencies, career competencies, global competence, transnational competence, and international competencies. Studies such as Opper, Teichler, and Carlson (1990) and Maiworm, Steube, and Teichler (1991) on learning competencies, Maiworm and Teichler (1996) and Bremer (1998) on career competencies, Yershova, DeJaegher, and Mestenhauser (2000) on intercultural competencies, IIE (1997) on transnational competence, Lambert (1994) on global competence, and D. Wilson (1998) on international competencies fall under this category.

There is little difference between the elements attributed by the authors to the four terms intercultural, transnational, global, and international competence. Using the meaning given in an Institute of International Education study (1997, 5) to transnational competence, one can say that these four competencies refer to the ability of individuals, organizations, communities, and governments to cope effectively with the rapidly changing transnational–intercultural–global–international environment and to realize their goals. One might wonder if these are new terms used to describe the same concepts and ideas, or if there are differences in reality. Looking at the different elements described, my perception is that there is more overlap than difference.

Process Approach

The process approach frames internationalization as a process that integrates an international dimension or perspective into the major functions of the institution. Terms such as infuse, integrate, permeate, and incorporate are used to characterize the process approach. A wide range of academic activities, organizational policies and procedures, and strategies are part of this process. This can be described as the most comprehensive approach to describing internationalization, and is reflected in the working definition.

Studies in this area include (comparative) studies on the internationalization strategies of institutions of higher education (Knight and de Wit 1995; Back, Davis, and Olsen 1996), on national policies (Kälvermark and van der Wende 1997); on the link between globalization and internationalization (P. Scott 1998, 1999), and on quality assurance and internationalization (Knight and de Wit 1999c).

CONCLUSIONS

In this chapter, an overview has been given of the different meanings of and approaches to international education and the internationalization of higher education. Jane Knight (1999d) addresses the opportunities and challenges for internationalization of higher education in relation to new societal trends: globalization and regionalization, and related to them, the knowledge society, information and communication technologies, the labor market, and lifelong learning. She links these trends to the rationales for internationalization and the way they change and become more diversified. Based on these trends and changing rationales, she reflects on the concept of internationalization. She tries to define international education in relation to global education, regional education, and transnational education. She distinguishes between "ism" (principle, value), "ization" (process), and "al" (kind of): internationalism, internationalization, and international, and the same for global, regional, and transnational. International means of, between, or among nations; transnational means extending across borders or over nations; regional means a group of nations based on physical proximity or a particular part of the world; and global means relating to the world as a whole.

Knight (1999d) applies these meanings to education in the following way: International education involves and/or relates to the people, cultures, and systems of different nations; transnational education occurs across borders of nations; regional education involves and/or relates to nations that are in close proximity to one another and can be seen as a subset of international education; and global education involves the world and relates to worldwide issues. This seems solid and logical, but her framework for analysis of the different terms remains rather abstract and generic, which is also the case with her definition of international education, as she herself admits: "a kind of education where the purpose, outcomes, activities, content or participants relate to or involve the people, culture and systems of different nations" (p. 12).

Knight (1999d) is correct to observe that, as the rationales shift, as the types of activities diversify, as outcomes take on increasing importance, and as the nature of the interactions among the participants changes, then so will the terminology. In this study, a historical development and a related development in terminology can also be observed: international dimension, international education, and internationalization of higher education. What is not sufficiently emphasized in Knight's analysis is this notion of development and historical analysis in the interpretation of the differences and relationships between these terms, as presented in this chapter and previous chapters. International dimension is used as a generic term to cover all aspects of higher education that have an international aspect or dimension, regardless of whether they are programmatically or strategically organized. The term international education refers to a more developed form of international dimension, a program or organization. Internationalization is an extension of international education and refers to a more strategic process approach. All three forms are present in higher education today and are not mutually exclusive.

Like Peter Scott (1998, 109–113), emphasis is placed on the historical dimension of the internationalization of higher education, an aspect to which only lip service has been paid in most studies, mainly linking it to the "myth" of the international university of the Middle Ages and to the current transition to globalization. A combination of a historical analysis and a conceptual framework—Parts I and II of this study—allows us to approach a better understanding of the term.

After having dealt with the "what," the next chapter analyzes strategies for internationalization of higher education and organizational models, the "how" of internationalization of higher education.

NOTES

1. Knight and de Wit (1995) gave an overview of this debate, elements of which are used here in a revised and extended version.

2. Crossley (1999) also refers to the distinction between applied and theoretical in relation to international and comparative education.

3. This distinction is not unique for the sector. Teichler (1996b, 436) makes reference to "a relatively vague distinction between the researcher and practitioner" in higher education in general.

4. According to Husén (1994), a term introduced in 1985 by Soedjatmoko, at that time rector of the U.N. University, Tokyo.

5. In line with these arguments, Crossley (1999) calls for a reconceptualized field of comparative and international education to position it better for the study of globalization, culture, and identity.

6. Harari's work, together with that of others, such as Sven Groennings, Richard D. Lambert, Barbara Burn, and Joseph Mestenhauser, has heavily influenced the further debate in the United States. The debate only came to life again in the 1990s (in particular in Europe, Canada, and Australia), partly as a reaction to the American interpretations (de Wit 1993, 1998b).

7. The same is true for Ellingboe (1998, 199), who also defines internationalization as a process.

8. See, for instance, van der Wende (1996, 8), Back, Davis, and Olsen (1996, 15), Mallea (1996, 113), Gacel-Avila (1999), Bond and Lemasson (1999), and Wächter (1999).

9. Jane Knight (1994) also mentions four approaches, not including the rationale approach but instead an ethos approach, which in my view is part of the rationale approach. See also Knight and de Wit (1995).

Chapter 7

Strategies and Organization Models for the Internationalization of Higher Education

The overview of meanings, definitions, approaches, and rationales in previous chapters demonstrates that various elements play a role in the internationalization process. These elements are described in a variety of different ways: mechanisms, facilitators, activities, barriers, factors, and strategies. For the purposes of this discussion, Knight and de Wit (1995) have used the term strategies to characterize those initiatives that are taken by an institution of higher learning to integrate an international dimension into research, teaching, and service functions as well as management policies and systems. In recent years, several attempts have been made to structure organizational strategies into different models of the internationalization process. This chapter provides an updated overview and critical analysis of strategies and organizational models for the internationalization of higher education, based on Knight and de Wit (1995).

STRATEGIES

In the process approach, the many different activities identified as key components of internationalization are divided into two major categories: program strategies and organizational strategies. The program strategies refer to those academic activities and services of an institution of higher education that integrate an international dimension into its main functions. Organizational strategies include those initiatives that help to ensure that an international dimension, or in other words the activities already discussed, are institutionalized through developing the appropriate policies and administrative systems.

Program Strategies

In their study in 1995, Knight and de Wit identified four categories of program strategies: research-related activities, education-related activities, activities related to technical assistance and development cooperation, and extracurricular activities and institutional services. Jane Knight (1997a, 1999a) later changed them into academic programs, research and scholarly collaboration, external relations and services, and extracurricular activities. Knight (1999a, 25) motivates the change from technical assistance and development cooperation into external relations and services by the change in orientation from "aid" to "trade." Nonetheless, this category, of the four, is the least clear. If we look at the activities listed in this category (p. 24), it is a mix of unrelated strategies, including transnational education strategies, development cooperation strategies, international alumni programs and community services, intercultural projects, and community-based partnerships. International students are placed under academic programs, although, as a trade, they could also be placed under external relations and services. Preference is given to distinguish between technical assistance strategies, export of knowledge (inward-oriented), and transnational education (outward-oriented) strategies, and to include international alumni programs and community-based programs under extracurricular activities. An overview of program-strategy categories and related examples is given in the following list (Knight 1999a):

Academic programs
A. Student-oriented programs
   Student mobility schemes
   Student exchange programs
   International students
   Work–internship–study abroad
   Study visits
B. Staff-oriented programs
   Faculty–staff mobility programs for teaching
   Visiting lecturers–staff for teaching
   Joint and double appointments for teaching
C. Curriculum development programs
   Internationalization of the curriculum
   Foreign language study
   Local language and culture training
   Area and international thematic studies
   Teaching–learning process
   Joint and double degree programs
   Summer programs and universities

Research and scholarly collaboration

A. Ph.D.-oriented programs
International Ph.D. students
Ph.D. student mobility
B. Staff-oriented programs
Faculty–staff mobility programs for research
Visiting lecturers–staff for research
Joint and double appointments for research
C. Research development programs
International research projects
International research agreements
International conferences and seminars
International publishing and citation
Area and international theme centers
Joint research centers

Technical assistance

A. Student-oriented programs
Student scholarship programs (South–North)
Student-oriented training programs (North–South)
B. Staff-oriented programs
Staff training scholarship programs (South–North)
Staff-oriented training programs (North–South)
C. Curriculum-oriented programs
Institution-building programs
Curriculum-development programs

Export of knowledge (inward)

Recruitment of international students for economic reasons
Development of special profit-based courses and programs for international
students
Development of postgraduate training programs for the international market

Transnational education (outward)

Offshore programs and campuses
Distance education programs
Twinning programs
Branch campuses
Franchise arrangements
Articulation programs
Virtual, electronic, or Web programs and institutions

Extracurricular activities

Student clubs and associations
International and intercultural events
Community-based projects and activities, intercultural and international
International alumni programs

As Knight and de Wit (1995, 20) have noted, all the activities described in this list can be part of a strategy for internationalization. The activities do not exclude one another, but only in a few exceptional cases will an institution have an explicit strategy that covers all or even most of the activities mentioned. It is essential to state that an institution should not be judged for its internationalization strategy on the assumption that all or most of these activities are implicitly or even explicitly part of their policy plans. It is more important that institutions identify their priorities and how these can be integrated into strategic plans.

Organizational Strategies

The previous section illustrates the number and variety of activities and services that are part of integrating an international dimension into the teaching, research, and service functions of higher education institutions. Knight and de Wit (1995, 20) state that even if there is an increasing number of academic programs and activities, if they are not underpinned by a permanent organizational commitment and structure they may die when supporters leave the institution, resources become scarcer, or new priorities emerge. Internationalization needs to be entrenched into the culture, policy, planning, and organization processes of the institution so that it is not marginalized or treated as a passing fad. Giving equal attention to both the program-strategy and organizational-strategy types, as well as differentiating between the two, is essential.

Knight and de Wit (1995, 20–22) identify the following elements of organizational strategies: the commitment and support of the board of governors and senior administrators; the support and involvement of a critical mass of faculty and staff; the international office or position; adequate funding and support, both internally and externally; policy; incentives and rewards for faculty and staff; the existence of formal communication channels; and an annual planning, budget, and review process. Knight (1999a, 26) groups them together in four categories of organizational strategies: governance, operations, support services, and human resource development:

Governance	Expressed commitment by senior leaders
	Active involvement of faculty and staff
	Articulated rationale and goals for internationalization
	Recognition of an international dimension in mission statement and other policy documents
Operations	Integrated into institutionwide and department planning, budgeting, and quality review systems
	Appropriate organizational structures

	Communication systems (formal and informal) for liaison and coordinator
	Balance between centralized and decentralized promotion and management of internationalization
	Adequate financial-support and resource-allocation systems
Support services	Support from institutionwide service units; that is, student housing, registrariat, counseling, fundraising, etc.
	Involvement of academic support units; that is, language training, curriculum development, library
	Student support services for international students studying on campus and domestic students going abroad; that is, orientation programs, counseling, cross-cultural training, student advisers, etc.
Human resource development	Recruitment and selection procedures that reorganize international and intercultural expertise
	Reward and promotion policies to reinforce faculty and staff contributions to internationalization
	Faculty and staff professional development activities
	Support for international assignments and sabbaticals

Different rationales and approaches will lead to different program and organizational strategies. The same is true for the organization models examined in the second part of this chapter.

ORGANIZATION MODELS FOR THE INTERNATIONALIZATION OF HIGHER EDUCATION

Six different organization models for the internationalization of higher education as identified in the literature on the internationalization of higher education are reviewed here. The first model, by Neave (1992b), presents a paradigmatic model for servicing and administering international cooperation. The second model, developed by Rudzki (1995a, 1995b, 1998), has a more programmatic approach to strategies, and tries to provide a framework for assessing levels of international activity within institutions. Davies's (1992) model gives more emphasis to the organizational strategies as a starting point. The fourth model, by van Dijk and Meijer (van Dijk 1995), is an attempt to refine Davies's model. Knight and de Wit (1995) have described these four models, and an updated account is given in the following sections. The fifth model is by van der Wende (1996) and resulted from a model she designed for the NUFFIC based on the process approach to internationalization. The last model is by Knight (1994), also based on the process approach and stressing the internationalization process as a continuous circle.

Neave's Model

Neave (1992b), using case studies at a global level written for UNESCO, developed two paradigmatic models, one "leadership driven" and a second "base unit driven." The first model has as its essential feature a lack of formal connection below the level of the central administration, while the second model sees such central administrative units mainly as service oriented to activities coming from below. Neave also casts them as "managerial rational" versus "academic consensual" models. He sees the two models "as opposite ends of a species of continuum," in which "structures administering international co-operation which mould around one paradigm may in certain specific conditions, move towards the opposite end of the continuum" (p. 166). Neave stresses that "the administrative structures of international co-operation (should be) continually provisional" (p. 168). He combines the leadership and base unit model for administration in a diagram with "definitional" and "elaborative" scopes of institutional strategy. Instead of definitional and elaborative, alternative terms that might be appropriate are proactive and reactive (see Figure 7.1).

In Neave's (1992b) paradigmatic approach, the widely used simple distinction between centralized and decentralized models of internationalization is implicit, although he adds the dimension of change to his matrix. Rudzki (1998, 184) criticizes Neave's model for its lack of practical application and self-evidence. The following three developmental models move away from this approach, which is based on distinguishing between centralization and decentralization.

Rudzki's Model

Another model is that of Rudzki (1998), who identifies four key dimensions of internationalization: student mobility, staff development, curriculum innovation, and organizational change. Originally, Rudzki (1995b, 1998, 216–218) outlined and contrasted reactive and proactive models of internationalization:

The reactive model of internationalization

Stage 1. Contact: Academic staff engage in making contacts with colleagues in other countries; curriculum development; limited mobility; links lack clear formulation of purpose and duration.

Stage 2. Formalization: Some links are formalized with institutional agreements being made. Resources may or may not be made available.

Figure 7.1
Task Analysis, Strategic Planning, and Administrative Models

Scope of Institutional Strategy

Administrative Orientation	Definitional	Elaborative
Leadership Model	Set institutional priorities. Lay down procedures. Set down student numbers. Evaluate applications. Negotiate agreements. Assign budget to dept. Determine which staff go abroad. Determine whether period abroad is recognized for accreditation purposes. Identify disciplinary priorities.	Apply national guidelines to institute. Ensure procedures set by government are adhered to. Screen and pass on applications. Implement agreements. Distribute budget to dept. and ensure it is utilized according to government guidelines. Present agreements for government confirmation. Monitor inflow/outflow of student numbers. Monitor inflow/outflow of staff numbers. Ensure disciplinary priorities are in keeping with government plan.
Base Unit	Coordinate departmental initiatives. Provide guidance/advice. Decide whether international cooperation is to be sustained and departmental commitment over time. Notify Center of initiatives at departmental level. Determine part of dept. budget to set aside for cooperation. Operationalize priorities. Negotiate cooperation agreements. Set maximum student numbers to be involved per year. Ascertain desirability of staff mobility and numbers per year.	Stimulate cooperation activities in priority fields laid down by government. Develop incentive scheme for departmental initiatives in cooperation. Transmit government guidelines, give advice on formulating departmental response. Make known whether additional governmental resources are available. Monitor and evaluate departmental responses in light of government priorities. Implement and evaluate cooperation agreements (suggest ways of improvement to departments). Set out and negotiate student number targets. Set out and negotiate staff movements within framework of institutional strategy for institutional planning horizon.

Source: Guy Neave, Managing Higher Education International Co-operation: Strategies and Solutions (unpublished reference document for UNESCO, Paris, 1992b), 168A.

Stage 3. Central Control: Growth in activity and response by management who seek to gain control of activities.

Stage 4. Conflict: Organizational conflict between staff and management leads to withdrawing of good will by staff. Possible decline in activity and disenchantment.

Stage 5. Maturity or Decline: Possible move to a more coherent, that is, proactive approach.

The proactive model of internationalization

Stage 1. Analysis: Awareness of what internationalization is and what it entails. Strategic analysis of short-, mid-, and long-term organizational objectives, answering the question "Should we internationalize?" "Why bother?" Staff training and discussions—understanding of options—what types of international activities are available. International audit of existing activities and staff audit. SWOT analysis. Cost–benefit analysis.

Stage 2. Choice: Strategic plan and policy drawn up in conjunction with staff and explicit use made of mutual interest of staff and organization. Performance measures defined. Resources allocated. Networking with internal and external organizations.

Stage 3. Implementation: Measure performance.

Stage 4. Review: Assessment of performance against policy and plan.

Stage 5. Redefinition of Objectives–Plan–Policy: Process of continual improvement and the issues of quality this entails. Return to Stage 1 in cycle of growth and development.

Rudzki (1995b) has used these models in a study of the internationalization of U.K. business schools, and comes to the conclusion "that the spectrum of activity ranges from those business schools who have positioned themselves on the global stage and are committed to internationalization, to one institution which has taken a strategic decision not to engage in international activity." He also concludes, "Internationalisation is clearly being driven by financial imperatives and incentives, in the form of external UK and EC funding" (p. 25). He redefined his models in 1998 into what he calls the fractal process model of internationalization (Figure 7.2; see also Rudzki 2000).

Under "context," Rudzki (2000) refers to the external environment; under "approach," such internal factors as the history and culture of the institution; and under "rationale," he refers to the political, economic, cultural, and educational rationales as described by Knight and de Wit (1995).

The model can be questioned for several reasons. In the first place, one can query his use of context and approach, instead of internal and external context. One can wonder also why context and approach are placed in a hierarchical order, which implies that the external environment is more important in strategic planning than the internal process. The four dimensions, which together form the internationalization process of an institution, are also questionable. First, because of the combination of the more generic dimension "organizational change" with three more concrete activities; second, because of his subjective choice of the three activities "curriculum development," "staff development," and "student mobility," excluding other program strategies or placing them under organizational change. Rudzki (1998) defines organizational change as "the process by which an educational establishment reacts to factors in its environment in order to ensure its continued survival for the purposes of maintaining teaching, research and related activities" (p. 240). As examples that show such change, he

Figure 7.2
The Fractal Process Model of Internationalization

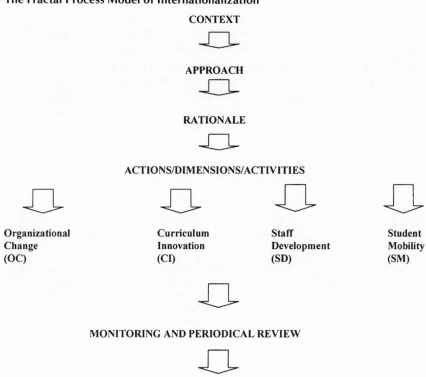

CONTEXT

APPROACH

RATIONALE

ACTIONS/DIMENSIONS/ACTIVITIES

| Organizational Change (OC) | Curriculum Innovation (CI) | Staff Development (SD) | Student Mobility (SM) |

MONITORING AND PERIODICAL REVIEW

CHANGE/REPOSITIONING/REALIGNMENT/REARRANGEMENT/
REAPPRAISAL/READJUSTMENT/RECONCEPTUALIZATION

Source: Romuald E. J. Rudzki, The Strategic Management of Internationalization: Towards a Model of Theory and Practice (Ph.D. diss., University of Newcastle upon Tyner, 1998), 220.

mentions such diverse activities as policy statements, twinning arrangements, joint research, networks, franchising, and joint degree programs (pp. 223–224). The distinction between and combination of program and organizational strategies as made by Knight and de Wit (1995) is a more useful way of describing the internationalization process of an institution.

Davies's Model

Davies (1995, 5) bases his model for internationalization strategies on the need for universities to develop a framework for their international activities in response to changes in the external environment (regionalization, globalization, and end of the Cold War). Two sets of factors are identified, internal and external to the university, and six elements, three related to the internal and three related to the external factor (see Figure 7.3). Davies refers to G. Keller (1983), *Academic Strategy*, as the basis for his analysis. Keeping these two factors and six elements in mind, Davies has developed an organizational model with a strongly prescriptive aspect: A university espousing internationalism should have clear statements of where it stands in this respect, as its mission should influence planning processes and agendas and resource-allocation criteria, serve as a rallying standard internally, and indicate to external constituencies a basic and stable set of beliefs and values.

According to Davies (1995), an institution can have

A: A central–systematic strategy, which means, "There is a large volume of international work in many categories, which reinforce each other and have intellec-

Figure 7.3
Elements in the Development of International Strategies in Universities

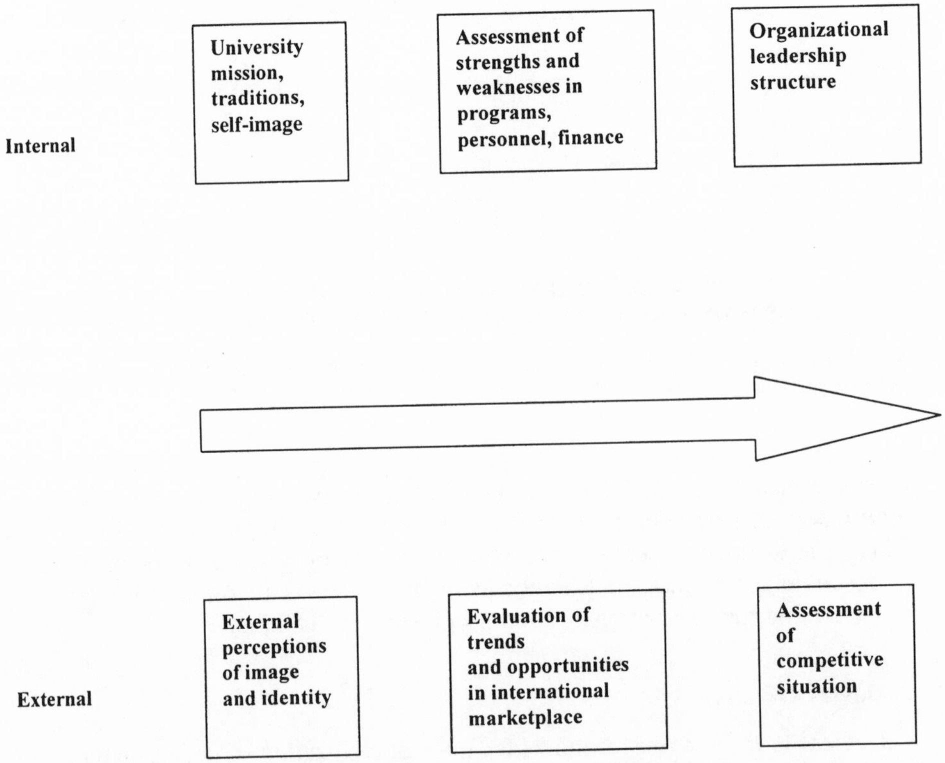

Internal

| University mission, traditions, self-image | Assessment of strengths and weaknesses in programs, personnel, finance | Organizational leadership structure |

External

| External perceptions of image and identity | Evaluation of trends and opportunities in international marketplace | Assessment of competitive situation |

Source: John L. Davies, University Strategies for Internationalisation in Different Institutional and Cultural Settings: A Conceptual Framework, in *Policy and Policy Implementation in Internationalisation of Higher Education*, ed. P. Blok (Amsterdam: European Association for International Education, 1995), 5.

tual coherence. The international mission is explicit and followed through with specific policies and supporting procedures" (p. 16).

B: An ad hoc–central strategy, where a high level of activity may take place throughout the institution but it is not based on clear concepts and has an ad hoc character.

C: A systematic–marginal strategy, which implies that the activities are limited but well organized and based on clear decisions.

D: An ad hoc–marginal strategy, where little activity takes place and is not based on clear decisions.

Davies has put his model together in a matrix, as shown in Figure 7.4. Davies's model has been used as the basis for further attempts to give structure to the organizational aspects of strategies for the internationalization of higher education.

Figure 7.4
Institutionalization of Approaches to Internationalization of Universities

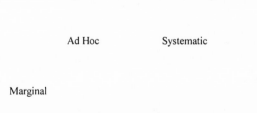

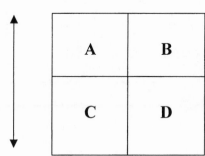

Source: John L. Davies, University Strategies for Internationalisation in Different Institutional and Cultural Settings: A Conceptual Framework, in *Policy and Policy Implementation in Internationalisation of Higher Education*, ed. P. Blok (Amsterdam: European Association for International Education, 1995), 16.

van Dijk and Meijer's Model

A fourth model, developed on the basis of an analysis of the internationalization of Dutch higher education by van Dijk and Meijer (1997), extends Davies's (1995) model by introducing three dimensions of internationalization: policy (the importance attached to internationalization aims), support (the type of support for internationalization activities), and implementation (method of implementation). A policy can in their view be marginal or priority, the support can be one-sided or interactive, and the implementation can be ad hoc or systematic. The model that is formed in this way is a cube with eight cells (Figure 7.5).

In their view (van Dijk 1995; van Dijk and Meijer 1997), this developmental model is an extension of the Davies model and makes it possible to distinguish different processes of development within an institution. They mention three routes through which it is possible to achieve internationalization as a real priority area in an institution:

Figure 7.5
Internationalization Cube

Cell	Policy	Support	Implementation
1	marginal	one-sided	*ad hoc*
2	marginal	one-sided	systematic
3	marginal	interactive	*ad hoc*
4	marginal	interactive	systematic
5	priority	one-sided	*ad hoc*
6	priority	one-sided	systematic
7	priority	interactive	*ad hoc*
8	priority	interactive	systematic

Source: Hans van Dijk, Internationalisation of Higher Education in The Netherlands: An Exploratory Study of Organisational Designs, in *Policy and Policy Implementation in Internationalisation of Higher Education*, ed. P. Blok (Amsterdam: European Association for International Education, 1995), 20.

- Route 1–2–6–8, indicating a thoughtful approach and a well-structured organizational culture, defined by them as "slow starters."

- Route 1–5–6–8, indicating a strong international commitment and an organized institutional culture, defined as "organized leaders."

- Route 1–5–7–8, indicating a quick response to external developments, a great variety of activities at different levels, and much commitment, which is only at a later stage organized in a more systematic way, defined as "entrepreneurial institutions."

van Dijk and Meijer (van Dijk 1995; van Dijk and Meijer 1997) have developed their model in relation to a survey by a consortium of Dutch organizations on the implementation of internationalization in Dutch higher education. They come to the conclusion that seven out of ten Dutch institutions can be placed in cells 7 or 8, which implies that they give high priority in their policy to internationalization and that support in the institution is well distributed at all levels. In most cases (5.5 out of 10) the implementation is not yet systematic but still ad hoc. It is significant that this conclusion applies to both universities and the nonuniversity sector, although the picture is more homogeneous for the first group. The nonuniversity sector represents a very heterogeneous group, ranging from extremely high priority to extremely marginal examples of internationalization.

The four approaches to the theoretical modeling of internationalization by institutions (Neave, Rudzki, Davies, and van Dijk and Meijer) complement one another in their prescriptive and descriptive aspects. They offer a means of measuring the formal, paper commitments of institutions against the practice to be found in concrete operating structures. Further, they offer a way to include in the theoretical frame the important fact that institutional strategies may be implicit as well as explicit. Knight and de Wit (1995) noted that one must be careful not to be too eager to strive for a model approach to the internationalization of higher education. The organizational models presented here provide useful information and tools, but should not be considered to be the new paradigm for strategies of internationalization. The models by Davies and van Dijk and Meijer are more consistent with our framework than Neave's and Rudzki's. Davies's model, although less refined, is particularly useful for a first rough assessment of the present organizational strategy of an institution and where it wants to move. Davies (1995) himself observes that "it is worth using a conceptual framework such as this to reflect on the dynamics of internationalization, rather than merely go hell-bent on the creation of new policies and structures and in beating the bushes for business" (p. 17).

The following two models by van der Wende (1996) and Knight (1994) take the process approach as their basis. They are not focused on the organization as such but on the process of internationalization strategy as a whole. The organizational model of an institution is directly linked to the process as a whole.

van der Wende's NUFFIC Model for the Internationalization of Higher Education

In this model of internationalization as a process taking place within a higher education institution, van der Wende (1996) identifies three important factors: goals and strategies as defined by the institution itself and by (inter)national policies; implementation of these goals and strategies (for which she identifies three categories—student mobility, staff mobility, and curriculum development); and the effects of the implementation on the short term—for students, staff, and education—and the long term—for the quality of education, output, and position of the institution (see Figure 7.6). An evaluation of the effects should have consequences for redefining goals and strategies.

van der Wende (1996, 9), who originally developed the model for NUFFIC, notes that the model concentrates on educational aspects of internationalization, excluding other aspects such as research and technical assistance. She also (p. 193) comments on her own model that it is too narrow in its description of motives, using only definitions from formal policy documents; and that it suggests that institutional policies are mainly inspired by (supra)national governmental policies, ignoring other factors.

Figure 7.6
NUFFIC Model for Internationalization of Higher Education

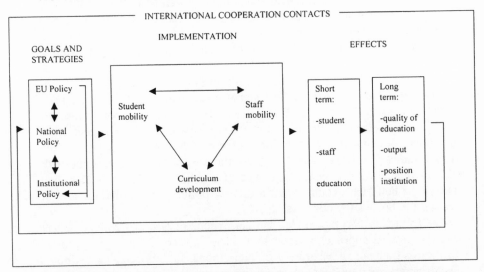

Source: Marijk C. van der Wende, Internationalising the Curriculum in Dutch Higher Education: An International Comparative Perspective (Ph.D. diss., Utrecht University, 1996), 8.

Knight's Model: Internationalization as a Continuous Cycle

A second alternative approach to the development of organizational models is to consider the internationalization process as a continuous cycle, not a linear or static process. The "Internationalisation Cycle: From Innovation to Institutionalisation," developed by Knight (1993), attempts to identify the steps or phases in the process of integrating the international dimension into the university–college culture and systems (Figure 7.7). The cycle has six phases, which an institution would move through at its own pace. While

Figure 7.7
Internationalization Circle

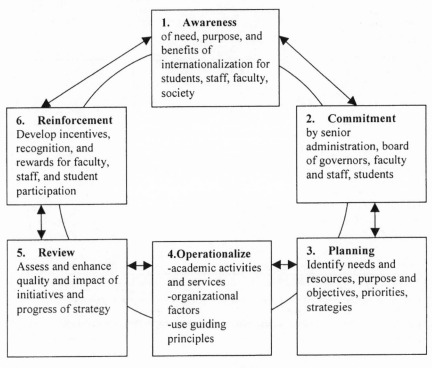

Internationalization Circle

Supportive Culture to Integrate Internationalization

Source: Jane Knight, *Internationalization: Elements and Checkpoints*, CBIE Research paper no. 7 (Ottawa: Canadian Bureau for International Education, 1994), 12.

it is clear that there is a sequence to the six phases, it is also important to acknowledge the two-way flow that will occur between the different steps.

CONCLUSIONS

If one compares the two models of van der Wende and Knight, we see a stronger emphasis by van der Wende (1998, 73) on the influence of the external and internal environment—comparable to Davies (1998), according to whom "internationalisation, almost more than any other domain of university activity, does call for environmental analysis of the highest order"—and also on implementation and the long-term effects (p. 73). In the circle of Knight one notices a stronger emphasis on awareness and commitment and on planning, operationalization, and review. Both lack the cen-

Figure 7.8
Internationalization Circle, Modified Version

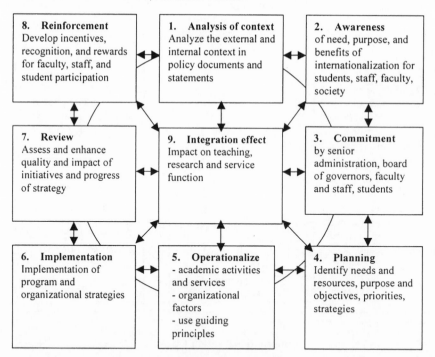

Internationalization Circle

Note: All phases address both the institution- and department-specific aspects and the relation between the two.

Source: Jane Knight, *Internationalization: Elements and Checkpoints*, CBIE Research paper no. 7 (Ottawa: Canadian Bureau for International Education, 1994), 12.

tral–departmental link, which is present in the organizational models of Neave, Davies and van Dijk, and Meijer.

Combining the six elements of Knight with three elements from van der Wende—analysis of context, implementation, and long-term effects—results in a modified version of the internationalization circle (Figure 7.8). In this model, the context analysis, the implementation phase, and the effect of internationalization on the overall functions of the institution have been incorporated. In all phases, both the institutional and the specific departmental aspects have to be addressed, as well as the link between the two. It is important to ensure that the specific circumstances of disciplines and departments get enough attention and are not forced into a general structure. The issue of differences among disciplines and academic fields in relation to internationalization is underrepresented in research on internationalization. Although there are many studies on the internationalization of specific academic fields, a comparative study is lacking. Kerr (1990, 14) makes some interesting observations on this topic. He identifies three types of areas: areas of worldwide uniformity in the content of knowledge, areas of intercultural similarity of knowledge, and areas of intranational particularity. Further comparative study on this issue would be useful, as current studies assume too much homogeneity among the disciplines, when in reality there are big differences in approaches, rationales, and strategies. An organizational model for the internationalization of higher education has to take this issue into account.

The integration effect is—although placed in its heart—outside the circle, for the following reason. It is possible to see internationalization as a strategy in itself, without a conscious and deliberate strategy to integrate it into the teaching, research, and service functions of the institution. In most cases, internationalization is assumed to have an integration effect, but is not primarily judged on that effect but on its own merits. However, in those cases where the main emphasis will be on the integrative factor of internationalization (i.e., internationalization as a strategy becomes a key factor in the overall strategy of an institution and/or department), the internationalization circle becomes part of an overall planning circle of the institution, with the integration phase as the central link. In this way, internationalization is no longer part of an external relations policy, but as van der Wende (1996, 195) also advocates, is an integral element of educational development and innovation.

Part III

Thematic Issues in the Internationalization of Higher Education

Chapter 8

Globalization, Regionalization, and the Internationalization of Higher Education

In the first two parts of this study a historical analysis of the development of the international dimension of higher education has been given, and a conceptual framework for the internationalization of higher education has been provided. In this third part, thematic case studies of relevant issues in relation to the internationalization of higher education will be presented. In this first chapter, the development of the internationalization of higher education will be related to the present context of globalization and regionalization.

First, the relationship between globalization and the internationalization of higher education will be analyzed. The knowledge society and transnational education will be related to globalization and higher education, as well as how they link with the internationalization of higher education. Then the different forms of regionalization in higher education and how this phenomenon is linked with both globalization and the internationalization of higher education will be handled.

GLOBALIZATION AND THE INTERNATIONALIZATION OF HIGHER EDUCATION

Although higher education is still predominantly a national issue, as several authors emphasize (e.g., P. Scott 1998; Haug and Race 1998; Teichler

1999), globalization is affecting this national competency of higher education (Altbach 1998, 349). As Magrath (2000) states, "If the globalization evident in business, communication, and finance is inevitable, how can universities that have provided so much of the intellectual capital for these developments not be affected—and indeed change themselves?" (p. 257). Altbach (1997c) describes universities as "international institutions, with common historical roots and also embedded in national cultures and circumstances . . . [that] despite remarkable institutional stability over time, have changed and have been subjected to immense pressures in the post–World War II period" (pp. 4, 17). These pressures are related to the globalization of our societies, economies, and technologies. According to P. Scott (1999) "Globalisation is perhaps the most fundamental challenge faced by the university in its long history." At stake is "the survival of the university as a recognizable institution" (p. 35). Slaughter and Leslie (1997), in their book, *Academic Capitalism*, argue that "the structure of academic work is changing in response to the emergence of global markets" (p. 209). According to Mason (1998), his research on global education shows an "increasing differentiation of the education market around the world, and hence the scrambling for position in that global market by existing as well as new education providers" (p. ix). Steven Muller (1995) argues that "with the end of the Cold War, the advanced technological societies of the information age seem to be well on the road toward a single global marketplace of ideas, data, and communication" (p. 65). Higher education is likely to be affected by this development, as P. Scott (1999) agrees.

So it is not surprising that the link between globalization and higher education has become a key topic of study in recent years. This is true in particular for Australia.[1] This strong interest among Australian academics in the link between globalization and higher education is, according to Pratt and Poole (1998a, 4); related to the fact that globalization is seen in analyses of Australian higher education as a major influence.

A large number of other publications deal with this issue or make at least ample reference to the importance of the phenomenon (Clark 1998; P. Scott 1998, 1999; Altbach and McGill Peterson 1999). The reason lies in the overall globalization of our societies and economies, described by Leyton-Brown (1996) in umbrella terms as "a wide variety of technological, economic, cultural, social and political trends, all pushing the boundaries of our social systems wider than the borders of our states" (p. 11).

Jan Sadlak (2000, 244) observes that globalization has become very rapidly part of higher education terminology, although the term is perceived by many as Anglo-Saxon "Westernization" or "Americanization." Peter Marcuse (2000) criticizes the use of the term globalization as a "nonconcept in most uses," cataloging "everything that seems different since, say, 1970." These comments look similar to the critique of the use of the terms international education and internationalization of higher education as Western and vague, as discussed in Part I of this study.

Sometimes, the terms globalization and internationalization of higher education are used interchangeably. An example of the use of the terms internationalization and globalization as synonyms is Lim (1995), who not only uses the terms international and global together, but also makes a plea for a gradual shift "from a concept of 'international' to one of 'global' or 'universal' in education, research, public service, and culture in universities" (pp. 1–2). "Global has," according to Lim, "a double meaning. In a geographical sense, it refers to more than issues or activities among (inter) nations. It describes the community on a larger scale and an ethos going beyond interactions among a given number of polities. In a conceptual sense, 'global' means 'general or universal'" (p. 10). Another example is Alladin (1992), who calls for "the globalization of universities, for the university is the only truly global institution that can promote international co-operation and understanding through educational exchanges" (p. 4). A third example is Kornpetpanee (1999), who defines internationalization of universities for her research as "the development process of universities into a more global aspect" (p. 5). Dubhasi (1995, 10) sees cross-cultural cooperation as an inherent part of the concept of globalization of knowledge. Warner (1992) also makes no distinction between the two terms. Mestenhauser (2000) uses internationalization as an umbrella concept of which global education refers to the worldwide context in which it works, and further uses the two terms internationalization and globalization in a confusing, alternate way. However, he also notes the need for clarification of the two terms and their links.

This interchangeable use of the terms internationalization and globalization, the proposed gradual shift from international to global, and the use of global in the meaning of general or universal are all highly questionable. They are not so because, as Wells and Pfantz (1999, 21) argue, globalization should be considered as a too complex and ideologically loaded term. Jane Knight (1997a) provides a more convincing view.

The description which is most relevant and appropriate to the discussion on the international dimension of the higher education sector is as follows:

- Globalisation is the flow of technology; economy, knowledge, people, values, ideas . . . across borders. Globalisation affects each country in a different way due to a nation's individual history, traditions, culture and priorities.

- Internationalisation of higher education is one of the ways a country responds to the impact of globalisation yet, at the same time respects the individuality of the nation.

Thus, internationalisation and globalisation are seen as different but dynamically linked concepts. Globalisation can be thought of as the catalyst while internationalisation is the response, albeit a response in a proactive way. (p. 6; see also 1999a, 13–14)

Peter Scott (1998) is also of the opinion that globalization and internationalization are not "simply words to describe the same process [but] radically different processes dialectically linked" (p. 108). He links internationalization with a world order dominated by nation-states, where the emphasis is on strategic relationships (pp. 126–127). Globalization, on the contrary, implies a reordering of this world order into new regional blocs and new allies and the breaking of national boundaries by high technology and world culture. Scott links these notions to higher education. The contemporary university is the creature of the nation-state: "Paradoxically perhaps, before it became an international institution the university had first to become a national institution—just as internationalization presupposes the existence of nation states" (p. 123). This way of linking internationalization and globalization was followed along general lines at a conference of the CRE in 1999 (van der Wende 1999a, 63).

According to P. Scott (1998), internationalization of higher education has taken two forms. The first was the export of ideas and systems, or academic imperialism. The second was that of exchanges and mobility, although not in structured form. In the present environment of processes of globalization, these forms have acquired new dimensions but have not yet been replaced by globalization. "Globalization cannot be regarded simply as a higher form of internationalization. Instead of their relationship being seen as linear or cumulative, it may actually be dialectical. In a sense the new globalization may be the rival of the old internationalization." It is also for that reason that Scott questions a possible link between the archaic notion of universalism and the new globalization, "because they both transcend, and are antithetical to, the dynamics of nationalism (and of internationalism as its logical extension)" (p. 124).

P. Scott (1999) gives three main reasons why globalization cannot be regarded as a higher form of internationalization:

1. internationalisation presupposes the existence of established nation states, where globalisation is either agnostic about, or positively hostile to, nation states;

2. internationalisation is most strongly expressed through the 'high' worlds of diplomacy and culture; globalisation in the 'low' worlds of mass consumerism and global capitalism; and

3. internationalisation, because of its dependence on the existing (and unequal) pattern of nation states, tends to reproduce—even legitimize—hierarchy and hegemony; globalisation, in contrast, because it is not tied to the past, because it is a restless, even subversive, force can address new agendas. (p. 37)

According to P. Scott (1999, 38), universities are challenged by globalization because of their close identification with national cultures, because of the standardization of teaching through the impact of communication and information technology and the emergence of global research cultures and networks, and because global markets undermine the welfare states that public universities depend on for the bulk of their income.

Teichler (1999) describes the relationship between the internationalization and globalization of higher education as "two more or less unconnected trends" of internationalization: "a growth of specific, visibly international, border-crossing operations" on the one hand, and "a trend towards universalisation, globalisation, internationalisation or 'regionalisation' of the substance and the functions of higher education" (p. 7). This is a confusing way of mixing terms and content. It is better to describe the first trend as internationalization and the second as globalization.

As argued by Jane Knight and Peter Scott, there is a fundamental difference and at the same time a dialectical link between the internationalization of higher education and globalization.[2] One example of this link is given by Kerr (1994b), who observes that "the international flow of information, of scholars, and of students is aided by what seems to be the convergence in the structures and policies of systems of higher education around the world" (p. 21). This relates to the trend for harmonization and uniformization of higher education, seen as one of the consequences of globalization of our societies. The dialectical relation expresses itself in two phenomena, referred to as the "knowledge society," also called the "knowledge economy," and "transnational education."

The Knowledge Society

The relationship between globalization, new technologies, and science finds its expression in the concept of the knowledge society, also—in a more narrow sense—referred to as the knowledge economy. The pace of knowledge is accelerating as a consequence of new technologies, and the university is changing in character and emphasis from sole production and dissemination of knowledge to technology transfer and the formation of incubator facilities and research centers with industrial participation. As analyzed in Chapter 1, globalization, the end of the Cold War, and the related development of a knowledge economy are calling the traditional role of the university into question. A "triple helix of university–industry–government relations" (Etzkowitz and Leydesdorff 1997), and the notion of the "innovative" or "entrepreneurial university" (Clark 1998) are expressions of the new relationship between science and economy in a global context that challenges the traditional notion of the "ivory tower." New paradigms of knowledge production are developing, emphasizing the importance of context and the proliferation of research communities. Greater emphasis is placed on knowledge transfer and applied research (P. Scott 1999, 41–42). The transformation into the entrepreneurial university, according to Clark (1998, 5), consists of at least five necessary elements: a strengthened steering core, an expanded developmental periphery, a diversified funding base, a stimulated academic heartland, and an integrated entrepreneurial culture.[3]

This change in emphasis and character for universities is described and analyzed by scholars mainly in the context of research and development or science. The same phenomenon, however, can be observed in the other core function of universities: teaching. Growing competition and collaboration with the private sector (in particular in the areas of specialized, professional training and lifelong learning, distance education, and the use of new technologies) are developments that are increasingly coming to the forefront in higher education. Where the notion of the knowledge society seems to be more research related; in teaching, the terms transnational education and, more recently, borderless education are normally used to describe this phenomenon.

Transnational Education

Transnational education, as Liston (1999) states, is not something of recent years or even of the past century, but has always been there.[4] It became a more visible phenomenon with the massification of higher education after World War II, and with the development of new technologies has, more recently, become a key factor in tertiary education. The term transnational education, however, is used by Liston in a confusing way, including both student mobility and the mobility of teaching and learning. The term transnational education is also used by other authors as a synonym for and modern version of international education, whereas, although there is a link, it should be seen in the broader context of globalization and the way this globalization impacts and is influenced by higher education.[5]

The Global Alliance for Transnational Education (GATE 1997) defines transnational education as follows: "Any teaching or learning activity in which the students are in a different country (the host country) to that in which the institution providing the education is based (the home country). This situation requires that national boundaries be crossed by information about the education, and by staff and/or educational materials (whether the information and materials travel by mail, computer network, ratio or television broadcast or other means)" (p. 1). A working group on transnational education of UNESCO–CEPES (1999) states, "Transnational education refers to those courses of study, parts of courses of study, or other educational services in which the students are located in a different country to the one where the institution providing the services is based. The institution or program in question may belong to the national education system of another country, or it may be independent of any national system" (p. I.1).[6] Machado dos Santos (2000) describes transnational education as "higher education activities in which the learners are located in a host country different from the one where the awarding institution is based" (pp. 5–6).

An alternative term, which recently has been used often instead of transnational education, is borderless education. According to Bjarnason and colleagues (2000), the term borderless higher education is used "to indicate developments which cross (or have a potential to cross) the traditional borders of higher education, whether geographical or conceptual" (p. 7). This description is broader than the one used for transnational education, but overlaps to a great extent with the activities falling under the last one.

Examples of transnational education are offshore programs and campuses; twinning programs; articulation programs; international institutions; franchise arrangements, and branch campuses; distance education; and virtual, electronic, or Web programs and institutions. Van der Wende (1999a, 61) makes an interesting implicit suggestion to include competition under globalization, implying that the recruitment of foreign students belongs to the domain of transnational education.

Following the argumentation of Peter Scott (1998), one can argue that transnational education is more a product of and related to the impact of globalization of higher education (breaking national boundaries by new technology) than internationalization (traditional strategic relationships). At the same time, transnational education and the internationalization of higher education are dialectically linked in the same way as globalization and internationalization, as rivals. L. Wilson and Vlâsceanu (2000, 76) describe it as a relatively new phenomenon sometimes with roots in more traditional forms of internationalization, sometimes taking completely new forms. See, for instance, the title of a special issue of *Higher Education in Europe* (1999), "The Changing Face of Transnational Education: Moving Education—Not Learners," that suggests a rivalry between international and transnational education.[7]

The dialectical link between globalization and transnational education on the one hand and internationalization of higher education on the other is an area of study that requires more attention in research. As transnational education becomes more central in this century as a result of the "information age" in which we live, it must be analyzed in its relationship with internationalization, the phenomenon of the 1990s, a relationship that in the future will become more closely connected.

Mason (1998, 139–141) comes to the following conclusions on transnational education, for which he uses the confusing term global education: predominance of English, very little real engagement with cultural issues, homogenization in large-scale global courses, custom-made characteristics of small-scale offerings, diverse forms of course delivery, attention paid to the learning process, role of the teacher, skills needed by students and institutional support systems, and dominant trend demands in the lifelong learning market of professional updating, IT skilling, and to a lesser extent leisure (see also Kahn 2000).

Several authors (for instance, Muller 1995; ACA 1997; Altbach 1997c; Currie 1998; Mason 1998; Kahn 2000; Machado dos Santos 2000; Task Force on Higher Education and Society 2000) point to the potential dangers of globalization for higher education and transnational education, such as the widening of the information gap, strengthening of Western dominance, and the related problems of access; the potential conflict between market forces and academic autonomy; transparency and regulation; and so on. The Task Force on Higher Education and Society (2000) describes some of the key elements of the knowledge revolution: Worldwide, the rate at which scientific papers are published has doubled in the past two decades, and the number of patent applications has been increasing steadily. However, at the same time, the Task Force observes that not a single developing country is included among the top fifteen of published scientific papers per capita, and industrial countries have about twenty times as many personal computers as middle-income countries and more than a hundred times as many Internet hosts. The Task Force concludes that countries that are only weakly connected to the rapidly emerging global knowledge system will find themselves at a disadvantage, in addition to rising inequality within countries. No easy solutions are available.

Others (T. Adams 1998; Knight 1999c; Machado dos Santos 2000) stress the specific need for quality assurance of transnational education programs. Machado dos Santos adds to this the need for mechanisms of regulation and recognition. Together, according to him, they must guarantee consumer protection.

In addition, there appears to be common agreement on the observation by Mason (1998, 15) that the established institutions of higher education are not leading the globalization movement, but that it is being led by the newer, less prestigious institutions and new educational providers from the private sector (telecommunications, computer and software, publishing companies).

The internationalization of higher education, in the sense that it emphasizes more the interaction between cultures than the homogenization of cultures, can play a counterbalancing role to the potential dangers of transnational education. This is one reason why it is important to relate these two trends and study the relationship between them.

REGIONALIZATION AND THE INTERNATIONALIZATION OF HIGHER EDUCATION

A related but specific aspect of both the internationalization of higher education and globalization is regionalization and higher education, a phenomenon that over the past two decades has become more evident in Europe but also elsewhere. Although globalization gets more attention in the literature, regionalization can be considered a more important trend in its impact on the national character of higher education.[8]

Regionalization takes several forms. First, a distinction should be made between interregional, regional, cross-regional, and supraregional forms of regionalization.

Interregional

Although according to Haug and Race (1998, 4) there is "more diversity than homogeneity" in characterizing interregional cooperation in higher education and for that reason no generic definition of it is possible, interregional should be defined as links between nations within one region, and interregional higher education as links between higher education (institutions) of nations within one region. Haug and Race (pp. 5–10) give a typology and examples of different forms of interregional cooperation in higher education in Europe: cooperation between homogeneous regions, neighboring as well as nonadjacent; cooperation between neighbors in a geographically limited area; and cooperation between less homogeneous areas for confidence building. Such forms of regional cooperation are to be found in other parts of the world as well.[9]

Regional

The clearest example of what we call regional is Europe and in particular the European Union. Another example is NAFTA, the regional cooperation between Canada, Mexico, and the United States. Haug and Race (1998) call this "regional co-operation with a continental dimension," but "continent" as a defining characteristic is too limited, as the cases of the European Union and NAFTA show (p. 10). The role of the regions has become more important with regard to internationalization and standardization and recognition.

Cross-Regional

Cross-regional can be defined as the links between different regions, such as European Union–ASEAN, Latin America–North America, or Asia–Pacific. Haug and Race (1998, 10) call this supracontinental cooperation, a term not found appropriate because continental limits this type of regionalization to continents and because supra lacks the interactive aspect that is more clearly present in the use of the term crossing. Cross-regionalization is an important foreign-policy instrument.

Supraregional

Supraregional covers the work of international bodies such as UNESCO and the Council of Europe. These bodies are involved in higher education as supraregional government pressure groups.[10]

A second distinction should be made between regionalization in the meaning of globalization with a regional character (i.e., standardization, homogenization, harmonization of rules, regulations, recognition, structures, and systems) and regionalization in the meaning of internationalization.

A clear example of the first meaning of regionalization is the Bologna Declaration of June 19, 1999, by twenty-nine ministers of education of Europe, and its predecessor, the Sorbonne Declaration of May 25, 1998, by the four ministers of education of France, Germany, Italy, and the United Kingdom, calling for an open European area for higher learning. These declarations (de Wit 2000b, 8–9) catalyze the reform of higher education throughout Europe.[11]

An example of the second meaning of regionalization is the so-called SOCRATES program—and its predecessor ERASMUS—of the European Commission, which is directed at international cooperation and exchange within the European Union and related countries in Europe.[12]

A close look at activities, programs, and studies on regionalization and higher education indicates that regionalization is at present more closely linked to internationalization than to globalization. Exceptions are the work of supraregional bodies such as UNESCO, and the work of regional entities such as the Council of Europe and the European Commission, which deal with both internationalization and globalization concerns in higher education. However, it is not difficult to see that we are in a transition period in which regionalization is becoming increasingly linked to globalization, while information technology, competition, and standardization are becoming essential elements of reforming higher education.[13]

CONCLUSIONS

In this chapter the development of globalization, its impact on higher education, and the different forms it takes in research (the knowledge society or economy) and teaching (transnational education) have been analyzed. This impact of globalization on higher education is directly linked to similar developments in our societies as a whole, and its manifestations in research and teaching take similar forms.

It is argued that the internationalization of higher education is different from this globalization development in the way that internationalization is based on relationships between nations and their institutions and for that reason takes differences as a starting point for linkages, whereas globalization ignores the existence of nations and their diversity and looks more for similarities than for differences. At the same time, the internationalization of higher education and the globalization of our societies are and will increasingly become linked phenomena, as institutions of higher education—privatized, deregulated, and more entrepreneurial—become active players in the global marketplace while still trying to maintain their autonomous position as academic institutions and focusing on diversification rather than harmonization. The same argument has been analyzed with respect to regionalization of higher education. This phenomenon is linked to the internationalization of higher education but is also a specific form of the way globalization impacts and is influenced by higher education.

The growing importance of knowledge and human capital and the development of information and communications technologies (ICT) as a consequence will make the link between the internationalization of higher education, globalization, and regionalization even stronger than before.

NOTES

1. Studies such as Slaughter and Leslie (1997) and Mason (1998), have been published on this theme.

2. The same applies to terms that are also used as alternatives for globalization, such as multinationalization (see, for instance, Altbach 1999). The danger of using this and other terms as synonyms for globalization is that the distinctive line between internationalization and globalization becomes even more obscured.

3. Although international and global aspects are clearly related to these elements, surprisingly enough, Clark (1998) does not acknowledge this and thus ignores the strong link between the entrepreneurial university and the context of globalization, in common with other authors.

4. The term transnationalization, a term frequently used interchangeably with globalization, will not be used. Jane Knight (1999d, 13) observes that transnational education does not appear to have been formalized or institutionalized. However, this is even more true for transnationalization of higher education.

5. Transnational education should not be confused with transnational competence, just as global education should not be confused with global competence (see Chapter 5).

6. Wilson and Vlâsceanu (2000, 75) indicate that the Working Group on Franchised Qualifications of the ENIC/NARIC network formulated this definition.

7. See also the remark by the working group of UNESCO–CEPES (1999) that "Student Mobility is replaced by the mobility of the study programmes" (p. I.6).

8. See, for instance, Blumenthal and colleagues (1996), referring to both global and regional trends. Hufbauer and Malani (1996, 20) describe regionalism as the trend at the end of the twentieth century.

9. See, for instance, CHEMS (1996, 8–9) on Commonwealth cases of regionalization, and IGLU (1996) on Latin American cases.

10. For instance, *World Declaration on Higher Education for the Twenty-First Century: Vision and Action*, adopted by the World Conference on Higher Education of UNESCO (1998).

11. See also Chapter 3, and Haug, Kirstein, and Knudsen (1999), *Trends in Learning Structures in Higher Education*, a project report prepared by CRE for the Bologna Conference on June 18–19, 1999.

12. A good illustration of how both interpretations of regionalization have affected national educational policy is the study by Aaro Ollikainen (2000) on the Europeanization of Finnish education policy discourses.

13. See, for instance, the contributions to *CRE-Action* by P. Scott (1999), Daxner (1999), and van der Wende (1999a), as well as Field (1998).

Chapter 9

Quality and the Internationalization of Higher Education

Quality and internationalization are closely related issues. They are both key strategic issues in higher education at the turn of the century. Quality relates to internationalization in the way in which internationalization contributes to the improvement of the quality of higher education, and in the way one assesses and enhances or maintains the quality of internationalization activities and strategies.

The increasing preoccupation with quality in higher education is linked to the call for accountability by national governments, the corporate world, and students. Not only are they the main sources of funding for higher education, they also have a vested interest in the products of higher education. This has recently become more evident as a result of the changing nature of the relationship between higher education institutions and national governments, the corporate world, and students. Sources of income for institutions are becoming more diversified (public funding, contract funding, and fees), and as the relationship between institutions of higher education and their governments becomes more distant (deregulation, lump-sum financing, long-term contracts), the contributions of the corporate world and students become relatively higher, and with that their demands for quality assurance increase. Audit, assessment, and accreditation as approaches to quality assurance have become terms in daily use in higher education.[1]

As institutions of higher education develop internationalization strategies, the assessment and enhancement of these strategies also becomes more important. This has resulted in a call for an internationalization quality review instrument. For that purpose, the Internationalisation Quality Review Process (IQRP) was designed as a pilot project of the program on Institutional Management in Higher Education of the OECD in cooperation with the ACA and implemented by these two organizations, together with the European Association of Universities, as a service, the Internationalisation Quality Review (IQR).

The development of new transnational forms of education delivery in response to the globalization of our societies and of higher education has also called for quality assessment. The instruments used for quality assurance of national education cannot be copied integrally to these transnational education forms. Given the different origin and nature of transnational education compared to internationalization, the same is true for internationalization quality review instruments. At the same time, there is a link and certain overlap between internationalization and transnational education, and for that reason between the quality assurance instruments used.

An important argument for the internationalization of higher education is the contribution it should make to improve the quality of higher education. In the academic context this argument is considered to be a crucial one, or even according to Wächter, Ollikainen, and Hasewend (1999), the only academic argument for internationalization, which is—as noted in Chapter 8—an overly narrow approach.

The truth of this argument is difficult to measure, as Overbeek (1997) has observed for Dutch internationalization policies, and is also dependent on its relevance in comparison to other rationales used. For instance, in study abroad programs of American institutions of higher education, the driving rationale is "social learning"—the confrontation of students with other societies and their languages and cultures—to overcome parochialism (institutional rationale) and to maintain a dominant position as a superpower in the world by understanding other societies (national rationale). One could argue that in this case the contribution to the quality of learning is not manifest, although within the concept of liberal arts and taking into account that these programs are mainly directed to liberal arts students, one can argue the opposite.

However, it is important to include the international dimension in the quality assessment of learning and research programs in order to measure the potential impact of internationalization on their quality, something still rarely done. When the international dimension becomes a more integrated part of the mission, planning process, and overall strategy of the institution, this dimension has to become a natural element of the quality approaches to higher education, as do the instruments used for its assessment.

In the first part of this chapter the focus will be on the quality assessment and assurance of internationalization, based on the experiences with the

IQRP. A brief description of the project and its concept and a reflection on the lessons learned are given. In the second part, the IQR service will be related to other instruments for quality assurance used in relation to transnational and international education. The chapter will close with reflections on the incorporation of the international dimension in higher education quality assurance approaches.

THE IQRP PROJECT AND PROCESS

The IQRP project is an initiative undertaken by the Programme on Institutional Management in Higher Education (IMHE) of the OECD in collaboration with the ACA. Since 1994, the IMHE has had an active program focusing on a cross-country analysis of institutional-level strategies for the internationalization of higher education.[2] Two important issues and concerns have emerged from this work: (1) quality assessment and assurance of these strategies, and (2) the contribution that internationalization has made to enhancing the quality of higher education. At an IMHE seminar on internationalization strategies held in October 1995 it was decided to proceed with a pilot project on quality assurance and internationalization and to cooperate with the ACA.

During the first phase of the project, 1995–1997, the IMHE and the ACA jointly developed the IQRP instrument and documents and tested the IQRP in three different institutions: University of Helsinki, Finland; Bentley College in Boston; and Monash University, Melbourne, Australia. Members of the IQRP project team participated in the pilots as external peer reviewers so that ways to improve the process could be noted. Based on the experiences and lessons learned from the pilots and the feedback from experts, the team was encouraged to revise the IQRP documents and to pilot the process in a wider group of institutions and countries. Thus, phase two of the project, 1997–1998, was planned and focused on two primary objectives: revising the original materials and testing the IQRP in different types of educational institutions in a wider variety of country and cultural contexts. During phase two, the IQRP was piloted in six more institutions: UNAM (National University of Mexico); Warsaw School of Economics, Poland; Tartu University, Estonia; Moi University, Kenya; Universiti Sains, Malaysia; and Royal Melbourne Institute of Technology, Australia.

Rationale for the Pilot Project

The key role of internationalization and its contribution to higher education is gaining more recognition around the world, in both developed and developing countries. As internationalization matures, both as a concept and a process, it is important that institutions of higher education address the issue of quality assessment and assurance of their international dimension. Most processes of quality assessment are focused on activities, projects, and programs.

Overbeek (1997, 57) observes this for the Dutch case, where monitoring and evaluation were restricted to the study abroad experience of Dutch students, and a check on the broader strategy of internationalization was lacking.

If the internationalization of higher education is understood to mean "the process of integrating an international/intercultural dimension into the teaching, research and service function of the institution" (Knight 1999a, 16), then it is critical to address the quality issue from three perspectives.

The first perspective refers to the inclusion of the international dimension as a key component in the general academic quality review systems operational at the institutional or system levels. This is based on the premise that an international dimension is part of the university or college mission and major functions and is thus included as one of many elements addressed in the quality review procedures.

The second perspective looks at the quality of specific internationalization policies, procedures, and programs (i.e., international students, work or study abroad, student and faculty exchanges, research, language instruction, technical assistance, etc.).

The third perspective concerns the internationalization of quality assurance procedures themselves. These procedures are in general nationally based. It is increasingly acknowledged that quality assurance procedures benefit from an international approach and input.

The purpose of the IQRP project is to bring attention to the importance and complementarity of the various perspectives and to develop a process that would guide institutions in undertaking a quality assessment and assurance review of their specific internationalization initiatives.

Objectives of the IQRP Pilot Project

Three major objectives have governed the activities of phases one and two of the project:

1. To increase awareness of the need for quality assessment and assurance in the internationalization of higher education.
2. To develop a review process whereby individual institutions can adapt and use a set of guidelines and a framework to assess and enhance the quality of their internationalization strategies according to their own aims and objectives.
3. To strengthen the contribution that internationalization makes to the quality of higher education.

Assumptions

There are a number of assumptions that have formed the foundation of the pilot project. They are listed here and complement a set of guiding principles that have guided and shaped the methodology and instruments of the IQRP.

The IQRP is based on principles of self-assessment and peer review and is guided by the institution's own mission and aims. While the review process and framework are intended to be international in application, acknowledgment and recognition of differences among institutions and countries is essential.

The self-assessment and external peer review reports on the pilot institutions are for their use only. There is no intention to publish the reports or make any comparisons across institutions. The development and refinement of the process and the self-assessment guidelines is the primary objective and intended outcome of the project.

It is important to recognize that higher education quality review systems, even at the institutional level, benefit from an international perspective and input. This is especially true for the IQRP and therefore importance was given to ensuring that the IQRP was developed by an international team, was tested in different countries, and was international in application.

Pilot Institutions

The IQRP project team worked with a small number of institutions from different countries in the testing of the IQRP instrument. With this group of selected pilot institutions the IQRP team members served as external peer reviewers in order to monitor the effectiveness of the document and guidelines. In choosing pilot institutions to test the IQRP, a number of factors were taken into consideration.

One element was the stage of the internationalization process at the institution. It was important to test the IQRP at different levels of the development of the international dimension. It became clear that the IQRP could also work well as a planning tool for those institutions in the initial phase of developing an institutionwide internationalization strategy.

It was also important that the IQRP was piloted in a diversity of country and cultural contexts, to ensure that lessons were learned from experience where there are different approaches and assumptions about evaluation. For instance, the fact that the IQRP is based on the concepts of self-assessment and peer review may not be appropriate or successfully used in certain cultural contexts. It was intended that the IQRP would be tested in institutions with different educational orientations or purposes (i.e., technical institutes, specialized colleges, comprehensive universities, undergraduate colleges, polytechnics, etc.).

The testing of the IQRP in eight countries in five different parts of the world provided valuable information for the design of the final guidelines. Three comprehensive institutions (Helsinki, Monash, and Tartu) and two specialized institutions (Bentley and Warsaw) with well-developed strategies for internationalization used the IQRP to assess their strategies. Two comprehensive universities (Mexico and Moi) used the IQRP to assist in moving from a marginal and implicit international dimension to a central and explicit internationalization strategy. One comprehensive university (Sains Malaysia) used the IQRP to create awareness of the importance of an internationalization strategy by assessing certain parts of the institution. The Royal Melbourne Institute of Technology used the IQRP to further the mainstreaming of the international dimension throughout all functions of the university, including their offshore programs.

The IQRP Framework

The IQRP pilot project followed a framework for self-assessment and peer review that was documented in the project document, "The Development of an Internationalisation Quality Review Process at the Level of Higher Education Institutions" (IQRP 1996) for pilot phase one, and the project document, "The Development of an Internationalisation Quality Review Process for Higher Education Institutions" (IQRP 1997) for pilot phase two. During the two phases changes were made in the framework based on the experiences in the pilot institutions. Some of the more important changes are described later. This section describes the principles of the IQRP, its operational framework, the outline for self-assessment, and the peer review.

The IQRP is a process whereby individual academic institutions assess and enhance the quality of their internationalization efforts according to their own stated aims and objectives. The review includes procedures and guidelines to be adapted and used in both a self-assessment exercise and an external peer review.

Purpose of the IQRP

The purpose of the IQRP is to assist institutions of higher education to assess and improve the quality of their international dimension by focusing on the identification of

- The achievement of the institution's stated policy (goals and objectives) for internationalization, and its implementation strategy.
- The integration of an international dimension into the primary functions and priorities of the institution.
- The inclusion of internationalization as a key theme area in the institution's overall quality assurance system.

Guiding Principles of the IQRP

The starting point for the review is the institution's own stated aims and objectives. The review process assesses the extent to which institutions actually achieve the aims and objectives that they set for themselves. The assessment of the relationship between objectives and actual achievement is the core of the quality issue.

The purpose of the self-assessment process is to provide a critical self-evaluation of a variety of aspects related to the quality of the international dimension of the institution. The more emphasis given to self-assessment, the more self-assessment will function as a means of training and assisting the institution to take responsibility for its own quality improvement. Self-assessment should not be seen as an exercise to produce information for the external peer review team, but rather as an opportunity to conduct an analysis of the extent and quality of internationalization initiatives.

The purpose of the external peer review is to mirror the self-assessment process and to provide feedback and a complementary analysis to the self-assessment by the institution from a different, external, and international perspective. The emphasis is not on actual fact finding, inspection, or evaluation. While the review process is intended to be international in application, acknowledgment and recognition of differences among institutions and countries is essential.

The self-assessment and external peer review reports are for the use of the evaluated institution only. The reports are owned by the institution and can only be published by the evaluated institution or with its explicit approval.

The review process is not intended to prescribe practices or advocate uniformity or standardization of internationalization approaches or procedures. There is no explicit or implicit comparison with other institutions involved; it is an exercise for self-improvement.[3]

The review process is seen as part of an ongoing cycle of advocating, planning, implementing, rewarding, reviewing, and improving the internationalization strategy of the institution.

Who Should Conduct an IQRP?

The IQRP guidelines and framework are designed in such a way that they are applicable in a great variety of circumstances. Experience of the use of the IQRP has indicated that the IQRP can be used in

- University and nonuniversity sectors of higher education.
- Small and large institutions, comprehensive and specialized institutions, and private and public institutions.
- Institutions wishing to assess an existing strategy for internationalization, but also institutions wishing to initiate such a strategy.
- Institutions in both developed and developing countries.

The specific circumstances of the institution and the objectives have to be taken into consideration in the implementation of the IQRP. This implies a flexible use of the guidelines. While the IQRP is guided by the institution's own goals and objectives for internationalization, there are major areas that are common to many institutions and which the review process addresses.

The Operational Framework of the IQRP

The emphasis and orientation of a self-assessment exercise is on the analysis of the quality of the international dimension of the institution. It should not merely be a description of the various internationalization initiatives. At the same time, it is recognized that, in particular for those institutions that intend to use the IQRP to initiate an internationalization strategy, a qualitative and quantitative inventory of international activities will be an important basis for the assessment.

Self-Assessment

Role and Structure of the Self-Assessment Team

A self-assessment team (SAT) is formed at the institutional level and is given the mandate to

- Collect the necessary information.
- Undertake a critical analysis of the provision for and the quality of internationalization, as well of the contribution of internationalization to higher education.
- Prepare the self-assessment report (SAR).
- Engage the commitment of various parties inside and outside the institution to the whole process.

The institution chooses the members of the team to reflect the internal organization and aims of the institution. Ideally, the SAT should consist of (central and departmental level) representatives of both the administrative and academic staff, as well as of international and domestic students. In order for the team to be functional and accomplish its task in a relatively short period of time, the group should be relatively small and the members should be administratively supported to undertake the work. The full endorsement and active involvement of the institutional leadership is essential for the success of the self-assessment team.

The SAT has a chairperson and a secretary. It is recommended that the key person in the institution responsible for internationalization strategy and policy be the chair of the SAT. The secretary is responsible for organizing the work of the SAT and for coordinating the preparation of its report.

The SAT exchanges comments with the peer review team (PRT) on the self-assessment report prior to its visit, prepares the program of the visit in conjunction with the PRT, and discusses the draft peer review report with the PRT. The secretary of the SAT plays an important role as the liaison with the secretary of the PRT.

The Design of the Self-Assessment Process

It is important to emphasize that the whole purpose of the self-assessment is to analyze the international dimension, not merely to describe it. Collecting data to build a profile of all the different activities, programs, policies, and procedures related to the international dimension of the institution is only a first step. It is certainly an important and rather time-consuming step, in particular for those institutions that use the IQRP as an instrument to assist in the preparation of an internationalization strategy and that do not yet have mechanisms in place to make a quantitative and qualitative description of these activities, programs, procedures, and policies. But the analysis of an institution's performance and achievements according to their articulated aims and objectives for internationalization is critical to assess and eventually assure the quality of the international dimension and the contribution internationalization makes to the primary functions of the institution. The process must indicate directions for improvement and change of the internationalization strategy of the institution, which follow from the diagnosis itself.

The self-assessment report should give a reasonable profile of the institution, reflecting its particular directions and priorities and the effectiveness of its operations, and aimed at giving directions for improvement and change. The self-assessment should recognize and reflect the potential diversity of rationales and strategies between faculties and schools.

This self-assessment should not primarily be regarded as a descriptive exercise, but rather as a critical analysis of the institution's performance and achievements in the field of internationalization. Besides providing the necessary information, an analysis should be made of strong and weak points, indicating how well the various internationalization efforts are being realized and formulating potential avenues to improvement.

Terminology often differs from country to country and from institution to institution. Institutions should use the terminology they find appropriate for their situation. It is helpful to add a note of explanation so that the peer review team understands the use of these terms in their institutional context.

General Outline of the Self-Assessment

The self-assessment outline is designed as a template for the process of analyzing the aims and objectives, the performance and achievements, the strengths and the weaknesses, and the opportunities and threats with regard to the international dimension of the institution. It needs to be emphasized that it is the international dimension that is being reviewed and analyzed.

For instance, in the case of curriculum activities and research initiatives, it is how the international dimension is addressed and integrated that is under review, not the curriculum or research itself.

The outline is a starting point and a guide for the institution to undertake the preparation of their self-assessment. It is not intended to be a coercive structure. There may be questions and issues included in the outline that are not relevant or appropriate to the mandate of the specific institution. In other instances, there may be important items that have not been included in the outline that the SAT wants to address, and therefore these should be added.

The main categories of the outline for the self-assessment are as follows: context, internationalization policies and strategies, organizational and support structures, academic programs and students, research and scholarly collaboration, human resources management, contracts and services, and conclusions and recommendations.

The Self-Assessment Report

After the self-assessment exercise has been completed, the preparation of the self-assessment report is the next step in the IQRP. The report should be limited to a maximum of twenty to thirty pages plus possible annexes. It is most helpful if it follows as much as possible the general pattern of the self-assessment outline, with the caveat that not all the categories and questions in the outline may be appropriate or relevant for each institution. It is also important to stress that the self-assessment team may add issues not covered by the framework but considered relevant. Thus, the self-assessment outline should be considered as a guide only, intended to introduce many of the areas and issues to be considered and to encourage the teams to undertake an analytical approach.

The self-assessment report will be much more than a description of the type and extent of internationalization efforts; it is meant to critically assess and address ways to assure and improve the quality of internationalization of the teaching, research, and public-service functions of the institution in light of existing issues and forthcoming challenges.

The language of the self-assessment report will in part be guided by the makeup of the PRT. During the initial stages of the IQRP the secretary of the SAT decides in collaboration with the secretary of the PRT the working language of the PRT site visit and also the language of the self-assessment report. If a language other than the native language is used for the SAT report and PRT reports, it is assumed that the supporting documents, such as data annexes, can be in the institution's national language.

The peer review team members should receive the self-assessment report at least one month prior to the visit. The institution sends the secretary of the PRT one copy of the SAT report for each of the PRT members, plus two additional copies for the IQRP archive.

The Peer Review Process

Membership of the Peer Review Team

The peer review team can vary in size but requires a minimum of three members and usually consists of three or four members; all must be external and independent of the institution undergoing the IQRP. The experts appointed to the PRT should have a general understanding of quality assessment and assurance, have a particular expertise in the internationalization of higher education, and be knowledgeable and experienced in higher education.

The PRT chairperson should preferably be a senior academic with expertise in higher education governance and the development and management of international relations and programs of institutions of higher education. Knowledge of recent developments in the internationalization of higher education globally is also essential. The expertise and experience of the other members should relate to the priority areas of the institution's aims and objectives for internationalization. They should be knowledgeable in academic culture and governance. It is considered an additional asset to have a team member with prior experience in quality assurance review exercises.

The composition of the PRT is primarily international, but it may include one member from the institution's home country or a member with considerable experience in and knowledge of higher education in the country (but not related to the institution itself). At least one member of the PRT should come from another continent than the institution's home country. The former is likely to be able to provide the PRT with insight in the national context; the latter is likely to be able to provide the PRT with a perspective beyond the regional context.

One member of the PRT serves as secretary and is responsible for organizing the work of the PRT and for coordinating the preparation of its report. The secretary of the PRT is also the liaison person with the secretary of the SAT for the response of the PRT to the self-assessment report and the preparation of terms of reference for the site visit.

The secretary of the PRT prepares a written agreement with the institution on the terms under which the self-assessment and peer review reports will be placed in the IQRP archives of the IMHE. The following options are available:

- The documents will not be included in the archives.
- The documents will be included, but permission for use by parties other than the institution has to be granted by the institution on each occasion.
- The documents will be included and permission is granted by the institution to IMHE to provide a copy of the documents upon request.

In the last two cases the SAT secretary is responsible for providing two copies of the self-assessment and peer review reports to IMHE.

The institution is responsible for all costs related to the peer review. It is important to clarify and agree upon all the financial aspects of the review before individuals are invited to become members of the PRT.

Responsibilities of the Peer Review Team

The task of the PRT is to examine

- The goals for internationalization of the institution and whether they are clearly formulated.
- How these goals are translated into the institution's curriculum, research, and public-service functions, and if the institution is providing the necessary support and infrastructure for successful internationalization.
- How the institution monitors its internationalization efforts.
- The institution's capacity to change, and its autonomy in order to improve its internationalization strategies.
- The adequacy of its diagnosis and proposals for change and improvement.

The PRT members should receive the self-assessment report at least one month prior to the visit. After thoroughly reviewing it, the PRT may provide general comments to the self-assessment team prior to the site visit. The PRT then pays a three- to four-day visit to the institution and produces a detailed report (twenty to thirty pages) for the institution no later than two months after the site visit.

Design of the Peer Review Process

Ideally, the PRT meets once before the actual site visit to discuss the self-assessment report, finalize the terms of reference for the visit, and agree on the division of labor among the team members. It is preferable that this meeting takes place at the institution where the IQRP is being carried out, and also includes a meeting with the self-assessment team to discuss the comments on the self-assessment report and to prepare the program.

It is acknowledged that in many cases, for reasons of costs and time, such a preparatory visit will not be possible. In that case, the secretary of the PRT establishes active communication with the other PRT members to receive their comments on the self-assessment report and suggestions for the terms of reference and the program of the site visit. It is then also recommended that the secretary pays a preparatory visit to the institution to discuss the comments on the self-assessment report and finalize the terms of reference and the program with the SAT.

The PRT has, on-site, a half- or one-day planning meeting prior to the commencement of the official PRT program. Based on the initial review of the self-assessment report and discussions of the PRT, a decision is made as to whether additional information is needed before the site visit. Prior to the site visit a list of specific issues to be addressed and individuals or groups to be met is prepared by the PRT and forwarded to the self-assessment team.

The institution prepares a detailed schedule for the PRT visit, which may vary in length between three and four days. The team should meet key persons among selected administrative and academic staff, students, and graduates, and, if possible, representatives of other bodies (both inside and outside the institution) responsible for or involved in international activities. Where appropriate, it may be useful to visit the units where students or staff receive assistance and service, as well as other related facilities of the institution. In some cases it may be appropriate for PRT members to visit locations and programs of the institution in other parts of the world. The schedule also includes meetings with the self-assessment team, the leadership of the institution, chief academic and administrative staff responsible for international activities, and related support services.

At the end of the site visit, the PRT meets with the SAT to comment on the site visit and discuss the plans for the preparation of the PRT report and its presentation to the institution. The PRT also meets with the senior leaders of the institution to give a brief report, oral and preliminary, on the visit.

The Peer Review Team Report

The major issues to be addressed in the PRT report are the following:

- Is the institution's self-assessment report on internationalization sufficiently analytical and constructively critical?
- Are the strengths and weaknesses of the institution's international activities clearly articulated and the plans for improvements clearly presented and realistic?
- Is the institution achieving the aims and objectives it has set for itself?
- How do the institution's vision and goals relate to the development and sustainability of its international activities within the totality?
- What action is required of the institution in order to monitor progress and provide continuing impetus?

The PRT prepares a draft report and sends it to the chairperson of the SAT within two months after the site visit. The draft version of the PRT report is meant for review and comment before the final version is submitted. This provides the institution with the opportunity to correct any factual errors and errors of interpretation. The institution provides feedback to the PRT within two weeks of the receipt of the draft version of the report. It is up to the PRT to decide whether to include the recommended changes in the report or not. Any required changes are made by the PRT and the final report is sent to the institution. The institution receives five copies of the report. It is up to the institution to decide how many additional copies it will make for internal and external use. The institution has complete ownership of the report. The report is strictly confidential if the institution wishes to consider it as such.

The follow-up activities and other uses of the PRT report are the responsibility of the institution. It is suggested that both the self-assessment report and the PRT report be made available at least internally. Given that the self-assessment process has taken place with active participation by many individuals and groups in the institution, it is important that they are included in an open discussion or planning session on the comments and suggestions made in both the SAT and PRT reports. In other words, the use of and follow up to the reports is an integral part of the process of assessing, assuring, and improving the internationalization strategies.

Follow-Up Phase

The institution may add a follow-up phase to the IQRP, approximately one and a half to two year after the PRT report has been delivered. This is particularly important in those cases in which the IQRP is used to start a process for the development of an internationalization strategy within an institution. This follow-up phase can take place with or without involvement of an external peer review. As part of this follow-up phase the self-assessment team writes a document analyzing the progress in implementing the recommendations made by the SAT and PRT and the internationalization strategy. It makes recommendations for further actions. This report is the basis for a one- to two-day site visit by the PRT to give their views on progress and recommendations for further action. The decision to include a follow-up phase in the IQRP should preferably be taken at the beginning of the IQRP and at latest at the end of the PRT visit.

FROM THE PILOT PROJECT IQRP TO THE IQR SERVICE

In 1998, when the IQRP pilot project came to an end, discussions started about the implementation of the IQRP as an instrument to assess internationalization strategies of European universities. The Association of European Universities showed interest. The CRE already had an instrument for assessing institutions of higher education in Europe, the so-called Programme of Institutional Quality Audits. The CRE was also responsible for a project to evaluate the European Policy Statements that European institutions of higher education had been obliged to write as the basis for their applications under SOCRATES (Barblan et al. 1998). The growing importance of internationalization strategies in Europe, demonstrated, for example, by the institutional audits and the European Policy review, encouraged the CRE to decide to use internationalization as the first choice for a focused audit in European universities. Instead of developing a new instrument, it was decided to work together with the IMHE and the ACA in adapting the IQRP into an instrument relevant for the European context. It was agreed that the CRE would administer the IQR as a joint service with the IMHE and the ACA.[4]

The Universiteit van Amsterdam expressed interest in a review of its internationalization strategy and volunteered to use the IQR service. Because of time constraints, the university was not able to wait for the adaptation of the IQRP guidelines and offered to act as an IQR pilot project, using the IQRP guidelines as a basis. In this sense, the Universiteit van Amsterdam might be considered more as an additional pilot case for the IQRP than as the first institution undergoing the IQR, although the experiences of the Universiteit van Amsterdam are considered to be relevant for the further refinement of the IQR service.

REFLECTIONS ON USING THE IQRP

The pilot cases of the IQRP have provided insights and information on using the IQRP to assess and enhance the international dimension of higher education. Based on the original, the IQRP reflections, and the experience with the IQRP at the Universiteit van Amsterdam, the following is an updated version of the experiences gained and lessons learned from the use of the instrument, and a reflection on its future application to other institutions.

Application of the IQRP in Different Contexts

Use in Different Educational Contexts

One of the most complex issues in the design of the guidelines for the IQRP was to take into account the diversity of cultures and systems in higher education. As already stated a guiding principle for the project was that the review process be international in application . . . and that acknowledgment and recognition of differences among institutions and countries is essential. Therefore, a key factor in selecting the pilot institutions was diversity. The final selection included nine institutions in eight countries on five different continents.

During the review of the lessons learned from the pilot case studies, there was consensus that the IQRP was useful and effective in different types of institutions in different regions of the world. The pilot case studies demonstrated that the IQRP is relevant to and adaptable to the following differences in educational contexts:

- Differences between private and public institutions.
- Differences between the university and nonuniversity sectors.

- Differences between large, comprehensive universities and specialized institutions.
- Differences between undergraduate colleges, research universities, and professional schools.

During the revision of the IQRP guidelines, particular importance was given to ensuring that the guidelines were applicable and sensitive to different types of higher education institutions. Therefore, the revised IQRP guidelines have been crafted so that they are flexible enough to recognize and accommodate the variety of higher education institutions that are interested in assessing and assuring the quality of their internationalization efforts.

Use in Different Cultural Contexts

A key challenge in developing the conceptual and operational frameworks for the IQRP was its application in different cultural contexts. Because the IQRP is based on two fundamental principles—self-assessment and peer review—it was very important to be sensitive to different cultural orientations to these principles. The notion of "face" or "reputation" was of particular concern. Would the process of self-assessment result in a "promotional or public relations report" that would identify strengths and accomplishments only and gloss over areas needing improvement? Would the peer review report be credible and accepted if it focused on specific issues and activities that needed further development and enhancement? Would culturally based interpretations of the concepts of internationalization or globalization negatively influence the process of reviewing the international dimension? Would the need for an explicit rationale and clearly stated goals and objectives for an internationalization strategy be problematic in different cultures and regions of the world? These were the types of questions being asked during the design and revision stages of the IQRP.

The experiences of the pilot case studies have demonstrated that the flexibility of the IQRP makes it adaptable and useful in different cultural contexts. Of course, the most important principle is that the IQRP respects and adapts to individual situations and fundamental cultural values and beliefs. Therefore, the frameworks and guidelines of the IQRP have intentionally been developed to respect and accommodate different contexts; in particular, the cultural context. The discussion on approaches to self-assessment later in this chapter illustrates the way in which different institutions in different contexts have adapted the self-assessment process to suit their situation.

Use in Institutions at Different Stages of Internationalization

The IQRP project was originally based on the assumption that the IQRP would be most useful for institutions in which a variety of international activities and relationships were already operational and where a comprehensive internationalization strategy was in place to ensure that there was a holistic and integrated approach to the international dimension. In fact, the experiences of the IQRP at several institutions proved this assumption to be false. There were several institutions at which an explicit internationalization strategy had not been developed in spite of the many international initiatives and where the IQRP was instrumental in developing such a strategy.

It is interesting to refer to the actual experiences of the pilot institutions to elaborate on this point. This discussion on the different development stages of internationalization at the pilot institutions is used for illustrative purposes. There is no comparison inferred or intended among or between the institutions.

In institutions such as the University of Helsinki, Bentley College, Monash University, Royal Melbourne Institute of Technology, and the Universiteit van Amsterdam, as expected, a comprehensive internationalization strategy had been developed and was more or less operational. The cases of the National University of Mexico and Moi University in Kenya demonstrated that the IQRP could also be used as a planning instrument to help design the overall institution's strategy for internationalization. This was done by assessing the strengths and weaknesses, opportunities, and threats for a strategic internationalization plan and/or for the formulation of the international dimension in the overall strategic plan of the institution.

In the case of Moi University, the self-assessment exercise was used as an instrument to help create awareness of the international dimension of higher education and its possible contribution to the overall mandate and goals of the institution. The IQRP was a catalyst and a tool to raise awareness about the importance of the international dimension and to collect and analyze the existing but fragmented international activities, contacts, and projects. Through the IQRP, the strengths and weaknesses of the current state of international activities were analyzed and priorities for an internationalization strategy were identified. Thus, the first steps toward developing and implementing an overall internationalization plan were taken through the IQRP.

In the case of the National University of Mexico, one can speak of an ad hoc and marginal approach to internationalization, but must recognize at the same time an impressive range of international activities, linkages, and projects. The institution needed the IQRP to place the selection of international activities into a more explicit and coherent perspective and to explore the possibilities for making organizational and programmatic changes for the development of an internationalization strategy and for the incorporation of the international dimension in the overall strategic plan of the institution.

The case of the Universiteit van Amsterdam placed a question mark after the original assumption that the IQRP would be most useful to institutions where a comprehensive internationalization strategy was in place. The instrument might be more relevant for institutions that are in the process of developing a strategy or that are in the first stage of such a strategy and want to use the review in order to widen and deepen it than for institutions that want to move from a systematic internationalization policy of internationalization, disconnected from the core activities of the institution, to an integrated internationalization (Teichler 1999, 9–10), as was the case for the Universiteit van Amsterdam. For such an integrated internationalization, inclusion of the international dimension in other quality assurance systems and procedures of the institution might be more appropriate. In such a case, an institution might still consider an IQR focused on the program and organizational strategies for internationalization in place, but should not expect more than general references to the impact on the overall reform of the institution.

In summary, the experiences with ten case studies have shown that the IQRP can be used by educational institutions at different stages in the development and evolution of a comprehensive internationalization strategy. The case of the Universiteit van Amsterdam, however, has shown that it is important to analyze carefully the rationale for and the context in which the institution wants to use the IQRP. The educational context, the external environment of the institution, and the stage of development of its internationalization strategy and the relationship between the three are all most relevant. The rationale for and the context in which the institution places its review should be made explicit and clear in advance to both the self-assessment and peer review team. Only in this way can there be a mutual understanding of expectations.

Practical Issues in Using the IQRP

The Commitment to Undertake an IQRP

Implementing a quality review of internationalization strategy only makes sense under certain conditions. The institution must be clear about the rationale for undertaking a quality review of the international dimension. The different constituency groups, including the leadership and the academic and administrative staff as well as students of the institution, must be committed to all stages of the process of review. This includes the decision to undergo the review, the self-assessment, the peer review, and the implementation of conclusions and recommendations.

There must be a clear identification of the follow-up procedures to the review and how to implement any recommendations. Finally, there must be awareness about the resource implications of the review itself and of potential resource implications of the recommendations of the review.

Description versus Analysis in the Self-Assessment

One of the greatest challenges and perhaps striking aspects of the self-assessment exercise was the tendency for the SAT report to be more descriptive than analytical. This is easily understood and can happen for a variety of reasons. In some cases, preparing the SAT report was the first time that the institution attempted to collect information systematically on all international initiatives and policies. Developing a comprehensive picture of the nature and extent of internationalization activities can be both a very revealing and an overwhelming undertaking. In situations where this type of inventory did not exist, the SAT tended to focus more on the collecting of the data than on the analysis of the findings. In other cases, the membership of the SAT was too focused (i.e., international office only). In another instance, the team members were not experienced enough in dealing with academic planning and governance issues at the macro level.

For the SAT report to be a useful document for the institution and the PRT, it is necessary for there to be a clear articulation of goals and objectives or targets for internationalizing the institution. The importance of having an explicit rationale as well as clearly stated goals and objectives cannot be overstated. It is the rationale, goals, and objectives that will guide the SAT and PRT, as the whole exercise is driven by the institution's mission and aims. Given that the underlying principle of the IQRP is to assess and assure the achievement of the aims and objectives as identified by the institution itself, it is critical that they are clearly stated. They can also provide or drive the framework for the analysis. The analysis of the strengths, weaknesses, opportunities, and threats (SWOT) of internationalization strategies is at the heart of the IQRP. Therefore, a SWOT analysis is critical to ensuring that the SAT report is more than a catalogue of internationalization initiatives. The SWOT analysis helps to identify what works well, what can be improved, and what are new opportunities.

A second factor in ensuring an analytical approach to the IQRP is the selection of the chair and members of the SAT and the types of support that are available to the team. The next section will address the importance of selecting the right chair for the SAT and the composition of the team members.

Self-Assessment Team Members

The pilot case studies have indicated how important it is to select carefully the members of the SAT. It is important to have a senior leader of the university who is directly involved in or responsible for internationalization to head the SAT. This is important for a number of reasons. First is the strong message given to the community about the importance of the international dimension and the IQRP. Second is the leader's familiarity with the internationalization work in particular, but also the more general policy and governance of the institution. The third relates to the benefit of having a senior person's insight and influence for the implementation of the final recommendations for improvement. However, there is also a danger in having a senior leader chairing the SAT. This person could push his or her own agenda on the team and the report. Among the pilot case studies there were two in which, from within the institution or from the PRT, questions were raised about the role of the chair in pushing a private agenda. This potential conflict of interest should be taken into account and discussed beforehand. In the case of the Universiteit van Amsterdam, the president of the university chaired the broad SAT and the vice president for international affairs was one of the two members of the core SAT that wrote the report. Although this delivered the positive input as described, it also raised questions about the objectivity of the relationship between the team and the board of the institution, which had to accept the report. Although in the end, according at least to the PRT, there were no indications of lack of objectivity and critical analysis, one can still wonder if this is the right approach.

To ensure that different constituencies of the institution are involved and to avoid a top-down process, it is important to have representatives of teaching and administrative staff as well as students on the committee. Experience has shown that members of the SAT do not necessarily have to be champions and promoters of internationalization; indeed, this can give a skewed picture of the level of commitment and support for internationalization within the institution. The noninvolved and even the internationalization "naysayers" can make a very useful contribution. That being said, one has to be aware of the size of the SAT. Of course, it will greatly differ according to the institution, but a team of four to six is often the most effective. Consultation with the wider community within the institution is critical and this can be done in a variety of ways to ensure that a broad cross-section of views is heard. The views and voices of both domestic and international students play a central role in the self-assessment process. In some cases, it may also be appropriate for the SAT to have a member external to the institution.

In three cases explicitly, and probably implicitly in some other cases, a distinction was made between a core SAT and a broader SAT that acted as an advisory group to the core team and/or for endorsement of the report. For practical reasons, working on a self-assessment with a broad team is difficult. Most members would not be able and/or willing to give the time needed to collect data, perform many interviews, and write a report. An individual or a small team is therefore selected for this task. In general, this is the senior person in charge of international affairs, one of his or her staff members, or an outsider. In the case of the Universiteit van Amsterdam, for instance, a team consisting of the vice president for international affairs and a researcher hired on a temporary basis from the NUFFIC acted as the core SAT. In such cases, one has to be careful that the report truly reflects the views of the broad SAT. If the number of meetings between the core and broad team is too limited and/or if the core team pushes its own agenda too hard, this can be a problem.

Approaches to the Self-Assessment Exercise

The experiences of the pilot case studies have demonstrated that the IQRP framework is flexible enough to be adapted to different needs and characteristics of institutions. This is illustrated by the different approaches used to complete the self-assessment exercise. The guidelines outlined a process whereby the appointed SAT would consult with the different stakeholder groups on campus, collect information, conduct a SWOT analysis, and be fully involved in the preparation of the SAT report with recommendations. This process was successfully adapted to specific situations at different institutions. For instance, as we have already mentioned, in three institutions the SAT acted as an advisory committee to the leaders responsible for internationalization who undertook the preparation of the SAT report, and then consulted widely in the community for reactions and additions to the report. In another case, both the SAT and the PRT reports were prepared and then shared with the university for feedback and support for the recommendations. In another institution, seminars were held with representatives of the different stakeholder groups, the process was explained, and participants were engaged in the preparation of the SAT and the whole IQRP. It is impossible and ill-advised to indicate which is the best approach. The culture of each institution is different and must be respected. Therefore, the IQRP framework and guidelines are deliberately flexible and adaptable to enable them to be used in the most effective way according to the goals and characteristics of the institution. An important point, which bears repetition, is the necessity of the university community to be involved and committed to the process of internationalization. The IQRP, including both the self-assessment and peer review, can be a constructive way to increase awareness, involvement, and commitment to internationalization. It is for this reason that special attention needs to be given to the composition of the SAT and the best approach to the self-assessment exercise.

Peer Review Team Members

As with the SAT, the composition of the PRT is crucial. There are a number of factors to take into consideration when selecting the members and building the best team. However, experience has shown that there are two or three key factors. First, it is assumed that all members are external to the institution and do not have any vested interests or biases. It is important to have at least one member who is familiar with the local context and culture (i.e., national education policies, trends, and issues) and can brief the other team members if necessary on any critical local issues. This has been an especially important and successful feature in the pilot case studies. It is equally important to have at least one team member who comes from outside the country or region and is knowledgeable about different education systems and policies. Expertise and practical experience in internationalizing an academic institution is absolutely essential; theoretical understanding is not enough. Experience in a senior management position in academia is also advisable, so that both the macro governance and policy issues as well as operational issues are understood. At the Universiteit van

Amsterdam, a suggestion was made to include someone from outside academia, from the political or corporate world, in order to include insight from the external environment on the rationales and strategies of the university. This might be relevant in other cases as well.[5]

While it is an advantage to have quality assessment expertise represented on the team, it is not an absolute necessity. In fact, knowledge of best practices of internationalization in different types of institutions in various countries of the world is probably more useful to the peer review process. Experience has shown that a diversity of backgrounds in the team makes for a perceptive and robust review. In one case, the team was composed only of senior managers and researchers in higher education. Although this team appeared substantial and strong, lack of diversity was perceived as a problem. In this case, different views on internationalization strategies also had a negative impact on the final result.

Conclusions and Recommendations

The process of undergoing a self-assessment exercise is at the heart of quality assessment and assurance and improvement. The PRT is the second step and acts as a mirror to the findings and conclusions of the SAT process and report. The conclusions and recommendations are an essential part of the SAT report. In some pilot case studies there was some hesitation to draw any conclusions or make any recommendations before the PRT visit. This is understandable, as it is helpful to get feedback and external perspectives on the findings of the SAT exercise before the recommended changes are finalized. However, because the PRT serves as a mirror and a feedback mechanism, it is important for the PRT to be aware of the suggested recommendations and discuss them with the SAT and senior leaders of the institution. It is therefore highly recommended that the SAT thinks through and articulates the conclusions and recommendations prior to the PRT visit, then reviews and revises them after the PRT report has been received, and then finally makes a report on the recommendations for quality improvement. As already stated, ownership of and commitment to improvement is an important outcome of the IQRP, and this is especially true for the conclusions and recommendations.

Timing of the IQRP

There are three major points to be made with respect to the timing of the IQRP exercise. The first relates to the stage of development of the institution relative to internationalization. The original expectation was that institutions, which were well along the path of internationalization, would be most interested in undertaking an IQRP. However, as discussed in two of the case studies, one of the unexpected outcomes of the project has been the value of the IQRP guidelines as a tool for strategic planning for institutions that are in the early stages of internationalization. This has been one of the key lessons learned and has expanded the potential use and benefits of the IQRP beyond the initial design and objectives of the project. On the other hand, as we have indicated, the Universiteit van Amsterdam case suggests that the instrument might be less relevant for institutions that are in the process of moving from a systematic internationalization policy, disconnected from the core activities of the institution, to an integrated internationalization. For such an integrated internationalization, inclusion of the international dimension in other quality assurance systems and procedures of the institution might be more appropriate.

The second timing factor relates to the institution's priority and preoccupation with quality reviews. In recent years increasing importance has been given to quality reviews for reasons of both accountability and improvement. While this is a positive sign, there is also a greater risk of the "quality review fatigue" syndrome being experienced at the institution. It is therefore important to be sensitive to the timing of the IQRP with respect to other evaluation or audit exercises so that there is not undue pressure on the institution. However, another unexpected outcome of the project has been that the IQRP is compatible with other quality review systems and that there are potential benefits in combining the IQRP with other review exercises. Therefore, while attention needs to be given to other institutional reviews, one can also consider the possibility of undertaking an IQRP in conjunction with other exercises. An institution considering an IQRP should consider all factors that may positively or negatively influence the ability to consult a cross-section of the institution and its commitment to the process and the eventual improvements.

The length of time it takes to complete an IQRP—the third factor—is obviously influenced by many factors, which are usually institutionally based and therefore differ from institution to institution. Experience has shown that between three and six months is an appropriate period for completion of the exercise. Taking more time can result in review fatigue, and it may be hard to sustain a high level of commitment and participation. An extended self-assessment exercise may also be a sign of overemphasis on data collection rather than analysis. After completion and submission of the SAT report, it usually takes another three months at least before the peer review phase is finished and the final report is submitted. Therefore, one should aim to have the entire self-assessment and peer review finished within nine months, and then the institution can focus on implementing the recommendations for improvements.

Follow-Up Phase

At the start of the project, the IQRP was designed as a three-step process: (1) self-assessment phase, (2) peer review phase, and (3) improvement phase.

Several of the pilot studies have indicated that a fourth step, a follow-up peer reiview exercise approximately one to two years afterward, would be very useful in order to assess the impact of the changes made and the evolution of the strategic planning and institutionalization of the international dimension. To date, a follow-up exercise has not been undertaken, as it would be premature for most of the institutions in the pilot project. There have been some requests, and therefore serious consideration will be given to undertaking follow-up PRT visits. It is for this reason that the idea of a follow-up phase has been introduced into the IQRP guidelines. It may not be necessary for all the members of the original PRT to participate in the follow-up, but it would be important that at least one or two members of the original team guide the follow-up peer review process.

Focused or Comprehensive IQRP

It was clear from the pilot institutions in the project that there are different rationales for why a university or college is interested in doing an IQRP. This was anticipated, and for that reason the IQRP was designed to be flexible and adaptable to different types of institutions and different motivations for an IQRP.

An interesting aspect of two of the case studies (UNAM, Mexico, and Universiti Sains Malaysia) was their focus on only part of the institution, not the whole organization. In the focused approach, however, it is still important that both academic departments and central administrative or service units are included. In addition, it is essential that a wide selection of faculty members, senior administrators, students, researchers, and so on, are consulted by the SAT and PRT. When only the international office and other support units are included in the review, there are significant limitations to understanding the strengths, weaknesses, opportunities, and threats of integrating the international dimension into the teaching, research, and service activities of the institution. Similarly, when only administrators are consulted by the SAT or PRT one gets a very skewed view; the opinions and perceptions of faculty, staff, and students are important and should not be excluded. Therefore, for both a focused and a comprehensive IQRP it is essential that a cross-section of both academic (teaching and research) and administrative and support units is reviewed, and also that there is broad consultation across the institution.

Ad Hoc versus Coordinated and Integrated Approach

An interesting and encouraging trend is the gradual shift toward a more strategic approach to internationalizing an institution. The process approach to internationalization has emphasized the concepts of integration and coordination and has deemphasized the fragmented-activities approach. The key point is that there is awareness and a gradual but perceptible change in planning and managing the international dimension.

The fact that the IQRP has been used as a planning tool as well as a review instrument illustrates that institutions are ready to think about internationalization strategies and not just a series of isolated activities. Furthermore, institutions are ready and trying to develop an overall institutional action plan to integrate an international dimension into teaching, research, and service activities. The movement toward strategic planning is helping to make internationalization a central part of the university mission and mandate, not a marginal, ad hoc, optional group of activities.

IQRP Guidelines and Self-Assessment Outline

In the two phases of the IQRP pilot project, two different types of guidelines have been used. In the first phase, the team worked with an extensive checklist, addressing the following major areas: the (inter)national context, the institutional profile, governance and organization systems, academic programs, research and scholarly collaboration, students, faculty and staff, external relations and services, and conclusions.

In the second phase, the team worked with a more global self-assessment structure, covering six major areas without a detailed checklist: summary of the higher education system and the institutional profile, analysis of the (inter)-national context, analysis of the institution's policy and strategies for internationalization, analysis of the implementation and effects of the internationalization strategies, analysis of the organizational structure and procedures for internationalization, and conclusions.

The reason for this change was that when the first three pilot institutions used the checklist, there was a tendency for the self-assessment teams to follow it too closely and to be too descriptive when answering the questions. The checklist also created confusion through the terminology used. Some of the terminology was too culture and region bound, such as "off-shore programs," a term more familiar to Australian higher education than to Finnish higher education.

In the second phase, it was clear that several institutions found the new self-assessment structure too general and vague, and they started to use the checklist of the first phase to help them perform the self-assessment. This was true in particular for those institutions that used the IQRP more as a planning instrument.

The experiences with the two methods have resulted in the development of a third version of the IQRP guidelines. The guidelines include a detailed self-assessment outline that covers the following major categories: context, internationalization policies and strategies, organizational and support structures, academic programs and students, research and scholarly collaboration, human resources management, contracts and services, and conclusions and recommendations. Each category requires a SWOT analysis and contains a list of possibly relevant questions on the "what" and "how," the effectiveness, and the possibilities for improvement. The outline is designed in such a way that it is distinctive from and at the same time applicable in combination with other instruments of quality assessment and assurance, and that it can be used at different stages of development of internationalization, as well as in different regional, cultural, and educational contexts (Knight and de Wit 1999c).

With the start of the IQR service, it was discussed whether to adapt the guidelines to focus more on strategic aspects of internationalization in relation to the overall context of the institution and its policy for change. This discussion was influenced by the primary focus on Europe and the assumption that most institutions of higher education in Europe are moving from an isolated to an integrated strategy of internationalization. The experience of the Universiteit van Amsterdam, the first case study of the IQR service and an institution that claims to be moving from an isolated to an integrated internationalization strategy, could be used to support both sides of the debate. One can argue that the IQR of the Universiteit van Amsterdam failed to accomplish this objective because no other guidelines than those of the IQRP were yet available. But one can also argue that the instrument is less useful for such an objective.

OTHER QUALITY ASSURANCE INSTRUMENTS AND THEIR RELATIONSHIP TO THE IQRP

Other quality assurance instruments are being used to assess the international dimension of institutions of higher education: benchmarking, performance indicators, codes of practice, and the GATE certification process. Instruments such as Total Quality Management and ISO 9000 are also sometimes used to assess the international dimension. The Royal Melbourne Institute of Technology has used ISO 9002 and IQRP in combination, with the IQRP addressing the goals, objectives, and strategies for internationalization, and ISO 9002 the quality of the management systems and processes (Knight and de Wit 1999b, 220). Benchmarking is, for instance, used in the framework of a project of the Commonwealth Higher Education Management Service (CHEMS) to improve the quality of internationalization through comparisons between institutions of higher education in the Commonwealth.[6]

The codes of practice are used in particular by national organizations such as UKCOSA in the United Kingdom, CBIE in Canada, NAFSA in the United States, and AVCC in Australia, and are mainly statements of principles to which institutions and/or professionals adhere.

The Global Alliance for Transnational Education (GATE) certification process is designed to assess the quality of transnational education.[7] As has been experienced in the case of Monash University and described by Jane

Knight (1999c), the GATE certification process is conceptually and operationally complementary to the IQRP, with GATE addressing the transnational dimension and the IQRP the international dimension of the institution and its transnational education.[8]

THE INTERNATIONALIZATION OF QUALITY ASSURANCE AND THE QUALITY ASSURANCE OF INTERNATIONALIZATION

Several authors (A. Smith 1994b; P. Scott 1996; El-Khawas, DePietro-Jurand, and Hlm-Nielsen 1998; van der Wende 1999c) stress the relationship between the quality assurance of internationalization and the internationalization of quality assurance. Globalization, decreased government support for education, the knowledge economy, the rapid growth of information technologies: All are directly influencing higher education. It is resulting in major shifts in the rationales and motivations for internationalization. It is therefore very important that attention is given to developing new quality review instruments and that existing instruments are adapted and applied to internationalization. It is equally important and an ultimate goal that the international dimension becomes a regularized part of all institutional audits or program accreditations, as has been observed by Knight (1999c, 220–221).

Peter Scott (1996) identifies five different levels or models for the quality assurance of internationalization:

1. Conceding that quality rules imposed in the domestic context need not apply to the international arena.

2. Extending existing quality assurance systems designed for the domestic environment to cover the internationalization of higher education.

3. Adapting quality assurance systems to take better account of the special issues raised by internationalization.

4. Attempting to create a common currency for quality assurance.

5. Treating the internationalization of higher education not so much as a series of activities that must be policed, but a national project to be encouraged.

The first two levels are not so much models as policy implications that should be part of the assessment process. The other three are not mutually exclusive and should be seen not so much as models but as connected measures for improvement of the systems themselves by incorporation of internationalization as a key factor and by internationalizing the system itself. Two issues are crucial in making future quality assessments of internationalization relevant.

In the first place, it is important to distinguish between three types of quality assessments:

1. The assessment of program and organizational strategies for internationalization, for which instruments such as benchmarking, ISO, and TQM could be used. In this case, the assessment is focused on the improvement of the quality of the program or the organization as such.[9] The link to other program and organizational strategies of the institution and the overall strategy of the institution is extremely marginal. Using the IQR service for such cases makes little sense because of the limited strategic implications.

2. The quality assurance of institutional strategies for internationalization, for which the IQR service is a useful instrument. In this case the combined program and organizational strategies of an institution are the objective of the assessment. As the IQRP pilot cases have shown, one can identify different stages in institutional strategies. Although these strategies should be assessed in reference to the overall strategy of the institution, the assessment's primary focus is on the internationalization strategy as such.

3. The quality assurance of internationalization as a key factor in an institutional or departmental strategy, for which institution- or discipline-focused audits seem more appropriate. In this case the emphasis is on the integration of the international dimension in the teaching, research, and service function of the institution or a discipline, department, or faculty.

The IQRP case studies have shown that it is not always clear what type of quality assessment an institution wants. In one case, an institution used the IQRP to review its organizational structure for internationalization (type one). However, it failed to make this explicit to the peer review team, which resulted in a conflict of expectations as to the focus of the review and the recommendations made.

As the Universiteit van Amsterdam case has shown, the IQR service—although originally designed for that purpose—is of limited use in the third approach. In addition, the university was not sufficiently clear to the peer review team that this was the objective. Incorporating the international dimension into existing instruments and at the same time internationalizing these (still largely national) systems is a better approach in these cases.

Before deciding on a quality assessment and the instrument to be used, it is essential to decide what type of instrument is appropriate. In other words, an organization must define the scope of the assessment and the reasons why it wants to do the assessment. The relation between the "what," "why," and "how" of the assessment is not always clear at the beginning of the decision-making process on a quality assessment. It is also not always made explicit to the self-assessment and/or the peer review team. This can result in reports and recommendations that were not anticipated by the leadership of the institution when they decided to initiate a quality review.

A second important issue is that the quality assurance of internationalization has to move beyond national borders. In the words of Peter Scott (1996), a common currency for quality assurance at the regional or even global level should be looked for. Instruments such as GATE for transnational education and the IQR service for the internationalization of higher education are examples of attempts to design common currencies. The same applies to disciplinary and institutional quality assurance instruments, although here, given the diversity and complexity of educational systems and cultures, regionalization of the currency is more likely at first than globalization.

In summary and conclusion, the development of the IQR and other instruments to assess the quality of internationalization and related programs and strategies is a sign of the importance that institutions of higher education and (inter)national agencies and governments attach to the assessment of the quality of their international strategies and activities. The IQR is an instrument that, when used carefully, taking into account the observations made in this chapter, can be of use to institutions of higher education in a broad variety of contexts and settings.

NOTES

This chapter is based on the book edited by Jane Knight and Hans de Wit (1999c), *Quality and Internationalisation in Higher Education*, in particular Chapters 3 and 10. With permission of Jane Knight and the publisher, OECD, these two chapters have been incorporated into the text of this chapter in an updated version. The author, however, is solely responsible for the current text and the opinions expressed in it.

1. For an analysis of the trend to greater quality assessment in higher education and its meanings, see El-Khawas (1998), Woodhouse (1999), and Brennan and Shah (2000).

2. Two publications have been the result of this program: de Wit (1995b) and Knight and de Wit (1997). The authors have been consultants to IMHE for this project.

3. As will be described further on, this does not exclude the possibility for an institution to combine the IQRP with other quality assurance procedures such as benchmarking, ISO 9000, GATE certification, or TQM.

4. Originally, it was left open whether IMHE would administer the IQR service for the rest of the world or look for similar alliances elsewhere. In the end it was decided that the CRE, already using the institutional audit in Latin America under the Columbus program, would also administer potential interest from elsewhere. The IQRP guidelines, as published in Knight and de Wit (1999c), are, however, public domain.

5. At the Universiteit van Amsterdam the proposed candidate had to withdraw at the last minute, owing to another urgent obligation. Such factors and the potential financial implications can, therefore, make this option difficult to realize.

6. The CHEMS benchmarking project is now also promoted for European institutions in joint cooperation between CHEMS and ESMU. Internationalization is one of several issues institutions can use for benchmarking.

7. In the IQRP of the Royal Melbourne Institute of Technology (RMIT), members of the peer review team reviewed the international dimension of the offshore activities of RMIT.

8. Recently, the GATE certification process has come under fire because of a loss of independence from its funding source, Jones International, and for that reason "is unlikely to be considered an objective arbiter of quality programs" (Altbach 2000a, 4). See also Blumenstyk and McMurtrie (2000).

9. An example is the Eurostrat project of the CRE, evaluating European policy statements (Barblan et al., 1998). Another example is the instrument that the Council on International Educational Exchange has developed to assess its study abroad programs.

Chapter 10

The Emergence of English as the Common Language in Higher Education

The English language is becoming the global language of communication in technology, trade, culture, science, and education. There are about a dozen languages in the world that serve as (sub)continental central languages, languages that operate as third languages of communication in their regions. According to Swaan (1998a), "In this constellation of moons circling planets, and planets circling around suns, one language is at the galactic center, in the midst of a dozen solar systems: this center of the linguistic galaxy is, of course, English" (p. 65). Also according to Swaan (1998b, 118), this export of the English language is related to the position of its language and culture in the global network of cultural exchange, in itself a function of the global military, political, economic, and cultural hegemony of the United States and before that of the United Kingdom. Fishman (1998–1999) also argues that "languages have risen and fallen with the military, economic, cultural, or religious powers that supported them" (p. 27). He believes that the English language will eventually lose its present dominance because it is spoken only by a small minority, that globalization will stimulate the emergence of other regional languages, and that a counterbalancing effect of localization and local-language revival is taking place.

Although it is difficult to look into the long-term future, and although the three points mentioned by Fishman (1998–1999) are correct observations, they are not valid as arguments for the future waning influence of English. As Swaan (1998a) points out, the fact that only a small minority is speaking English is not relevant. In medieval Europe, the fact that "a major proportion of speakers who were competent in more than one language spoke Latin" (p. 64) was crucial for the influence of Latin, and that is even more the case for English today. The emergence of other regional languages that have the role of central languages in their (sub)continents is also not valid. What would be relevant would be the rise of a new hegemonic political and economic power related to another language that would be able to overthrow English. The fact that potential future dominant cultures (such as Chinese, Spanish, Arabic) are using English more and more as their second language of communication makes it more difficult for these languages to take over as the dominant world language of communication. As far as the emergence of localization and local languages is concerned, it is more likely that these will have a strengthening impact on the role of English as the global language of communication. Instead of using the dominant language of the surrounding region and elite, speakers of such local languages will be more inclined to use English as their second language of communication.[1]

Opposition to the use of a second language as the language of communication is generally, however, extremely strong for the following reasons: the potential threat to and perhaps disappearance of the local language, the related danger of the disappearance of local cultural practices and products, and the fear for cultural and linguistic hegemony and imperialism (Swaan 1998b, 110). Fishman (1998–1999) relates the prevalence of local languages to authenticity, "a central core of cultural beliefs and interpretations, that are not only resistant to globalization but are actually reinforced by the 'threat' that globalization seems to present to these historical values" (p. 32).

Will the growing dominance of English mean that national languages disappear? According to Fishman (1998–1999), "regionalization and globalization require that more and more speakers and readers of local languages be multiliterate," with each language having "its own distinctive function" (p. 35). There are, according to Swaan (1998b), "no signs of abandonment or neglect of the indigenous language" (p. 122), and the same appears to be true in the cultural sphere.

At the same time, British English or American English will become less dominant. "Spoken English acquires strong regional idiosyncrasies," says Fishman (1998–1999, 38), and gradually we can see the same happening to written English. English emerges as a second, third, or "sometime tongue," used for occupational or educational purposes (pp. 35–36). English as a language of teaching and learning also becomes more local specific, as Raman Singh (1998) of the American College of Greece noted in a presentation with the provocative title. "Whose English Is It, Anyway?"

The growing dominance of English as the language of communication is certainly apparent in science and higher education (Bollag 2000). In the domain of research, it is an accepted fact that scientific publications have to be written or translated into English to get published, acknowledged, and cited (Altbach 1988). However, also in the domain of teaching, the emergence of English as the second language of instruction in addition to the local language seems to be becoming more and more widespread. Opposition to the use of English for scientific purposes has always been marginal, but in the area of teaching it has been stronger, both in developing countries such as Malaysia and in continental Europe. At present, opposition appears to be fading away, even in countries such as Japan and France, which have strong national cultural identities (Bollag 2000).

TEACHING IN ENGLISH IN THE NETHERLANDS: A CASE STUDY

A case study of the development of teaching in English in The Netherlands illustrates this. Over the past ten years, a lively debate has taken place on the use of English in teaching at institutions of higher education. In this debate it was largely ignored that at the so-called international higher education institutes, such as the Institute of Social Studies (ISS) and the International Institute for Aerial Survey and Earth Science (ITC), which train students from developing countries, and at the private business school Nijenrode, teaching in the English language had already been common practice for many years. The history of international education in The Netherlands goes back to the beginning of the 1950s. An account of that period by the director of NUFFIC in 1970, H. Quik, describes the situation as follows:

At that time it had already become clear that an active policy directed at attracting foreigners for normal study at our universities was not justified, even if it had any chance of being successful. Factors to be considered in this respect were the language difficulties (Dutch of course is not a world language), coupled with the facts that the system and classification of study, the system of degrees, and the duration of the university courses are different in an important way from those, for example, of the Anglo-Saxon countries. (Franks and Kardoes 1970, 2)

For that reason, a number of institutes were founded after 1950 to provide training for students from developing countries. The characteristics of their programs of education and research were and still are strongly directed to the development process, at the postgraduate level, and use English as the common language.

Until the mid-1980s, the rationales for the establishment of these institutes have continued to dominate international education in The Netherlands and deferred both the national government and regular institutions of higher education from developing their own initiatives in international education. Only recently has their exclusive character, isolated from the rest of higher education, come into question.

As a result of the European mobility programs and the emergence of the "competitiveness" rationale, institutions of higher education started to develop courses and programs in English. Soon, they were outnumbering courses offered by the institutes of international education, although these maintained their strong position in relation to the developing countries, thanks to their long tradition and the financial support of the Ministry of Foreign Affairs.

The development of English-taught courses and programs in regular Dutch higher education was considered more threatening than the isolated institutes of international education. In a public debate in The Netherlands in 1989, which arose from a plea in a television interview (December 12, 1989) by Minister of Education J. Ritzen for more instruction in English at Dutch universities, the arguments used are mainly of the three kinds already mentioned: the potential threat to and perhaps disappearance of the local language, the related danger of the disappearance of local cultural practices and products, and the fear of cultural and linguistic hegemony and imperialism. The media and in particular politicians started a furious campaign to denounce the plea as fundamentally undesirable. Although the minister explicitly stated that not all degree programs but only more courses should be given in the English language in the context of growing internationalization of higher education, the media and politicians interpreted the plea as if all programs and courses in Dutch higher education should be taught in English.

On May 23, 1990, in Ghent, Belgium, the minister spoke again of the role of English as a common language for communication in science and to stimulate exchange of students. When the Universiteit van Amsterdam later that year announced that it predicted 25 percent of its courses would be taught in English in the near future, a second wave of opposition in the media and parliament started. This time the media outcry was not limited to The Netherlands. Using a news item of the Guardian News Service, which suggested that the Dutch education ministry had announced that Dutch would cease to be the official teaching language in schools and universities across The Netherlands, other media in the United Kingdom, Italy, the United States, and as far away as New Zealand gave their readers the impression that English would be the new exclusive language of instruction in Dutch education.

Parliament forced the minister to stop this supposed trend. The minister appointed a committee to explore if there was ground for anchoring teaching in Dutch in the law. The committee did not see the need for such a decision because of the deep social roots of Dutch and the fear that higher education would not be able or willing to apply the law. This was later confirmed in a report in 1994 by the Inspectie van het Onderwijs, which states that the important position of English in Dutch higher education is forced by external international developments. The Inspectie was more concerned about the state of foreign language education for Dutch students.

The minister agreed with the committee, but parliament forced him to change his mind. The Higher Education and Research Bill of 1993 decreed that all instruction and examinations are to take place in the Dutch language (Section 7.1). Permission to use another language is limited to the following situations (Section 7.2):

- The instruction and examinations pertain to a foreign language.
- The courses are conducted by a visiting lecturer whose mother tongue is a foreign language.
- Wherever necessary in view of the specific nature of the course or the students' origin, in accordance with a code of practice drawn up by the institution concerned (Ministerie van Onderwijs, Cultuur en Wetenschappen 1997; see also Vinke 1995, 2).

It is interesting to observe that after the public and political storm over instruction in English in Dutch higher education in the early 1990s, this debate—with the exception of a very small minority of language and culture puritans—has almost completely evaporated. This was not the result of institutions of higher education abandoning teaching in English as a consequence of the legal limitations. On the contrary, according to information by NUFFIC (2000b), at present some 500 courses are taught entirely in English, approximately 200 of which lead to an international master's degree. In Europe, only the United Kingdom offers a larger number of master's degree courses taught in English.

There appears to be a general acceptance now, although to a lesser extent in the political arena, that instruction in English is a necessary evil in order to be a player in the global educational market, as was already generally accepted for the scientific role of universities.[2] In the 1997 policy paper on the internationalization of education of the Ministry of Education, Culture and Science, *Talents Unlimited*, much attention was paid to the legal limitations of teaching a language other than Dutch. One sentence, however, indicates a change: "A more general view is that universities and colleges themselves have an interest in offering foreign language teaching as part of their courses" (Ministerie van Onderwijs, Cultuur en Wetenschappen 1997, 17–19). This is a subtle statement, indicating that, although the law says differently, accepted practice is that teaching in English is allowed. Higher education therefore follows several other examples of "tolerance" in Dutch politics, such as the attitudes toward soft drugs and euthanasia. The rationale might be that Dutch politics have accepted, as Dronkers (1993, 295) put it, that not the supply of internationally oriented education but rather the demand determines the degree of internationalization. The difference, however, is that where Dronkers in 1993 saw the demand coming from students and parents in The Netherlands itself—something that is certainly true for the success of bilingual primary and secondary schools in The Netherlands— for higher education that demand is driven more by the international market. In a trading nation, principles take second place to the opportunities for trade. Dronkers's (p. 304) conclusion that the pressure in The Netherlands for international education stems primarily from the demand from internationally oriented Dutch parents and is thus class related to the development of a cosmopolitan culture among a section of the Dutch elite, is based on a study among pupils in secondary education. Although the development of the international dimension at this level will have an impact on the internationalization of tertiary education, in particular on the mobility of its students, this does not provide an adequate explanation for the growth of international education programs in Dutch higher education. This growth has been—in particular in recent years—primarily based on the import of international students.

One concern is the limited participation of Dutch students in these programs. A study by van der Wende (1996) on the internationalization of the curriculum in Dutch higher education confirms this. The OECD (1994) has developed a typology with nine types of internationalized curricula (p. 45):

1. curricula with an international subject.
2. curricula in which the traditional–original subject area is broadened by an internationally comparative approach.
3. curricula that prepare students for international professions.
4. curricula in foreign languages or linguistics that explicitly address cross-communication issues and provide training in intercultural skills.
5. interdisciplinary programs, such as regional and area studies, covering more than one country.
6. curricula leading to internationally recognized professional qualifications.
7. curricula leading to joint or double degrees.
8. curricula of which compulsory parts are offered at institutions abroad, staffed by local lecturers.
9. curricula in which the content is especially designed for foreign students.

As van der Wende (1996, 193) observes, some of these types (1, 2, 4, and 5) refer directly to the content of the curriculum; types 3 and 9 to its orientation; and types 6, 7, and 8 to specific operational aspects. For that reason she suggests changing the typology to a more systematic analysis of curricula on content, orientation, and operation.

If we look at the programs offered by Dutch institutions of higher education in the English language, the emphasis lies on orientation and operation, not primarily on the international content. The 2000–2001 *Catalogue of International Courses in The Netherlands*, published by NUFFIC (2000a), presents almost 500 study and training programs taught in the English language, ranging from short training seminars to fully fledged bachelor's and master's degree programs. Some of these courses, around 150, are offered by the Institutes for International Education, introduced in the 1950s to offer specialized training for students from developing countries. The other 350 programs are offered by the fourteen universities and fifty-five *hogescholen* (which call themselves "universities of professional education" in English).

The rapid expansion in the 1990s of international English-taught courses by Dutch universities and *hogescholen* created a rather complex myriad of programs, levels, degrees, entrance requirements, and accreditation procedures, which does not help the marketing of Dutch higher education abroad. Universities offer certificate programs at the undergraduate and graduate level, bachelor's degree programs (American style at the University College Utrecht), master's degree programs integrated into the regular degree program, master's degree programs with a bachelor's degree as an entrance requirement and outside the regular degree structure, advanced master's degree programs that require a master's degree or doctorate for admission, and diploma programs that require a master's degree. *Hogescholen* offer bachelor's degree programs integrated into the regular degree structure, as well as master's degree programs outside the national degree structure, either accredited via a foreign institution (mostly British) or accredited by their own Dutch Accreditation Agency. The Institutes for International Education offer master's degrees and diploma programs.

Pressure both from inside the institutions of higher education themselves and from the Bologna Declaration has stimulated the minister of education, science, and culture to move in a direction that will give more structure to this myriad of degrees and programs. The introduction of the bachelor's and master's degree into Dutch higher education, the development of a national accreditation agency for degree programs, and the integration of the Institutes of International Education into universities are initiatives directed toward giving more coherence to Dutch higher education.

As far as the use of the English language is concerned, one can expect that at the graduate level (both Ph.D. and master's degree programs) English will become the dominant language of instruction, while at the undergraduate level Dutch will continue to predominate. There will be exceptions to this rule at both levels, but the general trend will be in this direction, following the pattern of the international courses already provided by Dutch higher education and implicitly accepted both by the higher education community itself and by the government.

In the latest document of the Ministry of Education, Culture, and Science on internationalization of education in The Netherlands (Ministerie van Onderwijs, Cultuur en Wetenschappen 1999), no reference is made to the growing number of courses taught in English, but this development is welcomed implicitly, given the emphasis in the document on raising the profile of Dutch higher education abroad and on investment in recruiting international students to The Netherlands. Significantly, no questions were raised about the growing number of courses taught in English and the related recruitment efforts abroad in either the media or parliament.

Similar trends can be observed in other small-language countries, such as Denmark, Sweden, Norway, and Finland, as well as some Central and Eastern

European countries. In Germany and Austria, teaching in the English language is no longer considered as something that is "not done." The situation is still different in Southern Europe, but even there the trend is to open higher education to instruction in languages other than the local language. The reason for this lies in the internationalization and globalization of higher education and the related notion of education as an export commodity, which was already present in Anglo-Saxon higher education but reached the European continent in the second half of the 1990s. At the opposite end of the spectrum, a similar situation can be observed in some countries in Asia, where the language of instruction is English but additional teaching in the native language is now on the national agenda. The tension between the need for teaching in the native language (as part of a national identity moving away from the colonial past) and the importance of English in the world of science (which implies a growing demand for teaching and research in English) is clearly felt in, for instance, Hong Kong, Indonesia, and Singapore (de Wit 1997a, 27; see also Kornpetpanee 1999, 102).

EDUCATIONAL ASPECTS OF TEACHING IN A FOREIGN LANGUAGE

Although the political opposition to teaching in English seems to be fading, two relevant issues are still raised, usually by the academic community itself: the academic performance of international students in relation to their English-language proficiency, and the performance of the instructor when teaching in a language other than his or her mother tongue. Instead of the political arguments already described, the concern is that teaching in a foreign language could affect the quality of education. Most of the research on these two issues has been done in the United States, which is understandable given the high number of international students and the widespread use of international teaching assistants and academic staff. In the continental European context, English is a foreign instructional language for both the teacher and the students, and little research has been done under these specific circumstances, which are becoming more common. One of the few studies is the work by Diana Vinke (1995) on English as the medium of instruction in Dutch engineering education. As far as the experiences of Dutch lecturers with teaching in English are concerned, Vinke (p. 140) concludes that switching from the mother tongue to English has certain negative effects: linguistic limitations, a reduced ability to improvise, an increased workload, a less-favorable view of their instructional quality, and an increased emphasis on their teaching skills. These negative effects tend to be fewer when the lecturer is more experienced, has a good command of English, and has had ample opportunity to practice and use these skills (p. 142). In teaching behavior, she observes a moderate, negative effect: "A change of instructional language tends to reduce the redundancy of lecturers' subject matter presentations, lecturers' speech rate, their expressiveness, and their clarity and accuracy of expression" (p. 145). For students, she concludes that a switch from the mother tongue to English as the medium of instruction moderately reduces Dutch students' learning (p. 149), and has a weak and inconsistent effect on Dutch students' perceptions of the instruction offered (p. 151). English-medium instruction, according to Vinke (p. 152), may require a slower rate of delivery compared to instruction in the mother tongue.

As measures to reduce these negative effects, Vinke (1995) proposes screening lecturers on their English-language proficiency prior to their teaching assignment. Those who do not pass the screening should be given the opportunity to improve their proficiency. Encouraging academic experiences abroad (teaching, research, conferences, academic reading, and writing) could stimulate the practice and use of English. Other measures would be to use only experienced teachers, to make teaching experience and qualifications part of the selection process for new academic staff, and to give staff temporary exemption from other duties when they conduct a course in English for the first time. For students, Vinke recommends screening on English proficiency and measures to improve their language skills also. As curriculum-related measures, she suggests reducing the content coverage or extending the number of contact hours and/or changing from a teacher-oriented to a student-oriented format of instruction (pp. 155–162).

Vinke's (1995) study is focused on engineering education and on the effect on Dutch lecturers and students, but it has wider implications; for instance, for non-English–mother-tongue lecturers teaching non-English–mother-tongue international students from other countries. This is important given the development of the international student market worldwide. Even in the United States this situation is becoming relevant, as more and more academic staff and students without English as their mother tongue meet each other in the classroom.

Although more implicitly and gradually than explicitly and actively, most Dutch higher education institutions are implementing the recommendations made by Vinke (1995) to avoid losing their potential share in the international student market.

CONCLUSION

The trend is clear that English is becoming the global language of communication in science and teaching. The emphasis on English as the language of instruction is a mixed blessing, however. Nana Rinehart (1999) correctly points to the "hazards of arrogance" that "the increasing use of English deprives monolingual Americans (and other Anglo-Saxons) of motivation for breaking out of their isolation and reinforcing their conscious or unconscious linguistic arrogance." She argues that instead of fighting the dominant role of English, emphasis should move on to the acceptance of the intrinsic value of language acquisition as such and the link between language and culture. Abram de Swaan, in an interview with NRC Handelsblad

(May 22, 1999), speaks of "de enorme, 'volstrekt onverdiende' bevoordeling van Engelse moedertaal sprekers" (the immense, "absolutely undeserved" favoring of native English speakers), and makes an appeal for the "de-Anglicization" of English to fight that privilege. Raman Singh (1998) states that we should not make standard English synonymous with standard values, or, to be more precise, allow standard English to become a transmitter of English or more broadly Anglo-Saxon values.

This chapter has dealt with the growing importance of English as the language of communication, distribution of knowledge, and instruction in higher education. The picture would not be complete without making reference to the important role of language learning as part of the internationalization of higher education. The role of English as the global language of communication is strongly linked to the existence of a multilingual society. While globalization is linked to the use of English as its lingua franca, internationalization of higher education is linked to the strengthening of multilingualism. Study abroad is an important instrument in developing the learning of languages, even in those institutions where English has emerged as the second language of instruction. A combination of courses taught in English with courses on local language, culture, and history appears to be one effective way of providing a multilinguistic and multicultural dimension in the education of those who might otherwise be very hesitant about a study abroad experience in a country and institution that only teaches in the local language. Programs to stimulate foreign language training as part of the home curriculum and via study abroad are becoming more and more important in maintaining a multilingual society in which English is not the only communication link. Universities that develop programs taught in English have an extra obligation to invest in strengthening study of the mother tongue and of other foreign languages as well. This applies to universities in the Anglo-Saxon world, as well as to universities in other regions.[3]

NOTES

1. Fishman (1998–1999, 37) himself gives an example to illustrate this: "For many Tamils—who maintain frosty relations with the central authorities in Delhi—English seems less like a colonial language than does Hindi."

2. A member of parliament for a small Christian Democratic opposition party, Dick Stellingweaf, criticized this attitude of tolerance to the use of English in Dutch higher education in the magazine *Academia* (Stellingweaf 2000, 13), but even he had to acknowledge that it is a fact that one cannot escape from.

3. This is not the place to deal in detail with language learning in a study abroad context. Reference is made to a special issue of the journal *Frontiers* (1998) on this theme, in particular the articles by Freed (1998), "An Overview of Issues and Research in Language Learning in a Study Abroad Setting" and Coleman (1998), "Language Learning and Study Abroad: The European Perspective." See also Lambert (1993a, 1993b).

Chapter 11

The Rise of Regional and International Academic Networks and Alliances

Associations, consortia, and networks are quite common in the academic world. In recent years, academic organizations have become increasingly international in nature as a result of the globalization of our economies and societies. The emergence of new international academic organizations is directly related to the growing importance of the internationalization of higher education and the impact of globalization on higher education. There are a great variety of such academic organizations, and it is not always clear what their objectives and goals are nor how successfully they operate. This chapter gives a typology of international associations, consortia, and networks in higher education and will concentrate on the functioning of the last type, institutional networks, which appear to be the latest trend in the international organization of higher education. As Hans van Ginkel (1996, 91) observes, networking has been one of the key words in higher education for the last ten years, and increasingly networks are of an international rather than a national character. Why has there been such a rapid growth in international networks in the past decade? What are the challenges in establishing, operating, and sustaining such organizations? What is the added value that such an organization provides compared to what is done at the individual or bilateral level? What are the success and failure factors for an international academic network? Answers to these questions will be provided in this chapter.

TRENDS IN ACADEMIC COOPERATION

The emergence of new academic networks and alliances is directly related to the growing importance of internationalization of higher education and the impact of globalization on higher education.

Never before have university networks been so numerous; never before has it been so technically easy to create them and use them. The telephone, the fax machine, and now e-mail and instantaneous data transmission have revolutionized linkages between network members. It can also be said that never before has it been so necessary for academics to work together in networks. The complexity of the questions asked of researchers, the obligation—in face of financial constraints—to work together rather than alone, allied to the realisation that the sum of the parts is often greater than the whole, are all factors which motivate people to establish different types of collaboration and, in particular, to create networks. (Tousignant 1996, 3)

The growth of associations, consortia, and networks in higher education in the second half of the twentieth century, and in particular in the last decade, is a reflection of the globalization of society and the response of higher education to this process. Ulrich Teichler (1996a) states, "We find increasing common elements between international networks of higher education institutions on the one hand and decreasing elements of national systems" (p. 89).

Traditionally, institutions of higher education establish their international linkages with a partner institution abroad via bilateral agreements, memoranda of understanding, and letters of intent. These agreements have the character of arrangements for educational cooperation (student and/or faculty exchanges, joint degree programs, and curriculum development), research cooperation, international development projects, and so on. Sometimes these agreements are quite concrete; sometimes they are more an expression of intent. They are made at the department, center, or school, or institutional level. The recent rise of multilateral associations, consortia, and networks in higher education reflects the multilateral character of the process.

MEANING

The words association, consortium, and network are used most commonly to describe different types of multilateral cooperation in higher education. Other terms one may encounter are, for instance, league, group, and alliance. There does not appear to be a relation between the use of the term and its original meaning. According to the Cambridge and Oxford dictionaries, the meanings of the three terms association, consortium, and network are as follows.

Both dictionaries give the following definition of an association: "A group of people who are united in a single organisation for a common/joint purpose."

The original meaning of consortium is "partnership," from the Latin, consort. According to the Oxford Dictionary it means "an association, especially of several business companies." The Cambridge Dictionary describes it as "an organisation of several businesses or banks joining together for a shared purpose." From these two definitions it is clear that a consortium is associated with the business sector. The Penguin Business Dictionary describes a consortium as "a group of companies or firms none of which is competent to fulfil a contract alone. Generally a 'once only' combination bringing together a number of quite different operational skills or areas of specialised knowledge."

Networks are described by the Oxford Dictionary as "a group of people who exchange information, contacts and experience for social or professional reasons," or as "a group or system of interconnected people or things." The Cambridge Dictionary defines a network as "a large system consisting of many similar parts that are connected together to allow communication between or along the parts or between the parts and a control centre."

These descriptions do not help much in distinguishing between the three terms. Certain common features can be identified: partnership, group, system, and connection. Some differentiating aspects can also be detected: common versus specific purpose, multipurpose versus single purpose, "once only" versus permanent, individual versus institutional membership, centered versus flat structure, people oriented versus object oriented, and complementarity versus commonality.

A TYPOLOGY

Guy Neave (1992b) distinguishes between proactive and reactive consortia. The fundamental purposes of the first type are to limit competition between the partners by coordination, and to seek greater external resources by "cornering" a portion of the market. The driving factor of the second type is more efficient coordination in order to be able to take advantage of proposals for linkages coming from outside. Neave links the first type to market-oriented countries such as the United Kingdom, the United States, and France, which seek the import of foreign students; and the second type, for instance, with the ERASMUS program. Suggesting that consortia are "a further stage in the intensification of international linkages between institutions of higher education," he describes them as the fifth point of a continuum: monodisciplinary bilateral linkages, exchange partnerships, network partnerships, multidisciplinary networks, and consortia (pp. 55–58).

Although Neave (1992b) is correct to identify proactivity and reactivity as factors of relevance for consortia, they are not an adequate basis for a typology. His five-stage typology of interinstitutional cooperation is a simple analysis of international cooperation and exchange in education, but does not clarify the notion of consortia.

Without meaning to make a judgement on the use of terms by various international academic organizations, it might be useful to distinguish between three types of international multilateral organizations in higher education: academic associations, academic consortia, and institutional networks. Ginkel (1996, 92–93) arrives at a similar typology for Europe: associations, institutional networks, interuniversity cooperation projects–joint European projects, and university–enterprise training partnerships (the last two are included as academic consortia in the typology here).

Academic Associations

An academic association is an organization of academics or administrators and/or their organizational units (departments, centers, schools, and institutions), united for a common purpose that is related to their professional development (information exchange, training, advocacy, etc.). This type of organization is quite common and has a long history in higher education, even at the international level. This is particularly true for those associations that are based on individual membership; are single purpose, academic, and discipline based; and are faculty driven.

Institutional, multipurpose, management-based, and leadership-driven associations and individual administrative associations are a more recent phenomenon. Examples of institutional associations are the International Association of Universities (IAU) and the Programme on Institutional Management of Higher Education. Examples of the individual administrative type of organizations are the International Association of University Presidents and the European Association for International Education. The latter group is tending to become more institution based. Another example is the Association of European Universities, originally the association of European Rectors.

Academic Consortia

An academic consortium is a group of academic units (departments, centers, schools, and institutions) who are united for the single purpose of fulfilling a contract based on bringing together a number of different areas of specialized knowledge. In principle their lifespan is limited by the terms of the contract. They can be either faculty or leadership driven, but with a strong faculty commitment in the case of consortia with an academic purpose. Examples of academic consortia are the Joint Study Programmes in the ERASMUS scheme (in the area of teaching); consortia in the Framework Programmes for Research and Development of the European Commission (research); and consortia tendering for technical assistance projects (service).

The multilateral Joint Study Programmes in the ERASMUS scheme were discipline-based, faculty-driven agreements focused on student and staff exchange and curriculum development. Their success was mainly the result of the existence of external funding from the European Commission and their strength was more in student exchange than in the other two areas. As soon as these programs were forced to integrate with the leadership-driven institutional agreements in the new SOCRATES program and the money coming from the European Commission was reduced, many of them came to an end. This was also true for research- and service-oriented consortia that were project based and externally funded.

Academic consortia can develop into institutional networks when the success of their joint contracts become the basis for more structural and multipurpose cooperation between the partners. An example is the Utrecht Network, a network of institutions that originated in a consortium for a Joint Study Programme of the ERASMUS program.

International academic consortia are a rather common phenomenon in higher education, in particular in research. They appear to come and go according to the needs of the different partner institutions to make use of their partners' complementary skills, experiences, and facilities. As the example of the Joint Study Programmes demonstrates, external funding is a crucial factor for their success.

Academic consortia are and will continue to be the most common form of international organization in higher education, and increasingly so as part of academic associations or institutional networks.

Institutional Networks

An institutional network is a group of academic units (departments, centers, schools, and institutions) who are united for, in general, multiple purposes (academic and/or administrative), are leadership driven, and have an indefinite lifespan. While academic consortia are usually "single mission," institutional networks tend to have a "general framework objective," as noted by Neave (1992a, 65).

Although they are less focused on objectives and goals than associations or consortia, owing to their multipurpose character, it is this type of organization that seems to be emerging most recently. There is a trend toward leadership-driven multilateral institutional networks, mostly within the European Union but also elsewhere, and recently examples of an international nature are also emerging.

The European networks resulted mainly from the success of the Joint Study Programmes. The Coimbra Group, an institutional network of the two oldest universities in each of the countries of the European Union, was the first of these networks. Later followed the Network of Universities in the Capitals of Europe (UNICA), the Santander Group, the Utrecht Network, the Santiago de Compostela Group, the European Consortium of Innovative Universities, the European Consortium of Universities of Technology, and others. They differ from the discipline-based networks in the sense that they are leadership driven (top-down) and multipurpose. Student exchanges, staff exchanges, administrator exchanges, joint tenders, and joint research cooperation are the activities that these networks most commonly undertake. Although these networks are strongly driven by European Union funding, they have extended their membership to the rest of Europe as well. Others have a more interregional scope. Examples are the ALMA scheme, uniting the Universities of Aachen (Germany), Liege (Wallonia, Belgium), Diepenbeek (Flanders, Belgium), and Maastricht (The Netherlands); and the European Confederation of the Universities of the Upper Rhine (EUCOR). Some of these networks do not limit themselves to the academic community, but are networks including chambers of commerce, industry, or local government.[1]

One can also find institutional networks in other regions of the world, such as the Association of East Asian Research Universities (AEARU); the Associación de Universidades Grupo Montevideo (AUGM), a group of twelve universities in Argentina, Brazil, Paraguay, and Uruguay; the Consejo Superior Universitario Centroamericano (CSUCA), a consortium of Central American universities; and the College of the Americas, an inter-American network of institutions cooperating in interdisciplinary teaching, research, and continuing education.

In the United States, institutional networks or consortia are mostly regionally based American consortia, even though they are oriented to international cooperation. Examples are the Midwest Universities Consortium for International Activities Inc. (MUCIA) of ten universities in the Midwest, the Consortium for International Development (CID) of twelve Western public universities, the Illinois Consortium for International Education (ICEI), and the Texas Consortium. The first two focus on tenders for development-assistance contracts, the others are examples of networks for study abroad and international curriculum development. Some of these consortia seek partners abroad, such as the ICEI and the Utrecht Network in Europe.

Some networks have a cross-regional character, such as the University of the Arctic, in which universities from Northern Europe and Canada work together.

Recently, new international networks have been emerging; some based on existing regional networks—such as the combination of ICEI and the Utrecht Network—others as new initiatives. Examples of the latter are Universitas 21, an initiative of the University of Melbourne; the David C. Lam Institute for East–West Studies (LEWI), an initiative of Hong Kong Baptist University; and the League of World Universities, an initiative of New York University, all three with different objectives.[2]

The last one, the League of World Universities, is a more informal global network of the presidents and rectors of large, comprehensive, urban universities, who meet every two years to exchange views on developments in their institutions and their environment. Attempts to make the league a more active network to discuss and take joint action on common issues in between the biannual meetings—for instance, on teaching, information technology, and public health—did not bear fruit. From the League, however, a strategic alliance between four of its members—New York University, University College London, Freie Universität Berlin, and the Universiteit van Amsterdam—is emerging, and is focusing on closer cooperation on strategic issues such as curriculum development, human resources, new technologies, and joint research.

The David C. Lam Institute is a membership network of originally five and at present twenty-eight universities from China, East Asia, Southeast Asia, Australia, North America, and Europe. It was founded in 1993 to reach out across oceans and cultures, to work together for the common good, and to increase, through interaction between its members, mutual understanding, and by this to contribute to human well-being. In 1995 its mission was stated as follows: "to promote mutual understanding between East and West, by way of intellectual discourse among scholars in the Eastern and Western worlds through research, academic exchange, and other scholarly activities" (Teather 2000, 3). An evaluation of LEWI by Teather indicates ambiguity between the objective of the institute as a universitywide research center of Hong Kong Baptist University and that of an international consortium. Looking at the composition of the membership and the activities of the institute, the institute appears to be a consortium in which the link between the individual members and the center institution, Hong Kong Baptist University, is stronger than between the other members. LEWI is caught somewhere between being a "single mission" consortium focusing on East–West studies in a more restricted sense and a "general framework" consortium.

Universitas 21, established in March 1997, is an international association of comprehensive research-intensive universities. The director of the Universitas 21 Secretariat, Chris Robinson (1998), describes it as "an active, effective association, small enough to permit high levels of commitment, familiarity, collaboration and inter-operability between the member institutions, yet large enough to capture the benefits of international diversity. The underlying concept is of a small, tightly knit association of kindred institutions with immense potential to secure and improve international opportunities and positioning for its members" (p. 96). In addition to the activities that are common in other networks, Universitas 21 strives for benchmarking and development of new teaching and learning technologies, modalities, and delivery systems. More than the other two cases, Universitas 21 is an example of an institutional network that crosses national and regional borders to better prepare its members for the competitive global market. Transnational or borderless education creates new incentives for global institutional networks or bilateral and multilateral alliances, such as the alliance between the universities of Amsterdam, London, Berlin, and New York already mentioned.

Another example of such an alliance—in this case a bilateral one—is the $135-million joint venture that the Massachusetts Institute of Technology and the University of Cambridge announced in November 1999. According to the president of MIT this joint venture will "establish a model for the globally linked research universities of the future" (Tugend 1999). The Cambridge–MIT Institute will be involved in collaborative research and education to improve British productivity and competitiveness, research programs to improve technology, stimulating spin-off companies, bringing MIT's business-executive programs to Britain, and developing shared courses in science and management. Mainly the British government ($109 million) funds the institute. This fact and the activities planned indicate that the initiative is primarily in the interest of the United Kingdom. "The institute will help place the UK at the cutting edge of the globalization of higher education," according to David Blunkett, Britain's secretary of education (Tugend 1999). But MIT also benefits from the project. "For MIT, this partnership offers an opportunity to participate in the education of the next generation of European technology leaders; to develop important relationships with European industry; and to expose its students to the culture of Europe," according to Lawrence Bacow, chancellor of MIT (Tugend 1999).

SUCCESS AND FAILURE FACTORS

Although institutional networks in higher education appear to have become rather popular, not many success stories can be told as yet. What are the factors that are relevant to the success or failure of such networks?

Ginkel (1996) states, "Unclear choices and reluctant commitment to networking will result in the loss of identity" (p. 100). He notes the following characteristics of successful strategic alliances, based on his experience with strategic alliances of the University of Utrecht with private multinationals in research cooperation: congruence of missions, the will to invest through budget allocation and extra resources, appointment of liaison officers to bridge the differences in culture between the partners, strong agreement on methodology and quality standards, agreement on intellectual property rights, and taking time getting to know each other (p. 101).

Roger Prichard (1996, 8–9) provides an overview of factors for successful networking that is relevant for institutional networks:

1. "Long-term relationships have to be built." This implies that a lot of time and energy has to be invested in making the network objectives and goals known and accepted within and among the member institutions. This also implies that time is needed to establish and build good person-to-person relationships, at both the level of the leadership of the institutions and at the level of the academics involved in the projects.

2. "It is important to pick winners." Many projects are created on an ad hoc basis by brainstorming at leadership assemblies and are based on superficial assumptions instead of well-thought-out plans. Picking winners can be stimulated by awards and by well-funded plans.

3. "Cultivate sufficient resources to enable the programme of work, and any obvious spin-off programmes to succeed." Successful projects need investment, both in time and money, of those involved. This is often ignored in the design of projects. Clear plans and awards can help to overcome this threat.

4. "Network projects need to have limited and realisable goals, appropriate to the level of development of the institutions." This aspect is frequently ignored in networks, resulting in failure and frustration among the members. Formulation of clear goals for the short, mid, and long term is essential for success.

5. "The projects must be built around people in the institutions with relevant experience and interest to make a medium to long term commitment." Given the fact that many projects are designed by the leadership of the institution and lack guaranteed commitment of the relevant persons in the institutions, they have a tendency to fail. Again, awards and plans are helpful instruments for making project commitment a success.

6. "In building networks, specific areas should be targeted, not the whole operation." Many institutional networks live by their institutional nature and not by the sum of objectives, goals, projects, and targets.

7. "To get the network off the ground, it is important to have some project champions in key institutions who will keep the project moving forward." If there are no project champions, it will be difficult to convince others in the institution to commit themselves to projects of the network.

8. "Set up a network listserv to keep as many participants in frequent contact as possible." Communication is important, but only if one has something to tell.

Prichard (1996, 8–9) also provides some warnings, "don'ts" that are relevant to institutional networks:

1. "Don't develop a network without significant involvement of the people who will be key players in the network." Given the fact that institutional networks are leadership driven, this is a crucial factor in the success or failure of the network.

2. "Don't take a short term perspective." Many networks look only at the possibilities and sources available in the short term and do not survive the fact that these opportunities will disappear.

3. "Don't try to do too many things at once." Networks try to satisfy the interests of all their members and end up with a long list of things to accomplish without having the guarantee that the organization can handle all these suggestions.

4. "Don't have too many players." Experience shows that networks tend to expand their membership too fast to be representative and to cover the political, regional, and individual interests of their members. Too many players are a danger for any network. In addition, the selection of members is not always based on criteria related to the mission and objectives of the network.

One should add to these warnings the following:

5. Base the mission of the network on more than a geographical or historical identity. Such an identity does not provide a sufficient basis for successful partnership in a network.

6. Emphasize the complementarity of the partners, not only the commonality. Institutional networks are based on commonality—oldest universities, research universities, regional focus—and tend to neglect complementarity, which is the basis of success for a network. Cooperation only makes sense when both similarities and differences in operational skills and areas of specialized knowledge are recognized and used.

7. Recognize potential discrepancies between the partnership of the institution in a network and the partnership needs at the decentralized level. An institutional network cannot and does not need to cover the whole institution. Accept the fact that departments, centers, and schools have their own networks, that these do not always overlap with the institutional network, and that for that reason there may be no interest in being involved in network activities.

8. At the same time, the choice of institutional network should cover enough interest at the decentralized level to create commitment. A network that only exists in the heads of the institutional leaders will not have sufficient grounds for survival.

9. The cost of the network organization should not become the main drive for maintaining the network and place the organization into direct competition with its members. When network organizations become too big and require overhead costs from contracts, this is a real danger.

10. Be aware of the differences in structure, funding, and culture among the partners. If the network is not aware of this diversity, it will create misunderstanding of the objectives and goals of the network as a whole and the projects planned within the network.

11. Be aware of the potential tensions between the interest of the founder and/or center institution of a network and those of the other members. There are cases of networks in which the founding and/or center institution has bilateral relations with each of the members without real links between the other members. Teather (2000) calls this the "hub-and-spokes model" or "single node network."[3]

12. Do not organize the network around external funding but around institutional funding, with external funding as an additional resource (see also Ginkel 1996, 94).

Institutional networks should be conscious of the following elements:

- mission of the network.
- description of the purposes, objectives, and goals of the network.
- geographical focus.
- size of the network.
- composition of the membership in relation to the mission and purposes.

- relation between the founder and/or center of the network and the other members.
- relation between leadership commitment and commitment within each of the institutions.
- financial resources, including membership fees and external and internal project funding.
- organizational structure.
- mechanisms for evaluation of the network and its activities.[4]

THE FUTURE OF INSTITUTIONAL NETWORKS

The institutional, multipurpose, and leadership-driven networks are facing many problems with their identity, their size, the commitment of their faculty and students, and their objectives and goals. Can these regional and international institutional networks become the keys to the next stage of internationalization, in which not only the mainstream activities and programs of the universities but the whole of the institutions become international? Can we expect that universities will finally follow the same path that banks, industry, and even nation-states have followed over the past century: move into joint ventures, merge across borders, share their human resources, and create common products? According to Magrath (2000, 255) the transnational linkages of universities will move from "cottage industries" to "multinational consortia" as a consequence of globalization, and in particular digital and information technologies. It seems a logical, unavoidable step, but even a network such as Universitas 21 is a long way from such a concept of internationalization, and still has a strong activity orientation. According to Robinson (1998),

Globalisation means that major universities have to be systematically and essentially international in character and function. However, it is clear that no institution, however strong or prestigious it may be, can continue to be entirely successful operating on its own. . . . Universities seeking to respond to these challenges can contemplate several different approaches to internationalisation. They can adopt strategies involving the international expansion of a single institution through the establishment of offshore campuses. Alternatively, an existing institutional "brand" can be franchised to agencies in other countries. Or, there is an option that already has proven itself in other multinational industries: a consortium organised as a network. (p. 92)

Peter Scott (1998), addressing the question, What is likely to emerge? also sees a diverse pattern:

Probably not, despite the evident power of the Murdochs and Gateses, global universities designed by News Corporation or Microsoft. . . . But nor are global universities to be simply extensions of existing universities, in which international activities have simply been given greater prominence. So perhaps the most likely outcome is a highly differentiated development—of a few world universities (or, more probably, of world-class elements within them); of networks of existing universities that trade in this global market place while maintaining their separate national identities . . . of the growth of hybrid institutions that combine elements of universities with elements of other kinds of "knowledge" organization . . . of the emergence of "virtual" universities organized along corporate lines . . . and, inevitably, of a few global universities on a News Corporation or Microsoft pattern. (p. 129)

There are and will be institutions of higher education that, deliberately or not, are oriented to the local environment and for which the international dimension will stay incidental, individual, or at most consist of a combination of unrelated activities, projects, and programs. Others will not evolve further than having a separate internationalization strategy, without affecting the functions of the institution. Only a few global players will emerge, old institutions but also new providers of higher education, making use of the opportunities that new technologies and the global market provide. Coalitions, networks, consortia, or alliances among institutions of higher education, and between them and industry, are and will be increasingly important factors in ensuring a role in this global arena.

As Robinson (1998) and Scott (1998) note, this century will see such a differentiated development of new models of higher education. As Ginkel (1996) states, universities that want to be global players must focus their attention on the fields in which they are excelling and therefore have "to find co-makers, other universities as well as other role players in society, in order to keep offering a broad variety of good courses and good research. It is this type of networking, the connecting of the best within reach, the linking of university services to societal change, that needs our attention" (p. 97). Davies (1997, 90) also observes an increasingly likely substantial importance of interinstitutional alliances as a lever in institutional change for marketing, new interdisciplinary connections, and regional and international services.

This century will see international mergers and joint ventures of institutions of higher education, first at the interregional level and later at the global level. At the same time, more and more faculties and schools will combine their efforts in consortia and alliances beyond such institutional mergers and joint ventures. This will be the result of the principle that partnerships at the institutional level cannot always and completely match the needs at the decentralized level.

Even though institutional networks at present seem to be rather weak, lacking commitment at the departmental and school levels, and not very effective in their operations, they are more likely to be the motor for future mergers than the discipline-based networks, consortia, and alliances. Only central leadership is able to make the radical decisions needed to move away from fragmented activity-oriented cooperation to real mergers and joint ventures. It is only a question of time before such decisions are made. Initiatives such as Universitas 21 and the joint venture between MIT and the University of Cambridge are examples of this trend. The strategic alliance developing between the Universiteit van Amsterdam, University College London, the Freie Universität Berlin, and New York University can also be seen in this perspective.

Strategic partnerships in research, teaching, and transfer of knowledge, between universities and of universities with business and beyond national borders, will be the future for higher education in order to manage the challenges that globalization will place on it.

NOTES

1. For a study of this type of network, see Haug and Race (1998, 3–35).

2. The UNITWIN/UNESCO Chairs Program could also be called a global network program, but it is an UNESCO-initiated project of programs directed at discipline-oriented cooperation. The same can be said of the United Nations University in the area of research.

3. Teather (2000, 148) has labeled two variations on this type of network the "dumb-bell" model and the "conduit" model, which he describes for the David C. Lam Institute in Hong Kong, in the center Hong Kong Baptist (HKBU), and around two groups of spokes, universities from the West and universities in China, separately linked to HKBU (dumb-bell), or HKBU linked to a pipe through which connections can occur between LEWI member institutions in the East and the West.

4. For characteristics of academic networks, see also Silvio (1996, 11–22).

Chapter 12

Internationalization of Higher Education as a Research Area

Ulrich Teichler (1996b), describing the potentials and limits of comparative higher education, remarks that "we might consider internationalization of higher education as the next theme which gives rise to a new focus of both higher education policy and higher education research" (p. 435). In this chapter the position of this theme in the area of educational research will be analyzed. Before doing so, it is important to clarify the inclusion of the addition "higher" in the term internationalization of higher education. The use of internationalization of education, would in principle be correct. The use of one and the same term for different levels of education is characteristic of the subdivisions used under the broad umbrella of comparative and international education. It also positions the research more clearly within the concept of comparative education, as described by Anweiler (1977) (see Chapter 6). In the present stage of internationalization of education there is, however, such a strong emphasis on higher education that there seems to be a general tendency to use the term internationalization of higher education.

This limitation might not be correct in the long run. Teichler (1996c) states that for now "the major thrust of activity is in the domain of higher education," but internationalization is also to be found "at other levels and in other sectors of education" (p. 344). In the past, other levels and sectors of education were marginally focused on internationalization other than of the curriculum (foreign languages, history, and geography). There are programs oriented toward short study visits, homestay projects, and exchanges of teachers at the primary and secondary level, as well as in vocational training. They are, however, relatively marginal, although there are strong signs that the interest in such programs is rising. Perhaps the most obvious examples are the COMENIUS program within the SOCRATES program and the emphasis on vocational training in the LEONARDO program of the European Commission.

It is becoming increasingly more accurate to leave out "higher" and focus on internationalization of education in the case of using the term international education. At the same time, by emphasizing "higher," the restriction of research to this level of education is more obvious. The research should be positioned within comparative higher education research, an area that might, in analogy with comparative and international education, better be called comparative and international higher education, thereby giving recognition to the growing importance of internationalization in higher education.

In this way it will also be possible to address the problem van der Wende (1997b) identified through a survey of the specialized literature on higher education policy: "We find that, although an international comparative approach in the description and analysis of national higher education systems and policies is quite popular, the issue of internationalization as a domain or context of higher education policy making is not really addressed" (p. 12), and in research and related literature on internationalization, "little use is made of the theories, concepts and insights used in and gained from higher education research" (p. 22).[1]

Another missing or at least undervalued aspect of the study of the internationalization of higher education, as is true for comparative and international higher education in general, is its multi- and interdisciplinary character. As the previous chapters have made clear, research in this field will include aspects of educational, political, economic, social, cultural, anthropological, historical, and legal study. As Goedegebuure and van Vught (1996, 390) state for research in higher education in general, it is not an individual discipline but subject to the methodological requirements of other disciplines (see also Altbach 2000b, 3). This does not imply, however, that higher education and its international dimension are not relevant as a theme of study.

During the past ten years internationalization has become recognized as an area of research by organizations such as the European Association for Institutional Research (EAIR), the Consortium of Higher Education Researchers (CHER), the Programme on Institutional Management in Higher Education, and the Centre for Educational Research and Innovation (CERI) of the OECD.[2] Perhaps this increased attention will help in establishing the missing link between higher education research and research on the internationalization of higher education.

The interest in the internationalization of higher education as a research area is a reflection of the growing strategic importance of internationalization for higher education. Before the beginning of the 1990s, educational journals did not include many articles related to this topic. Exceptions are articles on student mobility in journals such as *Higher Education in Europe* (UNESCO/CEPES). It was only in the 1990s that journals such as *Higher Education Management* (IMHE/OECD), *Tertiary Education and Management* (EAIR), and the *European Journal of Education* (European Institute of Education and Social Policy) started to publish articles on this subject on a regular basis. An example for the United States is *International Higher Education* of the Boston College Center for International Higher Education. The publication of several books and the emergence of specialized journals in the United States, such as *International Education Forum* (AIEA), *International Spectator* (NAFSA), and *Frontiers* (independent), and in the United Kingdom, such as *International Education* (UKCOSA) and *International Higher Education* (TEXT Consortium), are also indications of an emerging research interest, although most of these publications publish mostly practice and case studies. The launch of the *Journal of Studies in International Education* in 1997 was the first attempt to bring together practitioners and researchers in the field of international education on a global instead of a national or regional scale.

COMPARATIVE HIGHER EDUCATION RESEARCH AND THE INTERNATIONALIZATION OF HIGHER EDUCATION

The internationalization of higher education is still a long way from becoming the regular subject of substantial research-based academic studies, as noted by Ulrich Teichler (1996c, 341). This lack of a strong research tradition explains why this area lacks academic recognition in the field of comparative and international education and why it is marginalized under confusing terms within that field, as described in Chapter 5. Recognition of the internationalization of higher education as a special research area will be unavoidable and necessary in the coming years, given the growing importance, both in practice and in research, of this area, as Teichler (1996b, 435) predicts.

One can say that within the broad field of comparative and international education, comparative education research focuses on comparative study between systems, regions, countries, institutions, programs, curricula, and so on, and international(ization of) education research focuses on study of the internationalization of systems, regions, countries, institutions, programs, curricula, and so on. These studies can cover all levels of education or one specific level, such as higher education. Following this line of definition would position the internationalization of higher education within the area of comparative higher education research in a similar way to that used by Teichler (1996b, 435; 1996c, 369) and Altbach (1997d, 8), and this would support a broadening of this field to comparative and international higher education research. At the same time, one has to take into account that the same applies to the internationalization of higher education research as to higher education research in general; namely, that it is an interdisciplinary field of study (Altbach 1997d, 11; 2000b, 3) and that its researchers are the "non-genuine" dimension experts of higher education and do not address its core dimensions (Teichler 1996b, 437).

INTERNATIONALIZATION OF HIGHER EDUCATION: A RESEARCH NEED

The call for research on study abroad has been around since before the 1990s, but became stronger in that decade. The need for research and evaluation of study abroad was already being stressed in 1985 by Barbara Burn (Briggs and Burn 1985, 57–58), and this call was recognized by a broad coalition of American and European organizations, such as NAFSA, CIEE, and the IIE on the American side and the European Cultural Foundation, the European Institute of Education and Social Policy, the European Community, and several national agencies in Europe. This joint interest resulted in a comparative study of study abroad programs in the United States and Europe (Burn, Cerich, and Smith 1990; Opper, Teichler, and Carlson 1990).

In 1994 the International Research Centre for Cultural Studies (IFK) in Vienna, in cooperation with the ACA, organized a seminar, "The International Dimension of Higher Education: Setting the Research Agenda." Alan Smith (1994a) at that time director of the ACA, based the reason for the seminar on "a broad spectrum of 'stakeholder' interests in the qualitative and quantitative improvement of research on aspects of international cooperation and interaction in the higher education sector" (p. 4). Ulrich Teichler (1996c), in an article that draws on this seminar, observes that "most of the research available on academic mobility and international education seems to be coincidental, sporadic or episodic" (p. 341).

In the United States there is a longer tradition of research on the internationalization of higher education, or rather on international education. However, with several notable exceptions, in the 1990s practitioners mainly followed this research tradition. Their studies are generally focused on single programs and institutions (Teichler 1996c, 340–341), and are American biased (de Wit 1998b, 16). In August 1995 in Washington the need for a more coherent American research agenda was expressed at a meeting organized by the AIEA. The main motivation for *A Research Agenda for the Internationalization of Higher Education in the United States*, as proposed by the AIEA (1995) was the following:

The internationalization of higher education is moving into a critical phase in the United States. From one perspective, the degree and character of internationalization that has been achieved over the past several decades is one of the extraordinary success stories of American colleges and universities. . . . From another perspective, however, serious public policy questions are being raised about the value and importance of continued public contributions—from the federal and state governments and from private foundations—to international components of higher education. . . . A diversified set of research activities is urgently needed to inform that debate. (p. 4)

The arguments for a research agenda for the internationalization of higher education in the United States seem to have primarily a national political character, whereas the call for research on the internationalization of higher education in Europe seems to be of a more generic and scholarly nature. At the same time, a review by Richard Lambert (1995) of Smith, Teichler, and van der Wende (1994) can be read as a critique of European conceptual thinking and research on internationalization. He notices in the texts a dramatic tension that underlies much of the discussion:

On the one hand, several authors eloquently call for the development of a more satisfying research tradition that will correct what Teichler characterizes as "the lack of theory, the weakness of methodology, and small base of knowledge, achieved so far." . . . On the other hand, it is difficult to prevent the whiff of scholasticism from creeping into the field, where the elegance of the formulation and research design is more important than the use to which the results are put. (p. 10)

He also sees an uncertainty in the conception of what is being studied:

Several papers are principally concerned . . . with students going abroad. . . . Others are concerned with internationalization more generally. . . . Some of the papers look out to the external environment. . . . A number of papers view internationalization in the context of the current European interest in institutional quality. . . . A somewhat sharper focus on just what is being studied, or perhaps a partitioning of the field into the different segments being studied, may help clarify the development of a research agenda. (p. 10)

In other words, Americans may be biased, but Europeans still have to find out the "what" and "how" of internationalization of higher education. And that is not an incorrect analysis, as indicated in this study. One could add that the danger of European bias is also present, with so much of our research attention going to European programs (see de Wit 1998b).

Setting the differences in approach and focus aside, there appears to be a general consensus, encompassing more than just the United States and Europe and including, in particular, Canada and Australia, that more research on the internationalization of higher education is needed, as the calls from practitioners (ACA, AIEA) and from higher education researchers such as Altbach (1997d) and Teichler (1996b, 1996c) confirm.

As Altbach (2000b) states, this research is "of increasing relevance in a globalized academic environment" (p. 14). One must be realistic, however.

Most higher education scholars do not yet recognize internationalization as a research theme. If one were forced to give an assessment of the present level of research on the internationalization of higher education (Teichler 1996b, 444), it would be placed primarily in the category of being of interest to occasional researching practitioners and the applied higher education researchers and research units, not to higher education scholars, and focused more on practical than on methodological issues (p. 449).

The initiative for a *Journal of Studies in International Education*, launched in 1997, did not come from the research community but from practitioners with a research interest. After an initial period of three years in which the journal was published by one organization, the Council on International Educational Exchange, to promote the study of international education, the journal became recognized by other organizations in the field as an important instrument to disseminate research in their field. As of 2000, the journal is published by a new Association for Studies in International Education, a joint initiative of American organizations such as NAFSA, the AIEA, the Council on International Educational Exchange, and World Education Services (WES); together with the CBIE, IDP–Education Australia, the EAIE, NUFFIC, the United Kingdom Council for International Education (UKCOSA), and the International Education Association South Africa (IEASA). As of 2001, the journal will be published by Sage Publishing on behalf of the association, and will move from two to four issues a year, an indication of its acceptance as a research journal. Although based on the initiative of organizations of practitioners, members of the research community are represented in the membership of its editorial and advisory board.

The publication of this journal, the appearance of more articles in other academic journals, and the publication of a growing number of books on the international dimensions of higher education reflect the growing importance of this area in general and as a research theme in itself. Themes for interdisciplinary research on the internationalization of higher education that emerge out of this study include the historical development of the international dimension in higher education (history); political rationales for the internationalization of higher education, globalization and internationalization, and regionalization (political science, international relations); economic rationales for internationalization, such as competitiveness and labor markets (economics); social and cultural rationales (social sciences, psychology); and academic rationales and quality assessment (education). Comparative studies of developments in different countries and regions and in different sectors of education are also relevant for a better understanding of the internationalization of higher education.

There is still a long way to go, however, before the "missing link" between internationalization of higher education and comparative higher education studies has been established. This becomes clear if one looks at the overview by Teichler (1996b, 440) of the disciplinary and thematic structure of research in higher education. It not only demonstrates, as Teichler himself notes, that there is a lack of paradigmatic consensus on higher education as a field of research, but it also shows that the internationalization of higher education lacks recognition as a theme within higher education studies. Of the seven classifications presented, only two have reference to aspects of internationalization: Goldschmidt, Teichler, and Webler (1984) to study abroad, and Altbach (1991) to foreign students. Goedegebuure and van Vught (1996, 387), in their categorization of comparative higher education studies, only make reference to evaluation projects commissioned by the European Commission on the effectiveness of European programs and point out that the comparative component in those studies is more or less a side issue.

Acceptance of the relevance and stimulation of research on the internationalization of higher education by schools of education and other disciplines is needed to make this area more accepted by the community of higher education researchers and beyond.

NOTES

1. This missing link is remarkable, when, for instance Opper, Teichler, and Carlson (1990), in a comparative study of study abroad programs, observed that "the predominant characteristics and norms of the respective systems of higher education have an impact on the structure of the study abroad programs themselves" (p. 9).

2. Ulrich Teichler (1996b, 1996c) observes this for the first two organizations, and the work of Knight and de Wit (1995, 1997, 1999c) and van der Wende (1997b) indicate this for the other organizations.

Chapter 13

Summary and Conclusions

Internationalization has become an important issue in the development of higher education. At the same time, it is still a phenomenon with a lot of question marks regarding its historical dimension; its meaning, concept, and strategic aspects; its relationship to developments in society and higher education in general; and its status as an area of study and analysis. This book is an overall analysis of this phenomenon, from a historical perspective, as a conceptual framework, and in some of its key manifestations.

HISTORICAL ANALYSIS

From a description of the historical development of the international dimension of higher education, it becomes obvious that changes in the external and internal environment of higher education during the past centuries have been extremely influential in the way this international dimension has presented itself.

Until the twentieth century this dimension was rather incidental and individual: the wandering scholar and student, the Grand Tour, the student flows from South to North. The export of higher education models in the eighteenth and nineteenth centuries, seen by some as an important manifestation of the internationalization of higher education, is difficult to understand as such and is better seen as academic colonialism. The notion of knowledge as universal applied mainly to research and did not presuppose action; on the contrary, it assumed no need of action.

Before World War II and immediately afterward, these incidents became more structured into activities, projects, and programs, mainly in the United States and only marginally in Europe (the Soviet Union, Germany, France, and the United Kingdom). In the limited and mostly American research literature they are collectively referred to as international education. They were driven in particular by the Cold War. A second manifestation, appearing in the 1960s, is technical assistance and development cooperation, an area that in some countries, such as Australia, Canada, and The Netherlands, until the 1980s became the most dominant international program and is also strongly present elsewhere. In addition, though less organized, the international flow of students, mainly from South to North, continued and even expanded.

Major changes in internationalization took place in the 1980s. The move from aid to trade in Australia and the United Kingdom, the development of the European programs for research and development (the Framework Programs and their predecessors) and for education (SOCRATES, LEONARDO, and their predecessors), the development of transnational education, and the presence of internationalization in mission statements, policy documents, and strategic plans of institutions of higher education were clear manifestations of these changes. Globalization and the related knowledge society based on technological developments, as well as the end of the Cold War and the creation of regional structures (in particular the EU), influenced these changes. The need for an organized response by higher education to these external developments resulted in an internationalization strategy that was based on more explicit choices (rationales) and a more integrated strategy (process approach).

It was only in the 1980s that the internationalization of higher education became a strategic process. Competitiveness in the international market became a key rationale. Incidents, isolated activities, projects, and programs were still present at both the national and institutional levels, but internationalization as a strategic process became more central in higher education institutions.

However, this situation is one of transition. The globalization of our societies and markets and its impact on higher education and the new knowledge society based on information technology will change higher education profoundly and will also change the nature of the internationalization of higher education. It would be better to speak of a transition to an integrated internationalization of higher education; that is, a response of higher education to globalization and regionalization.

Internationalization of Higher Education in the United States

In the period between the two world wars, as well as after World War II and during the Cold War, the United States determined to a large extent the development and characteristics of the international dimension of higher education under the umbrella term of international education. After the Cold War, Europe and to a certain extent also Australia and Canada have taken over the leading role in developing internationalization strategies for higher education.

In the twentieth century, American higher education has become dominant. A sense of superiority is not absent in American higher education these days. On the other hand, another aspect of American international education is its emphasis on overcoming parochialism. A feeling of cultural parochialism prevails. This explains why international education in the United States, in particular study abroad, has been mainly an undergraduate issue, part of the general education that students have to receive in preparation for specialized education at the graduate level and for their future careers. This phenomenon is linked to the generally insular character of American higher education. It is this combination of parochialism on the one hand and sense of superiority on the other hand that determined for most of the twentieth century, and still to a large extent today, the worldview and motivation for international education in the United States.

The fragmented development of a large number of not directly related activities, projects, and programs (study abroad, international students, international studies, area studies, technical assistance), in general brought together under the umbrella name of international education, and the prevalence of political rationales (foreign policy, national security, and peace and mutual understanding) over other rationales determined the international dimension of higher education in the United States between the beginning of the twentieth century and the end of the Cold War. In the context of marginal federal policy for postsecondary education, the drive for internationalization has to come from other factors, both outside higher education and from inside the institutions. If one looks at the development of international education, both trends are clear. Foreign policy and national security on the one hand and a strong emphasis on personal development, peace and mutual understanding, and multicultural exposure on the other dominate among the rationales.

The post–World War II period and the Cold War drove American governments, for reasons of defense, public diplomacy, and security, to stimulate international exchange and cooperation. Even after the end of the Cold War these continue to be the main rationales for federal support, although competitiveness increasingly enters the arguments supporting internationalization. This context explains the strong ethos approach in American international education, present at both the institutional level and at the intermediate level between the federal government and the sector of higher education; the relatively strong presence of private foundations and organizations in international education; and the strong advocacy culture.

For longer, to a larger extent, and more professionally than anywhere else, American higher education has been developing a broad variety of activities, programs, and projects in international education, mainly at the undergraduate level: international curriculum development, area studies, foreign language training, study abroad, exchanges, foreign student recruitment and advising, and development cooperation and assistance. At the same time, however, most institutions of higher education do not have an internationalization strategy for the whole of the institution. This can be explained through the specific characteristics of American higher education and the role of the federal government and private foundations with respect to higher education.

Internationalization of Higher Education in Europe

Massification of the student flow and its bipolar nature (i.e., the dominance of the United States in the Western bloc and of the former Soviet Union in the Communist Bloc), were the main characteristics of the international dimension of higher education in Europe in the 1960s and 1970s. The open-door and laissez-faire policy and the one-way dimension were the other characteristics of the process of internationalization of higher education, at a global level and in Europe in particular. The universities themselves played a mainly passive role as receivers of foreign students. International activity was largely oriented toward the cooperation of European higher education with the United States (outward mobility) and with the Third World (inward mobility). A European policy for internationalization did not exist, and the same applied at the institutional level. At the national level, international cooperation and exchange was included in bilateral agreements between nations and in development cooperation programs driven by political rationales. Institutions were passive partners in these programs.

In the 1970s this changed. Outgoing mobility was given more emphasis than the previous open-door policy for foreign students. A change in pattern from South–North mobility to North–North mobility accompanied these changes. In 1976 the Council of the European Communities adopted an action program for education. This was the first such move, since the Treaty of Rome did not mention education as an area for community action. The Commission therefore had to justify its action program by noneducational, mainly economic criteria. In the rationales for the action plan we recognize the first signs of issues that are still dominant in the European policy for education: harmonization, Europeanization, and globalization. Although important in itself, the impact of the action program was marginal.

The 1980s produced four distinct changes: first in the open-door mobility of individual students, second in the development of a research and development policy for the EC, third in student mobility as an integrated part of study, and fourth in the widening of scope to other regions, such as third countries in Western, Central, and Eastern Europe, third countries outside Europe, and development cooperation.

With respect to the individual mobility of students, the European nations and universities began changing their benevolent laissez-faire policy to a more controlled reception and in some cases the active recruitment of fee-paying foreign students. At first this applied nearly exclusively to the case of the United Kingdom: the British decision in 1979 to introduce full-cost fees for foreign students. Higher education as an export commodity quickly became dominant in the United Kingdom. For most people on the European continent, considering the education of foreign students as an export commodity was still anathema at that time. On the European continent, the reception of foreign students was and in most cases still is based more on foreign policy arguments than on considerations of export policy. At the end of the twentieth century the international movement of students as an export commodity had spread over the European continent and became a more important element of higher education policy than it had been in the past, both at the national and institutional levels.

The technological needs of modern society demand very expensive research projects that individual research groups, institutions of higher education, companies, or even national governments cannot finance alone. Therefore, a logical role exists for the European Commission in international cooperation in science and research in the Union: to stimulate those activities in which European cooperation offers major advantages and generates the maximum beneficial effects. Another rationale was the challenge posed by new technologies and related competition with the United States and Japan. Europeanization, harmonization, and globalization are central elements in this policy. Although the R&D programs are more substantial in terms of quality and funding than the educational programs of the European Commission, they are considered in most institutional policies—with the exception of the United Kingdom and some of the newly entered members, in particular in Scandinavia—to be less closely related to internationalization strategies than are the educational programs.

In the late 1970s and early 1980s the notion of study abroad, in the sense of sending students to foreign institutions of higher education as part of their home degree programs, became an issue on the continent that overshadowed the developments in individual mobility of students. The action program of 1976 was the basis for future activities in academic cooperation and exchange within the European Community. The member states limited the role of the European Community in the field of education, however, to complementary measures, decided only with the authorization of the Council of Ministers. Education would remain the exclusive task of national governments, although from 1982 onward social and economic factors gave the Commission more room to extend its role in this area. One can observe in its objectives a more pragmatic and less ambitious approach. Pluralism and complementarity are more dominant than harmonization and Europeanization.

Ironically, the lack of a legal basis for action in the field of higher education gave the European Commission a great deal of freedom for creative programmatic action in the field of education in the period after 1982, a freedom and creativity that would have been less within a more formal legal structure. The launch of COMETT, a program for cooperation between higher education and industry, in 1986, and of ERASMUS—later integrated in SOCRATES—a program for cooperation within higher education, in 1987, took place in this period, followed by several other education programs.

The end of the 1980s also saw the development of an involvement of the EC in relation to other parts of the world as part of its foreign policy: with the rest of Europe, in particular Central and Eastern Europe, in anticipation of their future integration in the EU; with developing countries by way of technical assistance; and with Northern America, Latin America, the Middle East, and Asia.

In the 1990s the creative and informal period of educational policy of the European Community came to an end. The Maastricht Treaty, signed in 1992 and ratified on November 1, 1993, included education for the first time. The importance of strengthening the European dimension in education was placed high on the agenda. Related issues that were also given attention were the development of a European Credit Transfer System as part of ERASMUS–SOCRATES, recognition of diplomas, and the development of an open European space for cooperation in higher education. Together these new measures redirected step by step the scope of the debate to harmonization, integration, and Europeanization, moving gradually away from the previous direction of pluralism and complementarity, but without stating that explicitly as such.

This overview of the development of Europeanization of higher education in the period between the 1960s and the 1990s explains how it culminated in the 1990s in a broad range of programs and activities to stimulate a European dimension in higher education. The main focus lay on the Europeanization of higher education, with an emphasis on R&D, mobility of students and staff, curriculum development, and network building. At the turn of the century, Europe is preparing for a big step forward in Europeanization. It manifests itself in the Bologna Declaration on the European Higher Education Area of 1999. The creation of a European space for higher education, the prime objective of the Bologna Declaration, should be completed in 2010. A set of specific objectives has been formulated to make this happen: a common framework of understandable and comparable degrees, undergraduate and postgraduate levels in all countries, ECTS-compatible credit systems, a European dimension in quality assurance, and the elimination of remaining obstacles to mobility. The Bologna Declaration not only looks at the internal implications for higher education, but also explicitly refers to the need to increase the international competitiveness of European higher education and to make it more attractive to students from other continents. In that sense, the declaration follows the visible pattern everywhere, with competitiveness becoming a driving rationale for the internationalization of higher education.

ERASMUS and the other EC programs have placed internationalization high on the priority lists of national, institutional, and departmental strategic plans. Several national governments, private funds, and regional entities have established funds alongside the European programs to stimulate international cooperation and exchange. Since the creation of ERASMUS in 1987, one can state that institutions of higher education in Europe have largely learned to cope with its demands and those of the other European programs. In many institutions of higher education, offices of international relations, smaller or larger, have been established at the institutional and frequently also at the department levels. With due regard to variation and exceptions, the trend is for institutions to give internationalization a central place in their mission statements, strategic plans, and budgets. From a move imposed by the outside world, internationalization is becoming an integral part of higher education policy, though still as a separate strategy. Institutions of higher education, faculty, and students are increasingly placing international education at the center of their strategies.

At the turn of the century one can observe a gradual shift from internationalization as a separate strategy in the direction of internationalization as a natural element in the overall strategy of the institution. The role of national governments—already diminished by deregulation and privatization of higher education—is becoming more concentrated on removing barriers and obstacles and creating facilities. The same applies to the role of the European Commission. The Bologna declaration can be interpreted as part of this changing role of national governments and the Commission.

A Comparison

Differences in the development of the internationalization of higher education in Europe and the United States of America in general terms can be described as follows:

- In the United States the international dimension of higher education is older, and is founded on arguments of foreign policy and national security. In Europe the tradition is still rather young, only became more important as part of the European economic and political integration process, and is primarily motivated by arguments of economic competition.

- The international dimension of higher education has a longer tradition of organization and a higher level of professionalization in the United States than in Europe.
- In the United States the objective of international education is more directed to global and intercultural awareness in response to cultural parochialism, while in Europe the accent is more on the extension and diversification of academic performance.
- In the United States the emphasis in study abroad activities is on undergraduate mobility, while in Europe exchanges at the graduate level have more priority.
- The focus of international education in the United States is more directed to globalization of the curriculum, area studies, and foreign language study, while in Europe the focus is more on networking and mobility.
- In the United States study abroad and foreign student advising have a tendency to be seen more as different, unrelated activities, while in Europe they are seen as related parts of mobility schemes, with the emphasis on exchanges.
- In the United States study abroad has the tendency to take the form of faculty-supervised group mobility, while in Europe mobility is based more on mutual trust and is individual oriented.
- In the United States there is a lack of strategic approach and the tendency toward fragmentation. In Europe the different programs and organizational aspects are more integrated into an overall strategy, and at the professional level one can see a higher level of integration.

Explanations for these differences are as follows:

- In the United States internationalization is seen as part of general education, while in Europe it is seen more as an activity within academic specialization.
- In the United States undergraduate education has to compensate for the lack of global and intercultural education and foreign language training in primary and secondary education. In higher education this takes the form of international education. In Europe general education, including global and intercultural education and active foreign language training, are an integral part of primary and secondary education. Higher education can undergo internationalization more as an integrated part of academic specialization.
- In the United States area studies, foreign language training, the study of international relations, and development studies are externally added and sponsored programs, while in Europe they have developed as regular disciplines, no different from others, such as law, economics, and medicine.
- In the United States internationalization is more driven by political rationales of national security and foreign policy, while in Europe economic competition and academic quality are the main rationales for the internationalization of higher education.

These differences are the results of the following:

- Different cultures and structures in primary, secondary, and undergraduate education.

- Different emphases in foreign policy after World War II.
- A lack of national policy for higher education and its internationalization in the United States.
- A lack of private initiative in higher education and its internationalization in Europe.
- Different leadership traditions.
- Different funding mechanisms.

These differences have influenced to a large extent our perceptions and our strategies for internationalization. But in recent years our political and educational systems have moved toward each other. If we look to the future, in spite of all the differences mentioned, we are moving in each other's direction. America and Europe, although having the same higher education roots, come from a different starting point in international education. Globalization, competitiveness, and new forms of education are important factors influencing this development.

A CONCEPTUAL FRAMEWORK

The historical analysis of the internationalization of higher education makes clear that at certain moments different answers have been given to the "why" (rationales), "what" (meanings and approaches), and "how" (strategies and organization models) of this phenomenon.

Rationales

Why are institutions of higher education, national governments, international bodies, and increasingly the private sector so actively involved in international education activities? There is not one single answer to that question. Rationales can be described as motivations for integrating an international dimension into higher education. They address the "why" of internationalization. Different rationales imply different means and ends to internationalization.

Four groups of rationales can be identified, each with different subcategories: political (foreign policy, national security, technical assistance, peace and mutual understanding, national identity, and regional identity), economic (economic growth and competitiveness, the labor market, national educational demand, and financial incentives for institutions and governments), social–cultural, and academic rationales (providing an international dimension to research and teaching, extension of the academic horizon, institution-building, profile–status, enhancement of quality and international academic standards). When analyzing rationales, one has to take into account the following:

- The diversity of stakeholder groups in higher education and within each stakeholder group: the government, the private sector, and the educational sector.

- There is a strong overlap in rationales within and between different stakeholder groups. The main differences are in the hierarchy of priorities.

- In general, stakeholders do not have one exclusive rationale but a combination of rationales for internationalization, with a hierarchy in priorities.

- Rationales may differ between stakeholder groups and within stakeholder groups.

- Priorities in rationales may change over time and by country and region.

- Rationales have a strong influence on the internationalization of higher education but are seldom made explicit.

Meanings and Approaches

One of the fundamental problems one faces when dealing with the internationalization of higher education is the diversity of related terms. Sometimes they are used to describe a concrete element of the broad field of internationalization, but in other cases these terms are used as *pars pro toto* and as synonyms for the overall term internationalization. Each of these terms has a different emphasis and reflects a different approach, and are used by different authors in different ways. For a better understanding of internationalization of higher education it is important to place that term in perspective with approaches and other terms used, and to provide a working definition of its meaning.

Definitions by American authors generally sum up or emphasize activities, rationales, competencies and/or ethos, and they use the term international education rather than internationalization of higher education. Non-American authors, mainly from Europe, Canada, and Australia, tend to use more a process approach and their use of the term internationalization of higher education is a reflection of this emphasis on process.

From a historical point of view, international education reflects the period between World War II and the end of the Cold War and is more strongly observed in the United States than elsewhere. The internationalization of higher education reflects the period starting with the end of the Cold War, and is more predominant in Europe, as well as in Australia and Canada. The differences in meanings accepted by American authors and others for that reason can be explained by the fact that most practice and analysis in the period before the end of the Cold War was done by Americans and still dominates American practice, whereas most practice and analysis of the international dimension of higher education now takes place outside of the United States, in particular in Europe, Canada, and Australia.

"The process of integrating an international or intercultural dimension into the teaching, research, and service functions of the institution" has become quite generally accepted as a working definition for internationalization of higher education. If one looks at the literature and practice of the internationalization of higher education, in many cases its meaning is linked to its rationales, its means, its content, and/or its activities. This has contributed to the confusing overlap in terms used to describe (elements of) internationalization. The various definitions of international education and internationalization of higher education reflect different approaches to the role of the international dimension in higher education: activity, rationale, competency, and process approaches. While each approach has a key aspect that distinguishes it from the others, it is important to recognize that they are not mutually exclusive. It may be more appropriate to think of them as different strands in a cord that integrates the different aspects of internationalization.

Strategies and Organization Models

The overview of meanings, definitions, approaches, and rationales demonstrates that various elements play a role in the internationalization process. These elements are described in a variety of different ways: mechanisms, facilitators, activities, barriers, factors, and strategies. For the purposes of this discussion the term "strategies" is used to characterize those initiatives taken by an institution of higher learning to integrate an international dimension into research, teaching, and service functions, as well as management policies and systems.

In the process approach, the many different activities identified as key components of internationalization are divided into two major categories: program strategies and organizational strategies. Program strategies refers to those academic activities and services of an institution of higher education that integrate an international dimension into its main functions. Organizational strategies include those initiatives that help to ensure that an international dimension (or, in other words, the activities already discussed) are institutionalized through developing the appropriate policies and administrative systems.

Six different organization models for internationalization of higher education are reviewed. The first four approaches to the theoretical modeling of internationalization by institutions (Neave 1992b; Rudzki 2000; Davies 1995; van Dijk and Meijer 1997) complement one another in their prescriptive and descriptive aspects. They offer a means of measuring the formal, paper commitments of institutions against the practice to be found in concrete operating structures. Further, they offer a way to include in the theoretical frame the important fact that institutional strategies may be implicit as well as explicit. They provide useful information and tools, but should not be considered to be the new paradigm for strategies of internationalization. The two models by van der Wende (1996) and Knight (1994) take the process approach as their basis. They are not focused on the organization as such, but on the process of internationalization strategy as a whole.

Combining the six elements of Knight (1994)—awareness, commitment, planning, operationalize, review, and reinforcement—with three elements from van der Wende (1996)—analysis of context, implementation, and long-term effects—a modified version of the internationalization circle of Knight is presented. In this model the context analysis, the implementation phase, and the effect of internationalization on the overall functions of the institution have been incorporated. In all phases both the institutional and the specific departmental aspects have to be addressed, as well as the link between the two. It is important to recognize that specific circumstances of disciplines and departments will get enough attention and will not be forced in a general structure. The integration effect is, although placed in its heart, outside the circle for the following reason. It is possible to see internationalization as a strategy in itself, without a conscious and deliberate strategy to integrate it into the teaching, research, and service functions of the institution. In most cases, internationalization is assumed to have an integration effect, but is not primarily judged on that effect, but on its own merits.

KEY ISSUES

Globalization and Regionalization

Although higher education is still predominantly a national issue, globalization is affecting this national competency. Sometimes the terms globalization and internationalization of higher education are used interchangeably. This interchangeable use of terms, the proposed gradual shift from international to global, and the use of "global" in the meaning of "general or universal" are all highly questionable. There is a fundamental difference and at the same time a dialectical link between internationalization of higher education and globalization. Internationalization is different from globalization in that internationalization is based on relationships between nations and their institutions, and for that reason takes differences as a starting point for linkages, while globalization ignores the existence of nations and their differences and looks more for similarities than for differences. At the same time, internationalization of higher education and globalization are becoming more and more linked phenomena, in the sense that institutions of higher education (privatized, deregulated, and more entrepreneurial) become active players in the global marketplace but are trying to maintain their autonomous position as academic institutions, holding strong to diversification more than harmonization.

The dialectical relation expresses itself in two phenomena referred to as the knowledge society or economy and transnational or borderless education. The relationship between globalization, new technologies, and science finds its expression in the concept of the knowledge society or economy. The same phenomenon, however, can be observed in the other core function of universities, teaching. Growing competition and collaboration with the private sector (in particular in the area of specialized, professional training and lifelong learning, distance education, and the use of new technologies) are developments that are increasingly coming to the forefront in higher education. Where the notion of the knowledge society or economy seems more research related, in teaching the term transnational education, and recently also borderless education, is normally used to describe this phenomenon.

Examples of transnational or borderless education are offshore programs and campuses; twinning programs; articulation programs; international institutions, franchise arrangements and branch campuses; distance education; and virtual, electronic, or Web programs and institutions. Given the fact that transnational or borderless education becomes more important as a result of the information age we live in, it also has to be analyzed in its relationship with internationalization, the "phenomenon" of the 1990s, a relationship that in the future will become more closely connected. The internationalization of higher education, in the sense that it emphasizes more the interaction between cultures than the homogenization of cultures, can play a counterbalancing role to the potential dangers of transnational education, and this is one reason why it is important to relate these two trends and study the relationship between them.

A related but specific aspect of both the internationalization of higher education and globalization is regionalization and higher education, a phenomenon that over the past two decades has become more evident in Europe, but also elsewhere. A first distinction in regionalization should be made between interregional, regional, cross-regional, and supraregional. A second distinction should be made between regionalization in the meaning of globalization with a regional character (i.e., standardization, homogenization, harmonization of rules, regulations, recognition, structures, and systems) and regionalization in the meaning of internationalization. A close look at activities, programs, and studies related to the regionalization of higher education indicates that regionalization is at present more closely linked to internationalization than to globalization. However, it is not difficult to see that we are in a transition period in which regionalization is becoming increasingly linked to globalization, while information technology, competition, and standardization are becoming essential elements of reforming higher education.

Quality Review

Quality and internationalization are closely related issues. They are both key strategic issues in higher education at the turn of the century. Quality relates to internationalization in the way in which internationalization contributes to the improvement of quality of higher education, and in the way one assesses and enhances or maintains the quality of internationalization activities and strategies. The increasing preoccupation with quality in higher education is linked to the call for accountability by national governments, the corporate world, and students. Not only are they the main sources of funding for higher education, but they also have a vested interest in the products of higher education. As institutions of higher education develop internationalization strategies, the assessment and enhancement of these strategies also becomes more important. This has resulted in a call for an internationalization quality review instrument. For that purpose, the IQRP was designed in a pilot project of the IMHE, in cooperation with the ACA, and is implemented by these two organizations together with the European Association of Universities as a service, the IQR. The instrument and its development into a service have been described and lessons learned from the use of the instrument and service were presented.

The development of IQRP and other instruments to assess the quality of internationalization and related programs and strategies is a sign of the importance that institutions of higher education and (inter)national agencies and governments attach to the assessment of the quality of their international strategies and activities. The IQR is a service that—when used carefully, taking into account the observations made—can be of use to institutions of higher education in a broad variety of contexts and settings.

English as the Common Language

The English language is becoming the global language of communication in technology, trade, culture, science, and education. Opposition to the use of a second language as the language of communication is generally, however, extremely strong for the following reasons: the potential threat to and perhaps disappearance of the local language, the related danger of the disappearance of local cultural practices and products, and the fear for cultural and linguistic hegemony and imperialism. At the same time British English or American English will become less dominant, English as a language of teaching and learning also becomes more local-specific.

The growing dominance of English as the language of communication is certainly apparent in higher education. In the domain of research, it is an accepted fact that scientific publications have to be written or translated into English to get published, acknowledged, and cited. However, also in the domain of teaching, the emergence of English as the second language of instruction in addition to the local language seems to be becoming more and more widespread. Opposition to the use of English for scientific purposes has always been marginal, but in the area of teaching it is extremely strong.

A case study of the development of teaching in English in The Netherlands illustrates this. Over the past ten years, a lively debate has taken place on the use of English in teaching at Dutch institutions of higher education.

As a result of the European mobility programs and the emergence of the competitiveness rationale, institutions of higher education started to develop courses and programs in English. In a public debate in The Netherlands in 1989, the arguments used were mainly of the three kinds already mentioned. The outcome of the debate was that permission to use another language was limited to the following situations: the instruction and examinations pertain to a foreign language, the courses are conducted by a visiting lecturer whose mother tongue is a foreign language, or wherever necessary in view of the specific nature of the course or the students' origin, in accordance with a code of practice drawn up by the institution concerned. After the public and political storm over instruction in English in Dutch higher education in the early 1990s, this debate—with the exception of a very small minority of language and culture puritans—has almost completely evaporated. There appears to be a general acceptance that instruction in English is a necessary evil in order to be a player in the global educational market, as was already generally accepted for the scientific role of universities. The rationale might be that Dutch politics have accepted that not the supply of internationally oriented education but rather the demand by the international market determines the degree of internationalization. Although the law says differently, accepted practice is that teaching in English is allowed. Higher education therefore follows several other examples of tolerance in Dutch politics, such as the attitudes toward soft drugs and euthanasia.

Although the political opposition to teaching in English seems to be fading, two relevant issues are still raised, usually by the academic community itself: the academic performance of international students in relation to their English-language proficiency and the performance of the instructor when teaching in another than the mother tongue. Reference has been made to a study by Vinke (1995) on engineering education and the effects on Dutch lecturers and students. Her recommendations have wider implications than only for engineering education and The Netherlands.

Regional and International Academic Networks

Associations, consortia, and networks are quite common in the academic world. In recent years, academic organizations have become increasingly international in nature as a result of the globalization of our economies and societies. The emergence of new international academic organizations is directly related to the growing importance of the internationalization of higher education and the impact of globalization on higher education. There is a great variety of such academic organizations, and it is not always clear what their objectives and goals are, nor how successfully they operate. Why has there been such a rapid growth in international networks in the past decade? What are the challenges in establishing, operating, and sustaining such organizations? What is the added value that such an organization provides compared to what is done at the individual or bilateral level? What are the success and failure factors for an international academic network?

Three types of international, multilateral organizations in higher education have been identified: academic associations, academic consortia, and institutional networks. An academic association is an organization of academics or administrators and/or their organizational units, united for a common purpose, which is related to their professional development (information exchange, training, advocacy, etc.). This type of organization is quite common and has a long history in higher education, even at the international level. This is particularly true for those associations that are based on individual membership and are single purpose, academic and discipline based, and faculty driven. Institutional, multipurpose, management-based, and leadership-driven associations and individual, administrative associations are a more recent phenomenon. An academic consortium is a group of academic units (departments, centers, schools, and institutions) that are united for the single purpose of fulfilling a contract based on bringing together a number of different areas of specialized knowledge. In principle their lifespan is limited by the terms of the contract. They can be either faculty or leadership driven, but with a strong faculty commitment in the case of consortia with an academic purpose. International academic consortia are a rather common phenomenon in higher education, in particular in research. They appear to come and go according to the needs of the different institutions to make use of their partners' complementary skills, experiences, and facilities. Academic consortia are and will continue to be the most common form of international organization in higher education, and increasingly as part of academic associations or institutional networks. An institutional network is a group of academic units (departments, centers, schools, and institutions) that are united for, in general, multiple academic and/or administrative purposes, are leadership driven, and have indefinite lifespans. While academic consortia are usually single mission, institutional networks tend to have a general framework objective. Although they are less focused on objectives and goals than associations or consortia due to their multipurpose character, it is this type of organization that seems to be emerging most recently. There is a trend toward leadership-driven multilateral institutional networks, mostly within the European Union but also elsewhere, and recently also examples of an international nature emerge.

Although institutional networks in higher education appear to have become rather popular, not many success stories can be told as yet. Institutional networks should be conscious of the following elements: the mission of the network; the description of the purposes, objectives, and goals of the network; the geographical focus; the size of the network; the composition of the membership in relation to the mission and purposes; the relation between the founder and/or center of the network and the other members;

the relation between leadership commitment and commitment within each of the institutions; funding sources, including membership fees and external and internal project funding; the organizational structure; and the mechanisms for evaluation of the network and its activities. The institutional, multipurpose, and leadership-driven networks are particularly facing problems with their identity, their size, the commitment of their faculty and students, and their objectives and goals. Even though institutional networks at present seem to be rather weak, lacking commitment at the departmental and school levels, and not very effective in their operations, they are more likely to be the motor for future mergers than discipline-based networks and consortia. Only central leadership is able to make the radical decisions needed to move away from fragmented activity-oriented cooperation to real mergers and joint ventures.

There are and will be institutions of higher education that, deliberately or not, are oriented to the local environment and for which the international dimension will stay incidental, individual, or at most consist of a combination of unrelated activities, projects, and programs. Others will not evolve further than having a separate internationalization strategy, without affecting all the functions of the institution. Only a few global players will emerge, old institutions but also new providers of higher education, making use of the opportunities that new technologies and the global market provide. Coalitions, networks, and consortia among institutions of higher education and between them and industry are and will be increasingly important factors in ensuring a role in this global arena.

A Research Area

The interest in the internationalization of higher education as a research area is a reflection of the growing strategic importance of internationalization for higher education. The internationalization of higher education is still a long way from becoming the regular subject of substantial research-based academic studies. This lack of a strong research tradition explains why this area lacks academic recognition in the field of comparative and international education and why it is marginalized under confusing terms within that. Recognition of the internationalization of higher education as a special research area will, however, be unavoidable and necessary in the coming years given its growing importance, both in practice and in research.

In the United States there is a longer tradition of research on the internationalization of higher education, or rather on international education. With several notable exceptions, in the 1990s practitioners have mainly followed this tradition. The arguments for a research agenda for the internationalization of higher education in the United States seem to have primarily a national political character, while the more recent call for research on internationalization of higher education in Europe seems to be of a more generic and scholarly character. But if Americans may be biased in this sense, Europeans still have to find out the "what" and "how" of internationalization of higher education. One could add that the danger of European bias is also there, with so much of our research attention going to the European programs.

Setting the differences in approach and focus aside, there appears to be a general consensus, encompassing more than just the United States and Europe and including in particular Canada and Australia, that more research on internationalization of higher education is needed. One has to be realistic, though. Most higher education scholars do not yet recognize internationalization as a research theme. If one were forced to give an assessment of the present stage of research on the internationalization of higher education, it would be placed primarily as of interest to the category of occasional researching practitioners and the applied higher education researchers and research units, not to higher education scholars, and focused more on practical than on methodological issues. The publication of the *Journal of Studies in International Education*, the appearance of more articles in other academic journals, and the publication of a growing number of books on the international dimensions of higher education reflect the growing importance of this area in general and as a research theme in itself. There is still a long way to go, however, before the "missing link" between the internationalization of higher education and comparative higher education studies has been established.

CONCLUSION

This study addressed the following questions:

- What has been the historical development of the internationalization of higher education, in particular in the United States of America and Europe, and how are the differences in development between these two regions to be explained?
- What are the rationales behind this internationalization of higher education, its meaning and approaches, and the different strategies and organizational models?
- How can we interpret some of its key manifestations at the turn of the century?

It has been argued that the international dimension of higher education prior to the twentieth century was more incidental than organized, and that this international dimension as an organized activity, referred to in general by the term international education, is a product of the twentieth century, at first mainly in the United States for reasons of foreign policy and national security. Around the end of the Cold War this international dimension evolved into a strategic process, referred to as the internationalization of higher education, and became increasingly linked to the globalization and regionalization of our societies and the impact of this on higher education.

In addition, with the further development of globalization, the international dimension will evolve into an integrated element of higher education and move away from its present position as an isolated set of activities, strategies, or processes. This is manifested in a shift in emphasis from more traditional forms of international education to strategies more directly related to the core functions of the university, and in a shift in emphasis from political to economic rationales. This is also becoming manifest in the way the globalization of our societies and economies influences the new direction of internationalization of higher education, in the attention to quality review of internationalization and the contribution that internationalization makes to the overall quality of higher education, in the emergence of English as the language of communication in higher education, in the rise of international and regional academic networks and consortia, and in the development of internationalization of higher education as a research area.

References

Abádi-Nagy, Zoltán. (1999). Internationalism and National Identity in Eastern Europe. *International Educator* 8, no. 1: 10–11.

Academic Co-operation Association (ACA). (1997). *Making the Case for International Co-operation in Higher Education: The Meise Consensus.* Proceedings of a meeting of chief executives of higher education co-operation agencies, Meise, 18–19 October 1996. Brussels: ACA.

————. (1999). *Profiles of the Academic Co-operation Association's Member Organisations.* Brussels: ACA.

Adams, Don, and Gary Theisen. (1990). Comparative Education Research: What Are the Methods and Uses of Comparative Education Research? In *International Comparative Education: Practices, Issues and Prospects*, edited by R. Murray Thomas. Oxford: Pergamon.

Adams, Tony. (1998). The Operation of Transnational Degree and Diploma Programs: The Australian Case. *Journal of Studies in International Education* 2, no. 1: 3–22.

Aigner, Jean S., Patricia Nelson, and Joseph R. Stimpfl. (1992). *Internationalizing the University: Making It Work.* Springfield, Va.: CBIS Federal.

Alladin, Ibrahim. (1992). International Co-operation in Higher Education: The Globalization of Universities. *Higher Education in Europe* 17, no. 4: 4–13.

Allaway, William H. (1994). Peace: The Real Power of Educational Exchange. In *The Power of Educational Exchange, Essays in Honor of Jack Egle.* New York: Council on International Educational Exchange.

Alliance for International Educational and Cultural Exchange. (1998). *International Exchange Locator: A Resource Directory for Educational and Cultural Exchange, 1998 edition.* New York: USIA/Alliance, IIE Books.

Altbach, Philip G. (1988). *The Knowledge Context: Comparative Perspectives on the Distribution of Knowledge.* Albany: State University of New York Press.

Altbach, Philip G., ed. (1991). *International Higher Education: An Encyclopedia.* 2 vols. New York and London: Garland.

———. (1994). NAFTA and Higher Education, the Cultural and Educational Dimensions of Trade. *Change,* July–August, 48–49.

———, ed. (1996). *The International Academic Profession: Portraits of Fourteen Countries.* Princeton, N.J.: Carnegie Foundation for the Advancement of Teaching.

———. (1997a). The Foreign Student Dilemma. In *Comparative Higher Education: Knowledge, the University, and Development,* edited by Philip G. Altbach. Boston: Center for International Higher Education.

———. (1997b). The New Internationalism: Foreign Students and Scholars. In *Comparative Higher Education: Knowledge, the University, and Development,* edited by Philip G. Altbach. Boston: Center for International Higher Education.

———. (1997c). Patterns in Higher Education Development. In *Comparative Higher Education: Knowledge, the University, and Development,* edited by Philip G. Altbach. Boston: Boston College Center for International Higher Education.

———. (1997d). Research on Higher Education: Global Perspectives. In *Higher Education Research at the Turn of the Century,* edited by Jan Sadlak and Philip G. Altbach. New York: Garland.

———. (1998). Comparative Perspectives on Higher Education for the Twenty-First Century. *Higher Education Policy* 11: 347–356.

———. (1999). The Perils of Internationalizing Higher Education: An Asian Perspective. *International Higher Education* 15 (Spring): 2.

———. (2000a). The Crisis in Multinational Higher Education. *International Higher Education* 21 (Fall): 3–5.

———. (2000b). Research and Training in Higher Education: The State of the Art. In *Higher Education: A World-Wide Inventory of Centers and Programs,* edited by Philip G. Altbach and David Engberg. Boston: Boston College Center for International Higher Education.

———. (2000c). What Higher Education Does Right. *International Higher Education* 18 (Winter): 2.

Altbach, Philip G., Robert F. Arnove, and Gail P. Kelly. (1982). Trends in Comparative Education: A Critical Analysis. In *Comparative Education,* edited by Philip Altbach, Gail Kelly, and Robert F. Arnove. New York: Macmillan.

Altbach, Philip G., and Hans de Wit. (1995). International Higher Education: America Abdicates Leadership. In *International Higher Education* 1 (Spring): 11.

Altbach, Philip G., and Patti McGill Peterson. (1999). *Higher Education in the 21st Century: Global Challenge and National Response.* IIE Research Report no. 21. New York: IIE.

Altbach, Philip G., and Viswanathan Selvaratnam, eds. (1989). *From Dependence to Autonomy: The Development of Asian Universities.* Dordrecht: Kluwer Academic.

American Council on Education. (1998). *Educating for Global Competence: America's Passport for the Future.* Washington, D.C.: American Council on Education.

Anweiler, Oscar. (1977). Comparative Education and the Internationalization of Education. *Comparative Education* 13, no. 2: 109–114.

Arum, Stephen, and Jack Van de Water. (1992). The Need for a Definition of International Education in U.S. Universities. In *Bridges to the Future: Strategies for Internationalizing Higher Education*, edited by Charles Klasek. Carbondale, Ill.: Association of International Education Administrators.

Association of American Universities. (1996). *To Strengthen the Nation's Investment in Foreign Languages and International Studies: A Legislative Proposal to Create a National Foundation for Foreign Language and International Studies*. Washington, D.C.: Association of American Universities.

Association of International Education Administrators (AIEA). (1995). *A Research Agenda for the Internationalization of Higher Education in the United States*. Recommendations and Report of the Association of International Education Administrators Working Group based on the 10–11 August 1995 meeting in Washington, D.C. Pullman, Wash.: Association of International Education Administrators.

Association of Universities and Colleges of Canada (AUCC). (1993). *Guide to Establishing International Academic Links*. Ottawa: AUCC.

Back, Kenneth, and Dorothy Davis. (1995). Internationalisation of Higher Education in Australia. In *Strategies for Internationalisation of Higher Education: A Comparative Study of Australia, Canada, Europe and the United States of America*, edited by Hans de Wit. Amsterdam: European Association for International Education.

Back, Kenneth, Dorothy Davis, and Alan Olsen. (1996). *Internationalisation and Higher Education: Goals and Strategies*. Canberra: Department of Employment, Education, Training and Youth Affairs.

Barblan, Andris. (1999). The Sorbonne Declaration: Follow-Up and Implications: A Personal View. Presentation to the XII Santander Group General Assembly, 17 April.

Barblan, Andris, Barbara Khem, Sybille Reichert, and Ulrich Teichler, eds. (1998). *Emerging European Policy Profiles of Higher Education Institutions*. Werkstattberichte 55. Kassel: Wissenschaftlich Zentrum für Berufs- und Hochschulforschung, Universität Gesamthochschule Kassel.

Barblan, Andris, and Ulrich Teichler. (2000). *Implementing European Strategies in Universities: The SOCRATES Experience* (Mise en oeuvre de strategies européennes dans l'université: l'expérience Socrates). CRE doc. no. 6. Geneva: Association of European Universities (CRE).

Baron, Britta. (1993). The Politics of Academic Mobility in Western Europe. *Higher Education Policy* 6, no. 3: 50–54.

Barrow, Clyde. (2000). NAFTA and Trilateral Co-operation in Higher Education: Policy Initiatives in the United States. *Educación Global* 4 (April): 95–120.

Baumgratz-Gangl, Gisela. (1993). Cross Cultural Competence in a Changing World. *European Journal of Education* 28: 327–338.

———. (1996). Developments in the Internationalization of Higher Education in Europe. In *Academic Mobility in a Changing World: Regional and Global Trends* (contributions to the Wassenaar Colloquium, 1992), edited by Peggy Blumenthal, Craufurd Goodwin, Alan Smith, and Ulrich Teichler. London: Jessica Kingsley.

Ben-David, Joseph. (1992). *Centers of Learning: Britain, France, Germany, United States*. New Brunswick, N.J.: Transaction.

Bender, Thomas. (1997). International Studies in the United States: The Twentieth Century. In *Conference of the Rectors of the League of World Universities*, 22 February, pp. 16–20.

Bjarnason, Svava, John Davies, Dennis Farrington, John Fielden, Richard Garrett, Helen Lund, Robin Middlehurst, and Allan Schofield. (2000). *The Business of Borderless Education: UK Perspectives*. Summary Report. London: CVCP and HEFCE.

Blume, Stuart. (1995). Extended Review on the Internationalisation of Research Training in the E.U. Report to DG XII of the European Commission (grant contract Pss* 0891) on behalf of the Department of Science and Technology Dynamics, University of Amsterdam. Amsterdam: University of Amsterdam.

Blumenthal, Peggy, Craufurd Goodwin, Alan Smith, and Ulrich Teichler, eds. (1996). *Academic Mobility in a Changing World: Regional and Global Trends* (contributions to the Wassenaar Colloquium, 1992). London: Jessica Kingsley.

Blumenstyk, Goldie, and Beth McMurtrie. (2000). Educators Lament a Corporate Takeover of International Accreditor, Critics Say a Much-Needed Watchdog Has Lost Its Bite Due to Conflicts of Interest. *The Chronicle of Higher Education*, 27 October.

Bollag, Burton. (2000). The New Latin: English Dominates in Academe. *The Chronicle of Higher Education*, 8 September, A73.

Bologna Declaration. (1999). *Declaration on the European Higher Education Area*, 19 June, Bologna University.

Bond, Sheryl L., and Jan-Pierre Lemasson, eds. (1999). *A New World of Knowledge: Canadian Universities and Globalisation*. Ottawa: International Development Research Centre.

Bremer, Liduine. (1997). Central and Eastern Europe and Russia. In *National Policies for the Internationalisation of Higher Education in Europe*, edited by T. Kälvermark and M. van der Wende. Stockholm: Högskoleverket Studies, National Agency for Higher Education.

————. (1998). The Value of International Study Experience on the Labour Market: The Case of Hungary. *Journal of Studies in International Education* 2, no. 1: 39–58.

Brennan, John, and Tarla Shah. (2000). *Managing Quality in Higher Education: An International Perspective on Institutional Assessment and Change*. Buckingham: Society for Research into Higher Education/Open University Press.

Briggs, Asa, and Barbara Burn. (1985). *Study Abroad: A European and an American Perspective*. Paris: European Institute of Education and Social Policy; Amsterdam: European Cultural Foundation.

Brouwer, J. (1996). *De Europese Gemeenschap en Onderwijs, Geschiedenis van de samenwerking en het communitaire beleid op onderwijsgebied (1951–1996)*. Baarn: BKE–Baarn.

Brown, F. J. (1950). Universities in World-Wide Cultural Co-operation. In *Universities of the World Outside U.S.A.*, edited by M. M. Chambers. Washington, D.C.: American Council on Education.

Bunt-Kokhuis, Sylvia G. M. (1996). Academic Pilgrims: Determinants of International Faculty Mobility. Ph.D. diss., Tilburg University.

Burn, Barbara. (1996). Strengthening Internationalism in U.S. Higher Education. *International Higher Education* 4 (Spring): 19.

Burn, Barbara, Ladislav Cerich, and Alan Smith, eds. (1990). *Study Abroad Programmes*. Vol. 1. Higher Education Policy Series no. 11. London: Jessica Kingsley.

Callan, Hilary. (1993). The Idea of Internationalisation in British Higher Education. In Internationalisation: What Does it Really Mean? *International Education Magazine* 9, no. 1: 9.

———. (2000). The International Vision in Practice: A Decade of Evoluation. In *Higher Education in Europe* 25, no. 1: 15–23.

Callan, Hilary, and Hans de Wit. (1995). Internationalisation of Higher Education in Europe. In *Strategies for Internationalisation of Higher Education: A Comparative Study of Australia, Canada, Europe and the United States of America*, edited by Hans de Wit. Amsterdam: European Association for International Education.

Carnegie Commission on Science, Technology and Government. (1992). *Partnerships for Global Development: The Clearing Horizon*. Princeton, N.J.: Carnegie Foundation.

Carnestedt, Eva. (1997). Internationalisation Strategies in Higher Education: A Comparative Study between Australian and Swedish Universities. Master's thesis, Institute of International Education.

Cerych, Ladislav. (1989). Higher Education in Europe after 1992. *European Journal of Education* 24, no. 4: 319–332.

———. (1996). East–West Academic Mobility within Europe: Trends and Issues. In *Academic Mobility in a Changing World: Regional and Global Trends* (contributions to the Wassenaar Colloquium, 1992), edited by Peggy Blumenthal, Craufurd Goodwin, Alan Smith, and Ulrich Teichler. London: Jessica Kingsley.

Chambers, M. M., ed. (1950). *Universities of the World Outside U.S.A.* Washington, D.C.: American Council on Education.

Chandler, Alice. (1989). *Obligation or Opportunity: Foreign Student Policy in Six Major Receiving Countries*. IIE Research Report no. 18. New York: Institute for International Education.

———. (1999). *Paying the Bill for International Education: Programmes, Partners and Possibilities in the Millennium*. Washington, D.C.: NAFSA and Educational Testing Service.

Clark, Burton R. (1994). The Insulated Americans: Five Lessons from Abroad. In *Higher Education in American Society*. 3d ed., edited by Philip G. Altbach, Robert O. Berdahl, and Patricia J. Gumport. New York: Prometheus Books.

———. (1998). *Creating Entrepreneurial Universities: Organisational Pathways of Transformation*. Issues in Higher Education. Oxford: IAU Press/Pergamon.

Coleman, James A. (1998). Language Learning and Study Abroad: The European Perspective. *Frontiers: The Interdisciplinary Journal of Study Abroad* (Fall): 167–204.

Commonwealth Higher Education Management Services (CHEMS). (1996). *The Management of International Co-operation in Universities: Six Country Case Studies and an Analysis*. London: CHEMS.

Council on International Educational Exchange (CIEE). (1995). *Global Competence*. A CIEE leaflet. New York: CIEE.

Crespo, Manuel. (2000). Managing Regional Collaboration in Higher Education: The Case of the North American Free Trade Agreement (NAFTA). *Higher Education Management* 12, no. 1: 23–39.

Crossley, Michael. (1999). Reconceptualising Comparative and International Education. *Compare* 29: 249–267.

Cummings, William K. (1993). Global Trends in Overseas Studies. In *International Investment in Human Capital: Overseas Education for Development*, edited by Craufurd D. Goodwin. IIE Research Report no. 24. New York: Institute of International Education.

Cunningham, Christopher G. (1991). *The Integration of International Students on Canadian Post-Secondary Campuses*. CBIE Research Paper no. 1. Ottawa: Canadian Bureau for International Education.

Currie, Jan. (1998). Globalization Practices and the Professoriate in Anglo-Pacific and North-American Universities. *Comparative Education Review* 42, no. 1: 15–29.

Davidson, Ann, and Chris Andrews. (1998). *Bridging the Atlantic: Forging People-To-People Links*. Surrey, U.K.: ERICA.

Davies, John L. (1992). Developing a Strategy for Internationalisation in Universities: Towards a Conceptual Framework. Presentation to the IMHE conference, 1992, Paris. Published in *Bridges to the Future: Strategies for Internationalizing Higher Education*, edited by Charles B. Klasek. Carbondale: Ill.: Association of International Education Administrators.

———. (1995). University Strategies for Internationalisation in Different Institutional and Cultural Settings: A Conceptual Framework. In *Policy and Policy Implementation in Internationalisation of Higher Education*, edited by P. Blok. Amsterdam: European Association for International Education.

———. (1997). A European Agenda for Change for Higher Education in the XXIst Century: Comparative Analysis of Twenty Institutional Case Studies. *CRE-action* 111: 47–92.

———. (1998). Issues in the Development of Universities' Strategies for Internationalisation. *MillenIum* 3, no. 11: 68–80.

Daxner, Michael. (1999). Notes on Europe, Globality and Higher Education. *CRE-action* 115: 67–82.

Delors, Jacques. (1994). Interview. *Le Magazine* 2.

de Ridder-Symoens, Hilde. (1992). Mobility. In *A History of the University in Europe*. Vol. 1: *Universities in the Middle Age*, edited by Hilde de Ridder-Symoens. Cambridge: Cambridge University Press.

———. (1996). Mobility. In *A History of the University in Europe,* Vol. 2: *Universities in Early Modern Europe (1500–1800)*, edited by Walter Rüegg. Cambridge: Cambridge University Press.

Desruisseaux, Paul. (2000a). As Exchanges Lose a Political Rationale, Their Role Is Debated. *The Chronicle of Higher Education*, 11 February.

———. (2000b). From Controversy to Quiet Prosperity: Federal Foreign-Study Effort Is a Survivor. *The Chronicle of Higher Education*, 7 April.

Deutsch, Karl W. (1997). Nationalistic Responses to Study Abroad. *International Educator* 6, no. 3: 33–41.

de Wit, Hans. (1991). Internationalisering van het onderwijs: beleidskeuzes voor de jaren negentig. In *Zeven artikelen over hoger onderwijs en internationalisering*, edited by Han Aarts and Vincent Piket. Visum Perspectief 2. Den Haag: NUFFIC.

———. (1993). On the Definition of International Education (book review). *European Association for International Education Newsletter* 11: 7–10.

————. (1995a). Education and Globalization in Europe: Current Trends and Future Developments. *Frontiers: The Interdisciplinary Journal of Study Abroad* 1: 28–53.

————, ed. (1995b). *Strategies for Internationalisation of Higher Education: A Comparative Study of Australia, Canada, Europe and the United States of America.* Amsterdam: European Association for International Education.

————. (1997a). Strategies for Internationalisation of Higher Education in Asia Pacific Countries: A Comparative Introduction. In *Internationalisation of Higher Education in Asia Pacific Countries*, edited by Jane Knight and Hans de Wit. Amsterdam: European Association for International Education.

————. (1997b). Studies in International Education: A Research Perspective. *Journal of Studies in International Education* 1 no. 1: 1–8.

————, ed. (1998a). *50 Years of International Co-operation and Exchange between the United States and Europe: European Views.* Amsterdam: European Association for International Education.

————. (1998b). Ducks Quack Differently on Each Side of the Ocean. In *50 Years of International Co-operation and Exchange between the United States and Europe: European Views*, edited by Hans de Wit. Amsterdam: European Association for International Education.

————. (1998c). Kennisexport, een kwestie van lange adem en goede afstemming. *Tijdschrift voor Hoger Onderwijs & Management (THEMA)* 5, no. 5: 25–30.

————. (1998d). National Policies for Internationalisation of Higher Education: A Book Review. *Journal of Studies in International Education* 2, no. 1: 87–89.

————. (1998e). Rationales for Internationalisation of Higher Education. *MillenIum* 3, no. 11: 11–19.

————. (1999). Changing Rationales for Internationalization. *International Higher Education* 15 (Spring): 2–3.

————. (2000a). Changing Rationales for the Internationalization of Higher Education. In *Internationalization of Higher Education: An Institutional Perspective.* Papers on Higher Education. Bucharest: UNESCO/CEPES.

————. (2000b). The Sorbonne and Bologna Declarations on European Higher Education. *International Higher Education* 18 (Winter): 8–9.

Dronkers, Jaap. (1993). The Causes of Growth of English Education in The Netherlands: Class or Internationalisation? *European Journal of Education* 28: 295–308.

Dubhasi, P. R. (1995). Globalisation and Local Roots. *University News*, 4 March, 10–11.

Dunnett, Stephen C. (1998). International Recruitment in U.S. Higher Education: A Brief History. *International Spectator* 7 (Fall): 28–32.

Ebuchi, Kazuhiro. (1990). Foreign Students and the Internationalisation of the University: A View from the Japanese Perspective. In *Foreign Students and the Internationalisation of Higher Education*, edited by Kazuhiro Ebuchi. Hiroshima: Research Institute for Higher Education.

Education Abroad Program (EAP). (1995). The Globalization of Knowledge and the Education Abroad Program, 1995–2000. Internal document, EAP/UCL, Santa Barbara.

El-Khawas, Elaine. (1994). Towards a Global University: Status and Outlook in the United States. *Higher Education Management* 6, no. 1: 90–98.

El-Khawas, Elaine, Robin DePietro-Jurand, and Lauritz Hlm-Nielsen. (1998). *Quality Assurance in Higher Education: Recent Progress; Challenges Ahead.* Washington, D.C.: World Bank.

Ellingboe, Brenda J. (1998). Divisional Strategies to Internationalize a Campus Portrait: Results, Resistance, and Recommendations from a Case Study of a U.S. University. In *Reforming the Higher Education Curriculum, Internationalizing the Campus*, edited by Joseph A. Mestenhauser and Brenda J. Ellingboe. American Council on Education/Oryx Press Series on Higher Education. Phoenix: Oryx Press.

Englesson, Ulrika. (1995). Co-operation in Higher Education and Vocational Training between the European Community and the United States of America/Canada. Document by the National Agency for Higher Education on behalf of the Academic Co-operation Association, Högskoleverket National Agency for Higher Education, Stockholm.

Epstein, E. H. (1968). Letter to the Editor. *Comparative Education Review* 12, no. 3: 377.

————. (1994). Comparative and International Education: Overview and Historical Development. In *The International Encyclopedia of Education*. Vol. 2, edited by Thorsten Husén and T. Neville Postlethwaite. Oxford: Pergamon.

Etzkowitz, Henry, and Loet Leydesdorff, eds. (1997). *Universities and the Global Knowledge Economy: A Triple Helix of University–Industry–Government Relations*. Science, Technology and the International Political Economy Series. London: Pinter.

European Association for International Education (EAIE). (1992). *International Education in Europe: A Professional View on the Memorandum on Higher Education in the European Community*. Occasional paper no. 2. Amsterdam: EAIE.

————. (1999). *Europe in Association: The First Ten Years of the European Association for International Education, 1989 to 1999*. Amsterdam: EAIE.

European Commission. (1991). *Memorandum on Higher Education in the European Community*. Brussels: European Commission.

Field, John. (1998). *European Dimensions: Education, Training and the European Union*. Higher Education Policy Series no. 39. London: Jessica Kingsley.

Fishman, Joshua A. (1998–1999). The New Linguistic Order. *Foreign Policy* 113 (Winter): 26–40.

Flatin, Kjetil. (1998). Same Roots, Different Climate: Personal Reflections on Educational Encounters. In *50 Years of International Co-operation and Exchange between the United States and Europe: European Views*, edited by Hans de Wit. Amsterdam: EAIE.

Francis, Anne. (1993). *Facing the Future: The Internationalization of Post-Secondary Institutions in British Columbia*. Vancouver: British Columbia Center for International Education.

Franks, H. George, and P. J. Kardoes, eds. (1970). *The Dutch System of International Education*. Handbook prepared for the Institutes of International Education by NUFFIC. The Hague: NUFFIC.

Freed, Barbara F. (1998). An Overview of Issues and Research in Language Learning in a Study Abroad Setting. *Frontiers: The Interdisciplinary Journal of Study Abroad* (Fall): 31–60.

Friedman, Jonathan. (1994). *Cultural Identity & Global Process*. London: Sage.

Friedman, Thomas L. (1999). *The Lexus and the Olive Tree: Understanding Globalization*. New York: Farrar, Straus, Giroux.

Fulbright, J. William. (1994). An Essay in Honor of Jack Egle. In *The Power of Educational Exchange: Essays in Honor of Jack Egle*. New York: Council on International Educational Exchange.

Gacel-Avila, Jocelyne. (1999). *Internacionalización de la Educación Superior en América Latina y el Caribe, Reflexiones y Lineamientos*. Guadalajara, Mexico: Organización Universitaria Interamericana, Asociación Mexicana para la Educación Internacional, Ford Foundation.

Galpin, Perrin C. (1943). Belgian Higher Education and Belgian-American Exchanges between the Two Wars. Overview by the president of the Belgium-American Educational Foundation in the Belgium-American Educational Foundation report for the years 1941, 1942, and 1943, pp. 15–22. Washington, D.C.

Gayner, Jeffrey. (1996). *The Fulbright Program after 50 Years: From Mutual Understanding to Mutual Support*. Washington, D.C.: Capital Research Center.

Gingras, Yves, Benoît Godin, and Martine Foisy. (1999). The Internationalization of University Research in Canada. In *A New World of Knowledge: Canadian Universities and Globalisation*, edited by Sheryl L. Bond and Jan-Pierre Lemasson. Ottawa: International Development Research Centre.

Ginkel, Hans van. (1996). Networking and Strategic Alliances: Dynamic Patterns of Organization and Co-operation. *CRE-action* 109: 91–105.

Global Alliance for Transnational Education (GATE). (1997). *Certification Manual*. Washington, D.C.: GATE.

Goedegebuure, Leo, and Frans van Vught. (1996). Comparative Higher Education Studies: The Perspective from the Policy Sciences. *Higher Education* 32: 371–394.

Goldschmidt, D., U. Teichler, and W-D Webler, eds. (1984). *Forschungsgegenstand Hochschule*. Frankfurt/M and New York: Campus.

Goodwin, Craufurd D., and Michael Nacht. (1988). *Abroad & Beyond: Patterns in American Overseas Education*. Cambridge: Cambridge University Press.

———. (1991). *Missing the Boat: The Failure to Internationalize American Higher Education*. Cambridge: Cambridge University Press.

Greenwood, Davydd. (1993). Setting International Education Agendas on Campus and in Washington D.C. *International Education Forum* 13, no. 2: 61–66.

Gribbon, A. (1994). Idealism or a Marriage of Convenience? An Examination of Internal Relationships in International Exchange Programmes. *Higher Education Management* 6, no. 1: 23–31.

Groennings, Sven. (1987a). *Economic Competitiveness and International Knowledge*. Staff paper no. 2. Boston: New England Board of Higher Education.

———. (1987b). *The Impact of Economic Globalization on Higher Education*. Boston: New England Board of Higher Education.

———. (1990). Higher Education, International Education, and the Academic Disciplines. In *Group Portrait: Internationalizing the Disciplines*, edited by Sven Groennings and David S. Wiley. New York: American Forum.

———. (1997). The Fulbright Program in the Global Knowledge Economy: The Nation's Neglected Comparative Advantage. *Journal of Studies in International Education* 1, no. 2: 95–105.

Grünzweig, Walter, and Nana Rinehart. (1998). *International Understanding and Global Interdependence: A Philosophical Inquiry into International Education*. NAFSA Conference Paper. Washington, D.C.: NAFSA.

Halliday, Fred. (1999). The Chimera of the "International University." *International Affairs* 75: 99–120.

Halls, W. D. (1990). Trends and Issues in Comparative Education. In *Comparative Education: Contemporary Issues and Trends*, edited by W. D. Halls. London: Jessica Kingsley/UNESCO.

Halpern, S. (1969). The Institute of International Education: A History. Ph.D. diss., Columbia University.

Hammerstein, Notker. (1996). The Enlightenment. In *A History of the University in Europe*. Vol. 2: *Universities in Early Modern Europe (1500–1800)*, edited by Walter Rüegg. Cambridge: Cambridge University Press.

Hanson, Katherine H., and Joel W. Meyerson. (1995). *International Challenges to American Colleges and Universities: Looking Ahead*. American Council on Education Series on Higher Education. Phoenix, Ariz.: Orix Press.

Harari, Maurice. (1977). Internationalization of Higher Education. In *The International Encyclopedia of Higher Education*, edited by Asa S. Knowles. San Francisco: Jossey-Bass.

———. (1989). *Internationalization of Higher Education: Effecting Institutional Change in the Curriculum and Campus*. Long Beach, Calif.: Center for International Education, California State University.

———. (1992). The Internationalization of the Curriculum. In *Bridges to the Future: Strategies for Internationalizing Higher Education*, edited by Charles B. Klasek. Carbondale, Ill.: Association of International Education Administrators.

Haug, Guy. (1998). Student Mobility Between the US and the Europe Region. In *50 Years of International Co-operation and Exchange between the United States and Europe: European Views*, edited by Hans de Wit. Amsterdam: Eureopan Association for International Education.

———. (2000). National Exchange Agencies in the Process Towards a European Space for Higher Education. *Journal of Studies in International Education* 4, no. 2: 21–32.

Haug, Guy, Jette Kirstein, and Inge Knudsen. (1999). *Trends in Learning Structures in Higher Education*. Project report prepared for the Bologna Conference on 18–19 June 1999 on behalf of the Confederation of European Union Rectors' Conferences and CRE. Copenhagen: Danish Rectors' Conference Secretariat.

Haug, Guy, and Julia Race. (1998). Inter-Regional Co-operation in Higher Education in Europe. *Journal of Studies in International Education* 2, no. 2: 3–34.

Heginbotham, Stanley. (1997). Rethinking Perspectives on Educational "Exchanges" with Japan. *Journal of Studies in International Education* 1, no. 2: 79–94.

Higher Education in Europe. (1999). The Changing Face of Transnational Education: Moving Education—Not Learners. Special issue, vol. 24, no. 2.

Holzner, Burkart. (1994). The International Challenge to Education. *International Education Forum* 14 (Spring): 3–10.

Holzner, Burkart, and Davydd Greenwood. (1995). The Institutional Policy Contexts for International Higher Education in the United States of America. In *Strategies for Internationalisation of Higher Education: A Comparative Study of Australia, Canada, Europe and the United States of America*, edited by Hans de Wit. Amsterdam: Europan Association for International Education.

Huebner, L. W. (1994). Thriving on a Sense of Dislocation: Global Competence among International Journalists and Corporate Leaders. In *Educational Exchange and*

Global Competence, edited by Richard D. Lambert. New York: Council on International Educational Exchange.

Hufbauer, Gary, and Anup Malani. (1996). Economic Dimensions of Regionalism. In *Academic Mobility in a Changing World: Regional and Global Trends* (contributions to the Wassenaar Colloquium, 1992), edited by Peggy Blumenthal, Craufurd Goodwin, Alan Smith, and Ulrich Teichler. London: Jessica Kingsley.

Huizinga, J. (1993). *Amerika Dagboek 14 april–19 juni 1926.* Bezorgd door Anton van der Lem. Amsterdam/Antwerpen: Uitgeverij Contact.

Humpfrey, Christine. (1999). *Managing International Students.* Buckingham: Open University Press.

Huntington, S. (1996). *The Clash of Civilizations and the Remaking of World Order.* New York: Simon and Schuster.

Husén, Thorsten. (1994). International Education. In *The International Encyclopedia of Education.* Vol. 5, edited by Thorsten Husén and T. Neville Postlethwaite. Oxford: Pergamon.

Inspectie van het Onderwijs. (1994). *Voertalen en vreemde talen in het hoger onderwijs.* Inspectierapport no. 1994-8. The Hague: Inspectie van het Onderwijs.

Institute of International Education (IIE). (1994a). *Investing in Human Capital: Leadership for the Challenges of the 21st Century.* New York: IIE.

———. (1994b). *Investing in People Linking Nations, 1919–1995: The First 75 Years of the Institute of International Education.* New York: IIE.

———. (1997). *Towards Transnational Competence, Rethinking International Education: A U.S.–Japan Case Study.* IIE Research Report no. 28, prepared by the Task Force for Transnational Competence. New York: IIE.

Instituto de Gestión y Liderazgo Universitario (IGLU). (1996). *Les Réseaux Universitaires: Des Leviers pour l'action.* Special Issue of *Revue Interamericana de Gestion Universitaire.* Sainte-Floy, Québec: IGLU.

International Association of University Presidents (IAUP). (1995). *Policy Statement on Internationalization of Higher Education in the World.* Sacramento, Calif.: IAUP.

IQRP. (1996). *The Development of an Internationalisation Quality Review Process at the Level of Higher Education Institutions.* Paris: IMHE/OECD.

———. (1997). *The Development of an Internationalisation Quality Review Process for Higher Education Institutions.* Paris: IMHE/OECD.

Jenkins, Hugh M. (1977). Exchange, International, 2. International Student. In *The International Encyclopedia of Higher Education*, edited by Asa S. Knowles. San Francisco: Jossey-Bass.

Johnston, Joseph, and Richard Edelstein. (1993). *Beyond Borders.* Washington, D.C.: Association of American Colleges.

Kahn, Abdul W. (2000). On-Line Distance Learning: A Model for Developing Countries. *Journal of Studies in International Education* 4, no. 1: 11–22.

Kallen, Dennis. (1991a). Academic Exchange in Europe: Towards a New Era of Cooperation. In *The Open Door: Pan-European Academic Co-operation, an Analysis and a Proposal.* Bucharest: CEPES/UNESCO.

———. (1991b). Internationalisering van het hoger onderwijs: praktijk, politieke context, trends en uitdagingen. *VISUM perspectief* 2: 32–48.

Kälvermark T., and Marijk C. van der Wende, eds. (1997). *National Policies for the Internationalisation of Higher Education in Europe.* Stockholm: Högskoleverket Studies, National Agency for Higher Education.

Kehm, Barbara. (2000). Strategic Management of Internationalisation Processes: Problems and Options. *Tertiary Education and Management* 5: 369–382.

Kehm, Barbara, and Bärbel Last. (1997). Germany. In *National Policies for the Internationalisation of Higher Education in Europe*, edited by T. Kälvermark and M. van der Wende. Stockholm: Högskoleverket Studies, National Agency for Higher Education.

Kelleher, Ann. (1996). *Learning from Success: Campus Case Studies in International Program Development*. New York: Peter Lang.

Keller, G. (1983). *Academic Strategy*. Baltimore: Johns Hopkins University Press.

Kerr, Clark. (1990). The Internationalisation of Learning and the Nationalisation of the Purposes of Higher Education: Two "Laws of Motion" in Conflict? *European Journal of Education* 25: 5–22.

———. (1994a). American Society Turns More Assertive: A New Century Approaches for Higher Education in the United States. Foreword in *Higher Education in American Society*. 3d ed., edited by Philip G. Altbach, Robert O. Berdahl, and Patricia J. Gumport. New York: Prometheus Books.

———. (1994b). *Higher Education Cannot Escape History: Issues for the Twenty-First Century*. SUNY Series Frontiers in Education. Albany: State University of New York Press.

Klasesk, Charles, ed. (1992). *Bridges to the Future: Strategies for Internationalizing Higher Education*. Carbondale, Ill.: Association of International Education Administrators.

Knight, Jane. (1993). Internationalization: Management Strategies and Issues. *International Education Magazine* 9, no. 1: 6, 21–22.

———. (1994). *Internationalization: Elements and Checkpoints*. CBIE Research paper no. 7. Ottawa: Canadian Bureau for International Education.

———. (1995). *Internationalization at Canadian Universities: The Changing Landscape*. Ottawa: Association of Universities and Colleges of Canada.

———. (1997a). Internationalisation of Higher Education: A Conceptual Framework. In *Internationalisation of Higher Education in Asia Pacific Countries*, edited by Jane Knight and Hans de Wit. Amsterdam: European Association for International Education.

———. (1997b). A Shared Vision? Stakeholders' Perspectives on the Internationalization of Higher Education in Canada. *Journal of Studies in International Education* 1, no. 1: 27–44.

———. (1999a). Internationalisation of Higher Education. In *Quality and Internationalisation in Higher Education*, edited by Jane Knight and Hans de Wit. Paris: IMHE/OECD.

———. (1999b). Issues and Trends in Internationalization: A Comparative Perspective. In *A New World of Knowledge: Canadian Universities and Globalisation*, edited by Sheryl L. Bond and Jean-Pierre Lemasson. Ottawa: International Development Research Centre.

———. (1999c). Quality Assurance and Their Relationship to IQRP. In *Quality and Internationalisation in Higher Education*, edited by Jane Knight and Hans de Wit. Paris: IMHE/OECD.

———. (1999d). *A Time of Turbulence and Transformation for Internationalization*. CBIE Research paper no. 14. Ottawa: CBIE.

———. (2000). *Progress & Promise: The AUCC Report on Internationalization at Canadian Universities*. Ottawa: Association of Universities and Colleges of Canada.

Knight, Jane, and Hans de Wit. (1995). Strategies for Internationalisation of Higher Education: Historical and Conceptual Perspectives. In *Strategies for Internationalisation of Higher Education: A Comparative Study of Australia, Canada, Europe and the United States of America*, edited by Hans de Wit. Amsterdam: European Association for International Education.

———. (1997). Asia Pacific Countries in Comparison to Those in Europe and North America: Concluding Remarks. In *Internationalisation of Higher Education in Asia Pacific Countries*, edited by Jane Knight and Hans de Wit. Amsterdam: European Association for International Education.

———. (1999a). An Introduction to the IQRP Project and Process. In *Quality and Internationalisation in Higher Education*, edited by Jane Knight and Hans de Wit. Paris: IMHE/OECD.

———. (1999b). Reflections on Using IQRP. In *Quality and Internationalisation in Higher Education*, edited by Jane Knight and Hans de Wit. Paris: IMHE/OECD.

———, eds. (1999c). *Quality and Internationalisation in Higher Education*. Paris: IMHE/OECD.

Kolasa, Jan. (1962). *International Intellectual Co-operation (the League Experience and the Beginnings of UNESCO)*. Series A. no. 81. Wroclaw: Prace Wroclawskiego Towarzystwa Naukowego.

Kornpetpanee, Suchada. (1999). *Internationalization of Universities*. PhD diss., University of Amsterdam.

Kroes, Rob. (1996). *If You've Seen One, You've Seen the Mall: Europeans and American Mass Culture*. Urbana: University of Illinois Press.

———. (2000). *Us and Them: Questions of Citizenship in a Globalizing World*. Urbana: University of Illinois Press.

Kyvik, Svein, Berit Karseth, Jan Are Remme, and Stuart Blume. (1999). International Mobility among Nordic Doctoral Students. *Higher Education* 38: 379–400.

Lambert, Richard D. (1989a). *International Studies and the Undergraduate*. Washington, D.C.: ACE.

———. (1989b). *Study Abroad: Where We Are, and Where We Should Be*. CIEE forty-first conference report, Cannes. New York: CIEE.

———. (1992). *Foreign Student Flows and the Internationalisation of Higher Education*. Working Paper no. 37. Washington, D.C.: NAFSA.

———. (1993a). International Education and International Competency in the United States. In *Language and International Studies: A Richard Lambert Perspective*, edited by Sarah Jane Moore and Christine A. Morfit. Washington, D.C.: National Foreign Language Center.

———. (1993b). International Studies: An Overview and Agenda. In *Language and International Studies: A Richard Lambert Perspective*, edited by Sarah Jane Moore and Christine A. Morfit. Washington, D.C.: National Foreign Language Center.

———. (1994). Parsing the Concept of Global Competence. In *Educational Exchange and Global Competence*, edited by Richard D. Lambert. New York: Council on International Educational Exchange.

———. (1995). The International Dimension of Higher Education: Setting a Research Agenda (book review). *European Association for International Education Newsletter* 19: 9–10.

———. (1996). Domains and Issues in International Studies. *International Education Forum* 16, no. 1: 1–19.

Larédo, Philippe. (1997). Technological Programs in the European Union. In *Universities and the Global Knowledge Economy: A Triple Helix of University–Industry–Government Relations*, edited by Henry Etzkowitz and Loet Leydesdorff. Science, Technology and the International Political Economy Series. London: Pinter.

Laureys, G. (1992). "Mobility Has Come to Stay": Management Strategies to Meet the Demands of Internationalisation in Higher Education. *Higher Education Management* 4, no. 1: 108–120.

Lazenby, Alex, and Denis Blight. (1999). *The Story of IDP: Thirty Years in International Education and Development.* Canberra: IDP Education Australia.

León García, Fernando, Dewayne Matthews, and Lorna Smith. (2000). Movilidad académica en América del Norte: hacia nuevos modelos de integración y colaboración. *Educación Global* 4 (April): 37–58.

Leyton-Brown, David. (1996). Political Dimensions of Regionalization in a Changing World. In *Academic Mobility in a Changing World: Regional and Global Trends* (contributions to the Wassenaar Colloquium, 1992), edited by Peggy Blumenthal, Craufurd Goodwin, Alan Smith, and Ulrich Teichler. London: Jessica Kingsley.

Liaison Committee. (1992). *Reactions of the Liaison Committee of EC Rectors Conferences and CRE to the Memorandum.* Brussels: Liaison Committee.

Light, Timothy. (1993). Erasing Borders: The Changing Role of American Higher Education in the World. *European Journal of Education* 28: 253–271.

Lim, Gill-Chin, ed. (1995). *Strategy for a Global University: Model International Department Experiment.* East Lansing: Michigan State University.

Liston, Colleen. (1999). Students in Transnational Tertiary Education. *Higher Education in Europe* 24: 425–437.

Littmann, Ulrich. (1996). *Gute Partner—Schwierige Partner, Anmerkungen zur akademischen Mobilität zwischen Deutschland und den Vereinigten Staaten von Amerika (1923–1993).* DAAD-Forum 18. Bonn: Deutscher Akademischer Austausch Dienst (also available in English version, *Partners—Distant and Close: Notes and Footnotes on Academic Mobility between Germany and the United States of America (1923–1993).* DAAD-Forum 19. Bonn: DAAD.)

Löwbeer, Hans. (1977). Internationalization of Higher Education—Sweden: A Case Study. In *The International Encyclopedia of Higher Education*, edited by Asa S. Knowles. San Francisco: Jossey-Bass.

Lyman, Richard. (1995). Overview. In *International Challenges to American Colleges and Universities: Looking Ahead*, edited by Katherine H. Hanson and Joel W. Meyerson. American Council on Education Series on Higher Education. Phoenix, Ariz.: Orix Press.

Machado dos Santos, Sérgio. (2000). Introduction to the Theme of Transnational Education. Unpublished paper, Conference of the Directors General for Higher Education and the Heads of the Rector's Conferences of the European Union, Aveiro.

Magrath, C. Peter. (2000). Globalisation and Its Effect on Higher Education Beyond the Nation-State. *Higher Education in Europe* 25: 251–258.

Maiworm, Friedhelm, Wolfgang Steube, and Ulrich Teichler. (1991). *Learning in Europe: The ERASMUS Experience, a Survey of the 1988–89 ERASMUS Students*. Higher Education Policy Series 14. London: Jessica Kingsley.

Maiworm, Friedhelm, and Ulrich Teichler. (1996). *Study Abroad and Early Career: Experiences of Former ERASMUS Students*. Higher Education Policy Series 35. London: Jessica Kingsley.

Mallea, John. (1996). The Internationalisation of Higher Education: Stakeholders Views in North America. *Internationalisation of Higher Education*. Paris: OECD.

Marcuse, Peter. (2000). The Language of Globalization. *Monthly Review* 52, no. 3.

Markert, Axel. (1997). The University of Tübingen: A Model Case in Europe? *Educación Global* 1: 61–63.

————. (1998). Co-operation and Exchange between the USA and Germany. In *50 Years of International Co-operation and Exchange between the United States and Europe: European Views*, edited by Hans de Wit. Amsterdam: European Association for International Education.

Mason, R. (1998). *Globalising Education: Trends and Applications*. Routledge Studies in Distance Education. New York: Routledge.

Mayor, Frederico. (1989). Culture and the University. *Higher Education in Europe* 14: 5–13.

McBurnie, Grant. (2000). Quality Matters in Transnational Education: Undergoing the GATE Review Process—An Australian–Asian Case Study. *Journal of Studies in International Education* 4, no. 1: 23–38.

Mestenhauser, Joseph A. (1998a). International Education on the Verge. *International Spectator* 7, nos. 2–3: 68–76.

————. (1998b). Portraits of an International Curriculum: Uncommon Multidimensional Perspective. In *Reforming the Higher Education Curriculum, Internationalizing the Campus*, edited by Joseph A. Mestenhauser and Brenda J. Ellingboe. American Council on Education/Oryx Press Series on Higher Education. Phoenix: Oryx Press.

————. (2000). Missing in Action: Leadership for International and Global Education for the 21st Century. In *Internationalization of Higher Education: An Institutional Perspective*. Papers on Higher Education. Bucharest: UNESCO/CEPES.

Mestenhauser, Joseph A., and Brenda J. Ellingboe, eds. (1998). *Reforming the Higher Education Curriculum, Internationalizing the Campus*. American Council on Education/Oryx Press Series on Higher Education. Phoenix: Oryx Press.

Ministerie van Onderwijs, Cultuur en Wetenschappen. (1997). *Talents Unlimited: The Internationalisation of Education*. (English version). The Hague: Ministerie van Onderwijs, Cultuur en Wetenschappen.

————. (1999). *Kennis geven en nemen. Internationalisering van het Onderwijs in Nederland*. The Hague: Ministerie van Onderwijs, Cultuur en Wetenschappen.

Moore, Sarah Jane, and Christine A. Morfit, eds. (1993). *Language and International Studies: A Richard Lambert Perspective*. Washington, D.C.: National Foreign Language Center.

Muller, Steven. (1995). Globalization of Knowledge. In *International Challenges to American Colleges and Universities: Looking Ahead*, edited by Katherine H. Hanson and Joel W. Meyerson. Phoenix, Ariz.: American Council on Education/Oryx Press.

NAFSA. (1998). *International Educator: Golden Anniversary Issue.* Washington, D.C.: NAFSA.

National Association of State Universities and Land-Grant Colleges (NASULGC). (1993). *Internationalizing Higher Education through the Faculty.* Washington, D.C.: NASULGC.

National Task Force on Undergraduate Education Abroad. (1990). *A National Mandate for Education Abroad: Getting on with the Tasks.* Washington, D.C.: NAFSA.

Neave, Guy. (1992a). Institutional Management of Higher Education: Trends, Needs and Strategies for Co-operation. Unpublished International Association of Universities document for UNESCO, Paris.

————. (1992b). Managing Higher Education International Co-operation: Strategies and Solutions. Unpublished Reference Document for UNESCO, Paris.

————. (1997). The European Dimension in Higher Education: An Historical Analysis. Background document to the Conference "The Relationship between Higher Education and the Nation-State," 7–9 April, Enschede.

Nederlands Bureau voor Buitelandse Studentenbetrekkingen (NBBS). (1982). *Niettegenstaande Eenige Gebreken, NBBS 55 Jaar Geboekt.* Leiden: NBBS.

NUFFIC. (2000a). *Catalogue of International Courses in The Netherlands, Conducted in English, for Participants from All Over the World, Edition 2000–2001.* The Hague: NUFFIC.

————. (2000b). *The Netherlands and Its Higher Education at a Glance.* The Hague: NUFFIC.

Ollikainen, Aaro. (1996). Conflicts, Status Competition, and Different Rationales for Mobility: A Finnish Experience on Some Neglected Issues in International Education. *Frontiers: The Interdisciplinary Journal of Study Abroad* 2, no. 1: 83–92.

————. (1998). Bringing in the Strategy: A Study on Finnish SOCRATES European Policy Statements. *Journal of Studies in International Education* 2, no. 1: 23–38.

————. (2000). Into the Single Market for Education: Europeanisation of Finnish Education Policy Discourses. *Journal of Studies in International Education* 4, no. 2: 33–54.

Opper, Susan, Ulrich Teichler, and Jarry Carlson. (1990). *Impacts of Study Abroad Programmes on Students and Graduates.* Vol. 2. Higher Education Policy Series 11. London: Jessica Kingsley.

Organisation for Economic Co-operation and Development (OECD). Centre for Educational Research and Innovation. (1994). *Curriculum Development for Internationalisation: Guidelines for Country Case Studies.* Paris: CERI/IEA.

Overbeek, Marjan van. (1997). On Internationalisation, Student Mobility and Quality Assurance. *Higher Education Management* 9, no. 1: 49–57.

Parker, Christine S., and Erwin H. Epstein. (1998). *Comparative Education Review: Cumulative Index (revised edition) Volumes 1–42, 1957–1998.* Chicago: University of Chicago Press.

Paulston, R. G. (1994). Comparative and International Education: Paradigms and Theories. In *The International Encyclopedia of Education.* Vol. 2, edited by Thorsten Husén and T. Neville Postlethwaite. Oxford: Pergamon.

Pickert, Sarah M. (1992). *Preparing for a Global Community: Achieving an International Perspective in Higher Education.* ASHE–ERIC Higher Education Reports no. 2. Washington, D.C.: George Washington University Clearinghouse on Education.

Platt, James. (1977). Exchange, International, 4. Student Exchange Programs. In *The International Encyclopedia of Higher Education*, edited by Asa S. Knowles. San Francisco: Jossey-Bass.

Pratt, Graham, and David Poole. (1998a). Global Corporations R Us? Impacts of Globalisation on Australian Universities. Paper presented at Re-Working the University Conference, 10–11 December, Griffith University.

———. (1998b). Internationalisation Strategies as a Response to Market Forces: Direction and Trends. Paper presented at the annual conference of the Association for Institutional Research, 28 November, Melbourne.

Preston, Jill. (1991). *EC Education, Training and Research Programmes: An Action Guide*. London: Kogan Page.

Prichard, Roger. (1996). Networking for Research and Development: Necessity or New Religion. *Inter-American Journal of University Management* 10 (April): 5–10.

Rahman, Tannaz, and La Marr Kopp. (1992). Administration of International Education. In *Bridges to the Future: Strategies for Internationalizing Higher Education*, edited by Charles B. Klasek. Carbondale, Ill.: Association of International Education Administrators.

Rice, Condoleezza. (2000). Promoting the National Interest. *Foreign Affairs* 79, no. 1: 45–62.

Rinehart, Nana. (1999). Presentation at session, "Imperial Discourse or Lingua Franca? The Question of Language in International Exchange." Eleventh annual conference of the EAIE, Maastricht, 2–4 December.

Roberts, John, Agueda M. Rodrígues Cruz, and Jurgen Herbst. (1996). Exporting Models. In *A History of the University in Europe*. Vol. 2: *Universities in Early Modern Europe (1500–1800)*, edited by Walter Rüegg. Cambridge: Cambridge University Press.

Robinson, Christopher D. (1998). Universitas 21: A Network for International Higher Education. *International Workshop on Academic Consortia*. David C. Lam Institute for East–West Studies (LEWI), workshop report. Hong Kong: LEWI.

Roeloffs, Karl. (1994). Global Competence and Regional Integration: A View from Europe. In *Educational Exchange and Global Competence*, edited by R. D. Lambert. New York: CIEE.

Rooijen, Maurits van. (1998). *No Business like International Education*. Unpublished IDP Education Australia Conference Paper. Canberra: IDP Education Australia.

Rudder, Helmut de. (2000). On the Europeanization of Higher Education. *International Higher Education* 19 (Spring): 4–6.

Rudzki, Romuald E. J. (1995a). The Application of a Strategic Management Model to the Internationalization of Higher Education Institutions. *Higher Education* 29: 421–441.

———. (1995b). Internationalisation of UK Business Schools: Findings of a National Survey. In *Policy and Policy Implementation in Internationalisation of Higher Education*, edited by P. Blok. Amsterdam: European Association for International Education.

———. (1998). The Strategic Management of Internationalization: Towards a Model of Theory and Practice. Ph.D. diss., University of Newcastle upon Tyne.

———. (2000). Implementing Internationalisation: The Practical Application of the Fractal Process Model. *Journal of Studies in International Education* 4, no. 2: 77–90.

Rupp, Jan C. C. (1997). *Van oude en nieuwe universiteiten, De verdringing van Duitse door Amerikaanse invloeden op de wetenschapsbeoefening en het hoger onderwijs in Nederland, 1945–1995.* The Hague: SdU.

———. (1999). The Fulbright Program, or the Surplus Value of Officially Organized Academic Exchange. *Journal of Studies in International Education* 3, no. 1: 57–82.

Sadlak, Jan. (2000). Globalization versus the Universal Role of the University. *Higher Education in Europe* 25: 243–249.

Schoorman, Dilys. (1999). The Pedagogical Implications of Diverse Conceptualizations of Internationalization: A U.S.-Based Case Study. *Journal of Studies in International Education* 3, no. 2: 19–46.

Scott, Peter. (1992). *Mass Higher Education in Europe: Implications for Student Mobility and International Education.* EAIE Occasional Paper 1. Amsterdam: European Association for International Education.

———. (1996). Internationalisation and Quality Assurance. In *Internationalisation and Quality Assurance: Goals, Strategies and Instruments*, edited by Urbain DeWinter. EAIE Occasional Paper 10. Amsterdam: European Association for International Education.

———. (1998). Massification, Internationalization and Globalization. In *The Globalization of Higher Education*, edited by Peter Scott. Buckingham: SRHE and Open University Press.

———. (1999). Globalisation and the University. *CRE-action* 115: 35–46.

———. (2000). Globalisation and Higher Education: Challenges for the 21st Century. *Journal of Studies in International Education* 4, no. 1: 3–10.

Scott, Robert A. (1992). *Campus Developments in Response to the Challenges of Internationalization: The Case of Ramapo College of New Jersey (USA).* Springfield, Va.: CBIS Federal.

Serageldin, Ismail. (1994). Our Common Humanity. In *Europe and Beyond: Issues in North–South Co-operation*, edited by Han Aarts and Kjetil Flatin. EAIE Occasional Paper 6. Amsterdam: European Association for International Education.

Shaw, Martin. (1994). *Global Society and International Relations.* Cambridge: Polity Press.

Silvio, José. (1996). Introducción a la gestión de redes académicas en América Latina. *Inter-American Journal of University Management* 10 (April): 11–22.

Singh, Raman. (1998). Whose English Is It, Anyway? Presentation at the conference, "The International University: Local and Global Roles," American International University in London, Richmond, 3–5 April.

Slaughter, Sheila, and Larry L. Leslie. (1997). *Academic Capitalism: Politics, Policies, and the Entrepreneurial University.* Baltimore: Johns Hopkins University Press.

Smith, Alan. (1994a). *Academic Cooperation and Mobility: Trends, Issues and Challenges for the Next Millennium.* Unpublished report for discussion group I of the 11th General Assembly of the Association of European Universities (CRE) in Budapest. Geneva: CRE.

———. (1994b). *International Education: A Question of Quality.* EAIE Occasional Paper 7. Amsterdam: European Association for International Education.

Smith, Alan, Ulrich Teichler, and Marijk van der Wende, eds. (1994). *The International Dimension of Higher Education: Setting the Research Agenda* (Proceedings of an international research workshop jointly sponsored by the

Academic Co-operation Association and the International Research Centre for Cultural Studies, Vienna, 29–30 April). Vienna: IFK.

Smith, Ian, and Gillian Parata. (1997). Internationalisation of Higher Education in New Zealand. In *Internationalisation of Higher Education in Asia Pacific Countries*, edited by Jane Knight and Hans de Wit. Amsterdam: European Association for International Education.

Smuckler, Ralph H. (1999). Fifty Years after President Truman's Point IV Initiative: A Review of University Experience. *International Education Forum* 19, nos. 1–2: 1–14.

Sorbonne Declaration. (1998). *Joint Declaration on Harmonisation of the Architecture of the European Higher Education System*, 25 May. Paris: Sorbonne.

Stellingweaf, Dick. (2000). Nederlands als tweede taal. *Academia* 3, Vierdejaargang, Juni 13.

Swaan, Abram de. (1998a). A Political Sociology of the World Language System (1): The Dynamics of Language Spread. *Language Problems and Language Planning* 22: 63–75.

———. (1998b). A Political Sociology of the World Language System (2): The Unequal Exchange of Texts. *Language Problems and Language Planning* 22: 109–128.

Task Force on Higher Education and Society. (2000). *Higher Education in Developing Countries: Peril and Promise*. Washington, D.C.: World Bank.

Taylor, Mary Louise. (1977). Study Abroad. In *The International Encyclopedia of Higher Education*, edited by Asa S. Knowles. San Francisco: Jossey-Bass.

Teather, D.C.B. (2000). *David C. Lam Institute for East–West Studies, Five-Year Review 1995–2000*. Internal document. Hong Kong: Hong Kong Baptist University.

Teichler, Ulrich. (1996a). The Changing Nature of Higher Education in Western Europe. *Higher Education Policy* 9, no. 2: 89–111.

———. (1996b). Comparative Higher Education: Potentials and Limits. *Higher Education* 32: 431–465.

———. (1996c). Research on Academic Mobility and International Co-operation in Higher Education: An Agenda for the Future. In *Academic Mobility in a Changing World: Regional and Global Trends* (contributions to the Wassenaar Colloquium, 1992), edited by Peggy Blumenthal, Craufurd Goodwin, Alan Smith, and Ulrich Teichler. London: Jessica Kingsley.

———. (1999). Internationalisation as a Challenge for Higher Education in Europe. *Tertiary Education and Management* 5: 5–23.

Thullen, Manfred, Martin J. Tillman, David D. Horner, Susan Carty, and Steven Kennedy. (1997). *Cooperating with a University in the United States: Nafsa's Guide to Interuniversity Linkages*. Washington, D.C.: NAFSA.

Tierney, James F. (1977). Exchange, International, 1. Overview. In *The International Encyclopedia of Higher Education*, edited by Asa S. Knowles. San Francisco: Jossey-Bass.

Tonkin, Humphrey, and Jane Edwards. (1990). Internationalizing the University: The Arduous Road to Euphoria. *Educational Record* (Spring).

Tousignant, Jacques. (1996). University Networks: Leverage for Action. *Inter-American Journal of University Management* 10 (April): 3.

Tugend, Alina. (1999). MIT and U. of Cambridge Announce $135-Million Joint Venture. *The Chronicle of Higher Education*, 19 November, p. A71.

UNESCO. (1998). *World Declaration on Higher Education for the Twenty-First Century: Vision and Action.* Declaration adopted at the World Conference on Higher Education, 9 October. Paris: UNESCO.

UNESCO–CEPES. (1999). *Recognition of Qualifications in Transnational Education.* Working Group on Transnational Education. Bucharest: UNESCO–CEPES.

Université Libre de Bruxelles. (1996). *ULB USA, Passé, présent et futur d'une fructueuse collaboration (Past, Present and Future of a Fruitful Friendship).* Bruxelles: ULB.

U.S. Advisory Commission on Public Diplomacy. (1995). *Public Diplomacy for the 21st Century.* Washington, D.C.: U.S. Advisory Commission on Public Diplomacy.

van der Wende, Marijk C. (1996). Internationalising the Curriculum in Dutch Higher Education: An International Comparative Perspective. Ph.D. diss., Utrecht University.

———. (1997a). International Comparative Analysis and Synthesis. In *National Policies for the Internationalisation of Higher Education in Europe*, edited by T. Kälvermark and M. van der Wende. Stockholm: Högskoleverket Studies, National Agency for Higher Education.

———. (1997b). Missing Links: The Relationship between National Policies for Internationalisation and Those for Higher Education in General. In *National Policies for the Internationalisation of Higher Education in Europe*, edited by T. Kälvermark and M. van der Wende. Stockholm: Högskoleverket Studies, National Agency for Higher Education.

———. (1998). Quality Assurance in Higher Education and the Link to Internationalisation. *MillenIum* 3, no. 11: 20–29.

———. (1999a). Final Report CRE Conference Valencia, 1999. *CRE-Action* 115: 61–66.

———. (1999b). An Innovation Perspective on Internationalisation of Higher Education Institutionalisation: The Critical Phase. *Journal of Studies in International Education* 3, no. 1: 3–22.

———. (1999c). Quality Assurance of Internationalisation and Internationalisation of Quality Assurance. In *Quality and Internationalisation in Higher Education*, edited by Jane Knight and Hans de Wit. Paris: IMHE/OECD.

———. (2000). The Bologna Declaration: Enhancing the Transparency and Competitiveness of European Higher Education. *Journal of Studies in International Education* 4, no. 2: 3–10.

van Dijk, Hans. (1995). Internationalisation of Higher Education in The Netherlands: An Exploratory Study of Organisational Designs. In *Policy and Policy Implementation in Internationalisation of Higher Education*, edited by P. Blok. Amsterdam: European Association for International Education.

van Dijk, Hans, and Kees Meijer. (1997). The Internationalisation Cube: A Tentative Model for the Study of Organisational Designs and the Results of Internationalisation in Higher Education. *Higher Education Management* 9, no. 1: 157–166.

van Hoof, Hubert B. (1999). The International Student Experience: A U.S. Industry Perspective. *Journal of Studies in International Education* 3, no. 2: 57–72.

Vestal, Theodore M. (1994). *International Education: Its History and Promise for Today.* Westport, Conn.: Praeger.

Vinke, Diana. (1995). *English as the Medium of Instruction in Dutch Engineering Education*. Delft, The Netherlands: Delft University Press.

Wächter, Bernd, ed. (1999). *Internationalisation in European Non-University Higher Education: A Project of the Academic Co-operation Association*. ACA Papers on International Co-operation in Education. Bonn: Lemmens.

Wächter, Bernd, Aaro Ollikainen, and Brigitte Hasewend. (1999). *Internationalisation in Higher Education: A Paper and Seven Essays on International Co-operation in the Tertiary Sector,* edited by Bernd Wächter. ACA Papers on International Cooperation in Education. Bonn: Lemmens.

Wallerstein, Immanuel. (1997). The Unintended Consequences of Cold War Area Studies. In *The Cold War & the University: Towards an Intellectual History of the Postwar Years*, edited by André Schiffain. New York: New Press.

Warner, Gary. (1992). Internationalization Models and the Role of the University. *International Education Magazine* 9, no. 1.

Welch, Anthony. (1997). The Peripatetic Professor: The Internationalisation of the Academic Profession. *Higher Education* 34: 323–345.

Welch, Anthony, and Brian Denman. (1997). Internationalisation of Higher Education: Retrospect and Prospect. *Forum of Education* 52, no. 1: 14–29.

Wells, Betty L., and Tamara Pfantz. (1999). Advancing the "Agenda for Research on the Internationalization of Higher Education in the U.S." *International Education Forum* 19, nos. 1–2: 17–30.

White House. (2000). *International Education Policy: Memorandum for the Heads of Executive Departments and Agencies by President Clinton*. Oklahoma City: Office of the Press Secretary.

Wilson, David N. (1994). Comparative and International Education: Fraternal or Siamese Twins? A Preliminary Genealogy of Our Twin Fields. Presidential address. *Comparative Education Review* 38: 449–486.

Wilson, D. (1998). *Defining International Competencies for the New Millenium.* Research Monograph no. 12. Ottawa: Canadian Bureau for International Education.

Wilson, Lesley A., and Lazâr Vlâsceanu. (2000). Transnational Education and Recognition of Qualifications. In *Internationalization of Higher Education: An Institutional Perspective*. Papers on Higher Education. Bucharest: UNESCO–CEPES.

Woodhouse, David. (1999). Quality and Quality Assurance. In *Quality and Internationalisation in Higher Education*, edited by Jane Knight and Hans de Wit. Paris: IMHE/OECD.

Yershova, Yelena, Joan DeJaeghere, and Josef Mestenhauser. (2000). Thinking Not as Usual: Adding the Intercultural Perspective. *Journal of Studies in International Education* 4, no. 1: 39–78.

Yugui Guo. (1998). The Roles of Returned Foreign-Educated Students in Chinese Higher Education. *Journal of Studies in International Education* 2, no. 1: 35–58.

Index

ABOUT THE AUTHOR

Hans de Wit is Vice President for International Affairs, University of Amsterdam, The Netherlands.